Introduction to Criminal Justice

*Current Perspectives
from InfoTrac®*

Todd Scott

Schoolcraft Community College

WADSWORTH
CENGAGE Learning™

Australia • Brazil • Japan • Korea • Mexico • Singapore • Spain • United Kingdom • United States

WADSWORTH
CENGAGE Learning

For product information and technology assistance, contact us at **Cengage Learning Customer & Sales Support, 1-800-354-9706**

For permission to use material from this text or product, submit all requests online at **www.cengage.com/permissions** Further permissions questions can be emailed to **permissionrequest@cengage.com**

ISBN-13: 978-1-111-82833-2
ISBN-10: 1-111-82833-4

Wadsworth
20 Davis Drive
Belmont, CA 94002-3098
USA

Cengage Learning is a leading provider of customized learning solutions with office locations around the globe, including Singapore, the Unitod Kingdom, Australia, Mexico, Brazil, and Japan. Locate your local office at: **www.cengage.com/global**

Cengage Learning products are represented in Canada by Nelson Education, Ltd.

To learn more about Wadsworth, visit **www.cengage.com/wadsworth**

Purchase any of our products at your local college store or at our preferred online store **www.cengagebrain.com**

Printed in the United States of America
3 4 5 6 7 15 14

TABLE OF CONTENTS

Preface

As a student in the criminal justice discipline, you are becoming aware that the criminal justice system is a highly complex, interconnected structure. The three main branches of the system, law enforcement, adjudication, and corrections affect and are affected by each other. These effects can take many forms. Most criminal justice scholars and professionals will agree that the criminal justice system is in a continuous state of change; change for the better, for the betterment of societal control so we all can live safely and pursue our freedoms.

This Reader contains works that focus on recent issues within the three main branches of the criminal justice system. This Reader is divided into four major sections:

1. Criminal Justice System
2. Police and Law Enforcement
3. Courts and the Adjudication System
4. Correctional System

Section One explains two major themes that all the branches of the criminal justice system have recently been affected by: the sustained crime rate decline and the integration of homeland security responsibilities. In Section Two, you will read about four major issues affecting law enforcement. You will also have a chance to read and think about the importance of an increased focus of ethical behavior by law enforcement officers. This topic of ethical behavior is so important it has been expanded to all sections of this Reader and as such you will explore the ethical issues related to prosecutors and correctional personnel.

How law enforcement officers use force, when they use force, and to what degree has always been controversial and has strongly influenced the training and education of law enforcement officers. You will have the opportunity to read about some emerging technologies law enforcement is utilizing and discover in depth a recent strategy in law enforcement, evidence-based policing.

In Section Three of this Reader you will have the opportunity to explore the ethical concerns related to prosecutors and how sentencing strategies are developed. You will also read about controversial activities related to the Miranda Rule of interrogation.

Finally in this section, alternative courts, or courts that focus upon the special needs of categories of defendants, are explored.

Section Four covers enforcement personnel of the correctional system: probation, parole, and correctional officers face many of the same difficulties as law enforcement officers. This Reader acknowledges the similarities and explores the ethical behavior of correctional personnel and the use of force used by correctional personnel. A recent development in the correctional field is the application of evidence-based corrections. Evidence-based corrections is used to determine behavior and action after examining empirical evidence of the problem being investigated. Special populations pose a host of challenges for the correctional system. As these special populations grow to be a larger element of the correctional population, they become the subject of more research and examination, this Reader is no exception.

This Reader has been developed to enhance your learning of the criminal justice system. Topics that address the most recent challenges in the criminal justice system are included. These challenges confront current criminal justice professionals and will continue to be critical issues for you as you develop into a criminal justice professional. Thank you for your interest in this Reader.

~Todd Scott

Section I

Criminal Justice System

The first two articles in this section address the issue of the continuous dropping crime rate in the U.S. Consider the reasons proposed from the perspective of the authors and contributors. Criminologists and government officials provide their suggestions for the crime drop in the articles. Consider the likelihood that the explanations each provide is a valid cause. As pointed out in the second article by the New American, geographic location seems to be a variable in the crime rate drop, as some areas of the U.S. did not experience dramatic crime rate drops. Consider your geographic location; is the area where you live experiencing the same crime rate drop as other areas across the U.S.?

The last three articles of this section focus upon the recent interdependence of homeland security and the criminal justice system, especially law enforcement. Should homeland security and the criminal justice system be separate entities or does it make sense to combine the two? Consider the authority possessed by homeland security personnel and contrast them with those of local law enforcement? Do you have any concerns in this regard? Is it right for fusion centers to be funded through homeland security dollars and used primarily for local crime issues?

Crime Decline

1

U.S. Crime Rate is Down

Six Key Reasons

Husna Haq

High unemployment, continuing layoffs, mounting debt, record foreclosures, tight household budgets.

Recessions can be the perfect storm for crime.

Yet preliminary crime figures from the Federal Bureau of Investigation for 2009 show that the crime rate is falling across America, across all categories. Violent crime was down 5.5 percent and property crime down 4.9 percent between 2008 and 2009, according to FBI statistics released Monday.

In fact, crime in every category decreased, says FBI spokesman Bill Carter. Murder, forcible rape, robbery, and aggravated assault all declined in 2009, he said. Robbery - which tends to boom in bust times - dropped 8.1 percent.

Which has a lot of criminologists scratching their heads.

"In theory, in times of recession, crime rates go up," says Ted Kirkpatrick, co-director of Justiceworks, a crime and justice research group at the University of New Hampshire in Durham. Tight finances, Mr. Kirkpatrick explains, tend to boost property crime and robberies, and financial stress often produces more domestic violence.

"In fact, that hasn't been the case," he says. "We've seen a pretty dramatic decline in crime rates."

Haq, H. US crime rate is down: six key reasons. The Christian Science Monitor, May 24, 2010. Reprinted by permission of the author.

Why is crime down, in spite of the recession? Criminologists have a number of theories to explain the decline.

First, says Shawn Bushway, a professor of criminal justice at the University at Albany in New York, it's important to recognize that crime has been on a downward trend for more than a decade. The recession's short-term effects may have been overwhelmed by the longer-term factors that have produced the long, steady decline in crime.

"Crime is not a cyclical beast, like business," Mr. Bushway says. "It experiences big long ups and big long downs, unlike the up-down-up-down of the business cycle." He adds, "Could that overall downward trend swamp what's going on with the business cycle? Sure."

There's a lot more to crime trends than whether the economy is booming or not, Bushway says.

"Crime went up a lot in the '60s - when the economy was booming," he says. "That had to do with social institutions, not the economy."

In this case, a number of other factors might be pushing crime down, even as the recession encourages more criminal activity. Here are the key reasons cited by three criminologists interviewed for this article:

Incarceration

The theory goes: The more criminals are put in jail, the fewer are on the streets to commit crimes. The United States has reached a critical point at which a majority of violent crime offenders are behind bars, many criminologists say.

"By building more prisons and incarcerating more people, we've taken criminals off the street," says Kirkpatrick of the University of New Hampshire.

Policing

"Policing is more proactive," asserts Bushway of the University at Albany.

One way it's more proactive, Kirkpatrick says, is surveillance.

"It's simply getting harder to commit crime," he says. "Cameras are everywhere. Anytime there's a bank robbery, you can bet there's a number of pictures taken. That's forcing illicit behavior underground where it's less detectable."

Social programs

Law enforcement has worked with community groups for years to develop programs to keep youths engaged, provide them outlets, and combat crime. Those efforts may finally be paying off, criminologists say.

"Efforts to attend to the needs of young offenders through community outreach programs has helped," Kirkpatrick says. "The more attention we pay in our communities to kids at risk, the better."

Demographics

One factor contributing to the downward trend in crime may be simple demographics: Young people commit the most crime, and young people make up a smaller percentage of society now.

"Median age has increased rather dramatically in last 25 years," Bushway says. "Crime tends to be committed by young folks."

The median age in the US has reached its highest point ever at 36.7 years, according to a 2010 estimate by the Central Intelligence Agency's World Factbook. This is up from 35.3 years in 2000 and 32.9 years in 1990, according to census figures.

Unemployment benefits

Some theories suggest that the more government support an individual can receive - through unemployment benefits, food stamps, controlled rent, and other forms of welfare - the less he or she may be encouraged to commit financial- or stress-motivated crime.

The government's stepped-up aid during this recession may have had an effect on crime, says Bushway. "The extension of unemployment benefits probably held off crime," he says.

Fewer opportunities

In at least one way, the recession may have actually staved off property crime, says Richard Rosenfeld, president of the American Society of Criminology and a professor of criminology at the University of Missouri in St. Louis.

"During severe recessions like the current one, with chronically high unemployment rates, more people are at home and can act as guardians for their home," Mr. Rosenfeld says. "That leads to a decline in residential burglaries."

Furthermore, people have less cash and valuables on hand and in their homes now, making them less-attractive targets, he says.

Will crime rates change as the US climbs out of recession? Probably, but they won't necessarily be tied to any recession-related factors, Bushway says.

"[The crime rate] has been leveling off lately following a long, slow decline," he says. "What's striking is it's looking like it might start going up. If I can predict anything, it's going to go up again."

2

FBI Says Violent Crime Fell in 2009, But ...

The FBI reported in September that for the third straight year incidents of violent crime have declined across the United States. According to the federal police agency, violent crime declined by 5.3 percent during 2009, accompanied by a nearly five-percent drop in property crimes.

The FBI study, which is derived from nearly 18,000 reports by government departments and college campuses across the nation, found that among violent-crime statistics for 2009, murder fell by 7.3 percent, robbery by eight percent, aggravated assault by over four percent, and rape by 2.6 percent. Nationally, approximately 1.3 million violent crimes were reported last year, which breaks down to less than 430 crimes for every 100,000 individuals.

As for property crimes, vehicle theft declined by slightly more than 17 percent, larceny by four percent, and burglary by 1.3 percent.

U.S. Attorney General Eric Holder attempted to tie the most recent crime decline to "investments in law enforcement" made by the Obama administration as part of its broad-ranging "economic stimulus" tax giveaway. "In 2009, the Obama administration provided over four billion dollars in support to law enforcement and criminal justice initiatives through the American Recovery and Reinvestment Act," noted Holder, "including one billion in COPS funding to keep police officers on the street," boasting that in all, "These investments have helped maintain public safety and encourage new criminal justice innovations in state and local jurisdictions across the country."

Apparently, however, Obama's "investment" in crime-fighting didn't find its way to areas where beefed-up law enforcement was most needed. While violent crime was down in suburbs and smaller

FBI says violent crime fell in 2009, but...The New American, Oct 11, 2010 v26 i20 p7(1).

communities, it was up in traditionally high-crime urban areas like Detroit, which reported a 2.2-percent increase in violent crime during 2009, with some urban areas bordering metro Detroit witnessing rates that exceeded four percent.

One criminologist, James Allen Fox of Northeastern University in Boston, told CNN, "Although homicides were down sharply in more affluent areas and among those 25 and over, the sound of gunfire was all too common in some poor neighborhoods." African-Americans continue to voice the greatest concern over crime in their neighborhoods. While blacks make up about 13 percent of the U.S. population, almost half of the 14,000 murder victims in 2009 were black, with a majority of the deaths occurring in urban centers.

The Criminal Justice System and Homeland Security

3

Report: Gov't has Huge Intelligence Force

WASHINGTON, Dec. 20 (UPI) -- The U.S. government, since 2001, has assembled a huge, secretive intelligence task force to prevent future terrorist attacks, The Washington Post reported.

The operation has grown so large and secretive since the terrorist attacks of Sept. 11, 2001, that no one knows how much it costs, how many people it employs or how many programs it has, the Post said in a report Monday it called "Top Secret America."

The newspaper said it spent months compiling its report from more than 100 interviews and 1,000 documents.

The Post said the government's plan is to have every state and local law enforcement agency report information to Washington to help the FBI, which is in charge of terrorism investigations in the United States.

Among the Post's findings:

- Some battlefield techniques and technologies used in Iraq and Afghanistan are being used by law enforcement agencies in the United States.

- The FBI is assembling a database with names and personal information on thousands of U.S. citizens and residents who local police officers -- or fellow citizens -- believe are acting suspiciously.

- Some law enforcement agencies are hiring, as trainers, self-described experts whose extremist views on Islam and terrorism are considered inaccurate and counterproductive by the FBI.

Report: Gov't has huge intelligence force. UPI NewsTrack, Dec 20, 2010.

Government intelligence officials say the information is needed to prevent homegrown terrorists and others from striking.

"The old view that 'if we fight the terrorists abroad, we won't have to fight them here' is just that -- the old view," Homeland Security Secretary Janet Napolitano recently told police and firefighters.

4

Intelligence-Led Policing in a Fusion Center

David Lambert.

Much writing and discussion have focused on fusion centers as a key element of a homeland security strategy within policing. These centers have proponents in the homeland security and public safety policy-making structures, as well as critics from civil liberties groups and privacy advocates. A great deal of misperception exists on all sides of the issue regarding the role of fusion centers and intelligence gathering within policing in general.

The concepts of fusion centers, data fusion, and the associated philosophy of intelligence-led policing are abstract terms often misinterpreted and poorly articulated both in and out of law enforcement. While police departments traditionally have had an intelligence- and information-sharing function, the term fusion may be new to some in the profession. (1) Similarly, intelligence-led policing, which has many similarities to community and problem-oriented policing, might prove relatively unfamiliar to some officers. (2) As a result, the incorporation of fusion centers and intelligence-led policing principles into routine law enforcement functions has been a slow and uneven process. However, doing so can make police agencies more effective.

DEFINITIONS

Data fusion is "the exchange of information from different sources--including law enforcement, public safety, and the private sector--and, with analysis, can result in meaningful and actionable intelligence and information" that can inform both policy and tactical deployment of resources. (3) Building upon classic problem-solving processes, such as the scanning, analysis, response, and assessment (SARA)

Lambert, D. Intelligence-led policing in a fusion center. The FBI Law Enforcement Bulletin, Dec 2010 v79 i12 p1(6). Reprinted by permission of the author.

model, data fusion capitalizes on a wide array of available data to examine issues ranging from terrorism to traditional street crime. Through data fusion, personnel turn information into knowledge by collecting, processing, analyzing, and disseminating intelligence based upon end users' needs.

A fusion center is a "collaborative effort of two or more agencies that provide resources, expertise, and information to the center with the goal of maximizing their ability to detect, prevent, investigate, and respond to criminal and terrorist activity." (4) Fusion centers can identify potential threats through data analysis and enhance investigations through analytical support (e.g., flow charting and geographic analysis).

Finally, intelligence-led policing (ILP) refers to a "collaborative law enforcement approach combining problem-solving policing, information sharing, and police accountability, with enhanced intelligence operations." (5) ILP can guide operational policing activities toward high-frequency offenders, locations, or crimes to impact resource allocation decisions.

ROLE OF FUSION CENTERS

Fusion centers allow for the exchange of information and intelligence among law enforcement and public safety agencies at the federal, state, and local levels. A variety of indicators, such as gang behavior, weapons violations, or metals thefts, span jurisdictions. The growth of fusion centers demonstrates that no one police or public safety organization has all of the information it needs to effectively address crime problems. Progressive fusion centers have access to a wide variety of databases, many of which previously were accessible only by individual federal, state, or local law enforcement organizations. Agency participation in multijurisdictional fusion centers diminishes "stovepipes" of information.

Pooling resources, such as analysts and information systems, can maximize limited assets at a time when all agencies face budget cutbacks. Collaboration across organizations blends subject-matter expertise in areas, such as homeland security, violent crime, and drug control. It builds trusted relationships across participating agencies, which encourages additional collaboration. Fusion centers foster a culture of information sharing and break down traditional barriers that stand in the way. (6)

Combining data from multiple agencies enables policy makers and police managers to see trends and patterns not as apparent when using a single information source. Employing multiple sources helps present a more credible picture of crime and homeland security issues, as when personnel examine field interview data in conjunction with crime incident reports. Personnel often underreport drug or gang offenses, while field interview cards collected by street officers with intimate knowledge of the community may provide a more valid measure of illegal drug use or gang behavior. Using multiple indicators strengthens the information and results in a more coherent and accurate intelligence product.

MASSACHUSETTS EXPERIENCE

Commonwealth Fusion Center

In October 2004, Massachusetts officials opened the Commonwealth Fusion Center (CFC) to focus on terrorism, homeland security, and crime problems across the state. While addressing homeland security challenges is the driving force behind the center, traditional street crimes occur more frequently. The CFC constitutes part of the Massachusetts State Police (MSP), Division of Investigative Services, and employs state troopers and intelligence analysts. Committed staff members from the National Guard, Massachusetts Department of Corrections, FBI, Department of Homeland Security, and Bureau of Alcohol, Tobacco, Firearms, and Explosives (ATF) reflect its multijurisdictional nature. Other agencies participate in the CFC on a part-time or as-needed basis. In addition, the CFC is colocated with the New England High Intensity Drug Trafficking Area (NE-HIDTA). This program also incorporates a number of federal, state, and local police agencies to focus on drug control, interdiction, and narcotics intelligence.

Targeting Violent Crime Initiative

As an all-crimes information-sharing and intelligence center, the CFC devotes a significant portion of its analytical resources to examining emerging crime trends. In this regard, the U.S. Department of Justice (DOJ), Bureau of Justice Assistance, sponsored the Targeting Violent Crime Initiative, a grant program giving police agencies an incentive to use an ILP approach to address violence. The CFC, responding to a call from state policy makers to examine violent and, specifically, firearms crime throughout the state, proposed to develop a fusion process around weapons offenses.

This effort centers around answering questions about firearms in Massachusetts. First, where do guns used in crimes come from? In other words, do firearms used by criminals--many prohibited from legally owning guns--originate from traffickers bringing them into the state, individuals stealing them from businesses or homes, or other sources? Second, are the lesser-known illegal firearms markets in Springfield, Worcester, and Brockton the same as in Boston? Finally, what are the trends of firearms crime in various parts of the state? Is it on the rise in most large communities or do patterns vary? Which areas have the most stress from firearms crime? Answers to such broad questions can inform policy making.

ILP for Firearms Violence

Like many other states, Massachusetts has a number of public safety entities involved in violent crime reduction efforts. To this end, one objective of the CFC's DOJ-funded Intelligence-Led Policing for Firearms Violence project is to supplement, not duplicate, existing violent crime programs. Through the development of tactical and strategic intelligence products, the fusion center has sought to help these public safety agencies arrive at informed, data-driven decisions. (7)

Working cooperatively with the U.S. Attorney's Office, Massachusetts State Police's firearms identification section and its crime laboratory, Boston Police Department, ATF, Massachusetts Criminal History Systems Board, and other local police agencies, CFC began collecting, processing, and analyzing crime and weapons-trace data to provide policy makers with data on firearms crime patterns, the types of weapons recovered at crime scenes or during arrests, and the source cities and states of these guns.

This project also has focused on leveraging existing information and supplementing it with new data to provide strategic and tactical intelligence to end users so that they can make informed decisions. The CFC serves as the state crime reporting repository using the FBI's Uniform Crime Reporting Program's National Incident-Based Reporting System (NIBRS) to collect crime information. This data provides details on crime incidents across jurisdictions on a year-to-year and month-to-month basis and offers specifics on types of crime, such as aggravated assaults by firearm type and offender age and gender. For instance, the NIBRS data set allowed the CFC to closely examine firearms offenses committed by youths aged 10 to 17 across various communities to study juvenile gun crime.

As another valuable source of information, the ATF's National Tracing Center collects and disseminates data on firearms recovered from crimes. Participating police departments submit a request to

ATF, which traces the origins of the firearm through various databases and then provides information on the first retail purchaser, the licensed dealer that sold the firearm, and the type and manufacturer of the weapon. This trace data provides both tactical and strategic intelligence to investigators, patrol officers, intelligence analysts, and decision makers. For instance, identifying the city and state of the first retail purchase of a firearm involved in a crime, as well as the amount of time elapsed between purchase and offense, provides a possible indicator of firearms trafficking.

In addition, the project has accessed summary data collected from the MSP crime laboratory and the state's criminal justice information system to track firearms patterns in the commonwealth. These sources provide information on the varieties of weapons, types of crimes, and patterns of ownership for guns used in offenses. Employing these data sources--rarely used for analysis prior to this-- the project determined the number of firearms recovered at crimes and identified the weapons' journey to crime.

Fusing this criminal offense data with information on gun tracing, recovered firearms, and state weapon sales information provides investigators, police executives, and policy makers with a more comprehensive picture of firearms crimes in the state. Over the last year, the project has produced a number of intelligence briefs and analytical reports that outline gun violence by youth offenders or violent trends across communities.

The CFC disseminates intelligence briefs, analyses, and crime maps to policy makers and police administrators across the state to assist with resource deployment and the design of best practices to address firearms crime. In addition, the fusion center feeds these products back to information collectors, such as investigators and patrol officers, to reinforce their information-gathering efforts. This creates buy-in from collectors and illustrates the need for high-quality, accurate data.

As the map indicates, this type of data illustrates the geographic journey to crime for guns used in crimes in Massachusetts. Rather than confirming the common wisdom that only southern states fuel gun trafficking in Massachusetts, the project found that crime-related guns can originate from a number of states within the Northeast, the South, and beyond. This has important statewide implications for criminal justice policy.

CONCLUSION

The fusion center concept involving various criminal justice agencies opens a number of possibilities for enhancing intelligence-led policing. It establishes relationships among federal, state, and local agencies, which leads to improved information sharing and access to data that often was isolated in a single agency. It also brings together subject-matter expertise that provides a more relevant and credible intelligence end product. It creates buy-in from various agencies because they had input into its design.

This particular ILP project outlines a practical application of data fusion for traditional violent crime policy, easily transferable to homeland security and terrorism issues. Using existing and newly acquired data, fusion center analysts collect, process, analyze, and disseminate timely intelligence to decision makers at the federal, state, and local levels. More knowledgeable operational, strategic, and tactical deployment choices can be made on the basis of these data-driven products. This initiative provides an example of how data fusion and fusion centers can assist in everyday law enforcement challenges.

ENDNOTES

(1) Bart Johnson, "A Look at Fusion Centers," FBI Law Enforcement Bulletin, December 2007. 28-32.

(2) David Carter, "The Law Enforcement Intelligence Function: State, Local, and Tribal Agencies," FBI Law Enforcement Bulletin, June 2005, 1-9.

(3) U.S. Department of Homeland Security and U.S. Department of Justice. Office of Justice Programs, Bureau of Justice Assistance, Fusion Center Guidelines: Developing and Sharing Information and Intelligence in a New Era (Washington, DC: 2006).

(4) Fusion Center Guidelines.

(5) U.S. Department of Justice, Office of Justice Programs, Bureau of Justice Assistance, Navigating Your Agency's Path to Intelligence-Led Policing (Washington, DC: 2009).

(6) Navigating Your Agency's Path to Intelligence-Led Policing.

(7) Navigating Your Agency's Path to Intelligence-Led Policing.

5

Palm Beach County's High-Tech Security Hub Tracks Terror Threats and Crime

Cynthia Roldan

Tucked among the winding hallways of the Palm Beach County Sheriff's Office headquarters, behind many closed doors, is a room called the Situation Room. It's where local and federal agencies gather to collect and share information.

A 12-foot-wide video wall presents direct feeds of radar and satellite images, newscasts from around the world and live feeds of cameras installed in government-owned buildings, such as Palm Beach International Airport and the Port of Palm Beach.

This hub, dubbed the Palm Beach Regional Fusion Center, also is capable of monitoring private entities, such as the Mall at Wellington Green, with the owner's consent.

With special radar capabilities, the hub is even beginning to help fight crime.

"I don't want the bad guys to know what we can do with this," said sheriff's Maj. Daniel McBride.

Originally, the center was designed to improve communication among all government agencies after the Sept. 11 attacks. It has been in the works for nearly three years and in full operation for about two months.

Roldan, C. Palm Beach County's high-tech security hub tracks terror threats and crime. Palm Beach Post (West Palm Beach, FL), Nov 30, 2010

But over time, it became clear that anti-terror efforts did not consume all of the agencies' time, McBride said. That's why the local fusion center has "morphed" into an "all-crime, all-hazards facility," he said, where its nifty tools help analysts identify patterns and trends in crime and share them with local agencies.

When the Delray Beach Police Department released the image of a bank robber a few months ago, McBride said it was a fusion center analyst who grabbed the image from a media outlet's site and used its face recognition software to map it to a person.

What came out of that match, however, is unknown to the analyst, because the privacy guidelines of the center prevent such follow-ups.

The analysts in the fusion center come from Palm Beach, Broward and Monroe counties.

Although the Miami-Dade Police Department has its own fusion center, Palm Beach County Sheriff Ric Bradshaw said Miami-Dade County representatives also participate in the regional center.

Bradshaw hopes the county's fusion center becomes part of the 72 Department of Homeland Security-approved fusion centers that are in service across the country.

Each person at the center is assigned to monitor his or her area of expertise. As a demonstration of what can be seen during an emergency situation, one analyst tapped into the security cameras at PBIA and displayed several feeds on the $150,000 video wall.

The center does not have access to cameras' zooming or panning capabilities. Nothing gets recorded at the situation room because it's used purely for surveillance purposes.

"With the cameras that we have access to, you cannot see people's faces," said Scott Nugent, fusion center director. "They are just not that kind of quality."

The center doesn't have enough personnel to watch all cameras at all times, but McBride said he would like to be able to tap into more cameras during an emergency situation. Ideally, he would like to have the capability to tap into cameras at the county's public schools, but that would require school district approval.

For those who can't be at the center, there is a Virtual Fusion Center, where agencies can enter information. McBride said the virtual center is so advanced that it has become the standard for all other fusion centers in the state.

Making the center operational cost about $700,000, Nugent said. About $400,000 was allocated from a Homeland Security grant to cover the technology costs, and $300,000 from the sheriff's office budget covered the modifications for what is now the situation room.

It costs about $100,000 a year to keep the center running, Nugent said.

An additional federal grant of about $1 million was invested in radar that allows the center to track boats throughout Palm Beach, Broward and Miami-Dade counties. McBride said the sheriff's office is the only local agency with such a system, but he did not detail its functions.

He credited the center with the rescue of three boaters who were lost at sea for two days, then found by the Navy on Aug. 8 near Jacksonville.

McBride said the center's analysts used the radar to pinpoint the last known location of the boaters and then estimated their current location if the boat had remained afloat. "We'd like to think we played a major role in bringing them back," McBride said.

Section II

POLICE AND LAW ENFORCEMENT

In Part 1, ethical behaviors of law enforcement officers and agencies are explored. As you read through the articles in this Part consider the difference between unethical behavior and criminal behavior, are these two behaviors always related? How should law enforcement agencies treat employees engaged in unethical behavior in contrast to criminal behavior?

In Part 2, the use of force by law enforcement is examined from several perspectives. Consider the following questions when reading these articles: In Eugene, OR are Tasers an effective device for officers? What appears to be the benefit? Are there any disadvantages? Are there aspects of a deadly force incident investigation that are more harmful to officer(s) involved in deadly force incidents than the use of deadly force? What can be done to reduce the harm? What are the important concerns to be addressed when teaching law enforcement officers when to use deadly force?

In Part 3, four examples of emerging technologies in law enforcement is introduced. After you read each of the articles think about which technology has the potential to be the most useful to law enforcement to accomplish their mission. Keep in mind that law enforcement agencies must consider cost, ease of use, durability, and sustainability. Considering all of these requirements, which technology should be investigated further?

In Part 4 of this section, you will read about many different approaches to make the crime prevention and reduction process more effective. Each of the articles questions our current methods of crime control. An important aspect of this Part is that crime control methods must be supported by empirical evidence that the crime control strategy is effecting some measurable change? Do any of the programs presented in the articles meet this challenge? When considering crime control strategies of your own, think about how you would propose to measure its effectiveness.

Ethical Behavior

6

Ramsey Beefs Up Philadelphia Police Ethics Strategies

Allison Steele

Faced with a growing number of officers in handcuffs, Philadelphia Police Commissioner Charles H. Ramsey announced plans Thursday to assign more officers to the department's Internal Affairs bureau, enhance officer training in ethics issues, and create new ways for officers to report misconduct among their colleagues. Ramsey said he was not sure how many officers would be transferred to Internal Affairs, but said they would be assigned to a joint task force that works with the FBI in investigating police corruption. The department is also looking at ways to make Internal Affairs a more attractive assignment for officers, Ramsey said. Much of the anticorruption plan focuses on preventing officers from making bad decisions. Whereas officers now receive most of their ethics training at the Police Academy, Ramsey said the department would create additional courses to help officers develop critical thinking and self-awareness throughout their careers.

Ramsey said the department would work to encourage officers to report colleagues when they see inappropriate behavior. "The Police Department continues to ask the public to step up and report wrongdoing," Ramsey said. "We will ask no less of its own members." The department is launching a hotline and e-mail address that go straight to Ramsey's office. Officers and the public can use them to anonymously report police misconduct. The phone number, which will be active Monday, is 215-686-3009. E-mails can be sent to police.commissioner@phila.gov.

Stelle, A. Ramsey beefs up Philadelphia police ethics strategies. Philadelphia Inquirer (Philadelphia, PA), August 6, 2010

Ramsey has tasked Patricia Giorgio-Fox, deputy commissioner for organizational accountability, with implementing the new strategies.

He was spurred to announce the plan after Kenneth Crockett, a 26-year veteran of the 6,600-plus force, was charged last week with stealing $825 from a Northeast Philadelphia bar. The announcement also followed the arrest of three police officers last month on federal charges of robbing a drug dealer. Eleven officers have been arrested since March 2009, including two on murder charges stemming from off-duty shootings. Another officer was fired this year after admitting that he fabricated a story about being shot by a black man. In fact, the officer had shot himself. Ramsey said Thursday that the department had opened investigations into several other officers, but declined to comment further. "It's a cloud," he said of the spate of scandals. "And it's going to take time for that cloud to lift. But we're not going to run from it." Ramsey has said attracting stronger recruits is a priority. Starting in 2012, new officers will have to be at least 21 and have three years of driving and two years of college classes under their belts. Standards now allow 19-year-olds with no college education and little driving experience to join the academy. The residency requirement has been modified in an effort to draw candidates from outside the city. Police experts said implementing an anticorruption plan would not be easy. Some officers arrested recently were veterans and had nothing in their backgrounds that would indicate a predilection toward criminal acts. A larger obstacle to fighting corruption is often a version of the "don't snitch" culture that officers battle when policing urban areas, said Rich Jarc, executive director of the Josephson Institute, a Los Angeles nonprofit that educates police departments on ethics. In many departments, Jarc said, it's all but demanded that officers stand together, and ratting each other out is discouraged.

"It doesn't mean that the department is totally corrupt," Jarc said. "But that cultural code of silence might be preventing some people from stopping this behavior." Ramsey said Thursday that many officers had reported misconduct by colleagues, but that the department needed to reach those who remained hesitant to do so. After Crockett's arrest on theft charges last week, Ramsey said, more information came to light from officers who knew or suspected Crockett was not always going by the book. "We've got to create an environment where people feel comfortable coming forward and reporting something," he said. "It's the right thing to do."

7

Breaking the Law to Enforce It

Undercover Police Participation in Crime

Elizabeth E. Joh

INTRODUCTION

I. UNDERCOVER PARTICIPATION IN CRIME: AN OVERVIEW
   A. The Difference Between Undercover and Conventional Policing
   B. The Contemporary Significance of Undercover Policing
   C. Types of Undercover Policing
      1. Surveillance
      2. Prevention
      3. Facilitation
   D. Participation in Crime
      1. Providing opportunities
      2. Maintaining cover and access
      3. Rogue cops

II. RULES FOR BREAKING RULES
   A. Direct Liability
      1. Mental state requirements
      2. The public authority defense
   B. The Prosecution of Targets
      1. Defenses raised by targets
         a. The entrapment defense
         b. Due process limits
      2. Eliminating barriers to conviction
   C. Internal Guidelines
   D. Authorized Criminality in Comparative Perspective

Joh, E. (2009). Breaking the law to enforce it: undercover police participation in crime. Stanford Law Review, Dec 2009 v62 i1 p155(44).

INTRODUCTION

Covert policing necessarily involves deception, which in turn often leads to participation in activity that appears to be criminal. In undercover operations, the police have introduced drugs into prison, (1) undertaken assignments from Latin American drug cartels to launder money, (2) established fencing businesses that paid cash for stolen goods and for "referrals," (3) printed counterfeit bills, (4) and committed perjury, (5) to cite a few examples. (6)

In each of these instances, undercover police engaged in seemingly illegal activity to gather evidence or to maintain their fictitious identities. Yet unless these acts are committed by "rogue cops" not authorized to participate in illegal activity, these activities aren't considered crimes. Indeed, they are considered a justifiable and sometimes necessary aspect of undercover policing.

This practice of authorized criminality is secret, unaccountable, and in conflict with some of the basic premises of democratic policing. (7) And to the extent that authorized criminality presents mixed messages about their moral standing, it undermines social support for the police. (8) While the practice isn't new, authorized criminality raises fundamental questions about the limits of acceptable police conduct and has been too long ignored.

What is authorized criminality? I define it as the practice of permitting covert police officers (9) to engage in conduct that would be criminal (10) outside of the context of the investigation. (11) We can then distinguish it from other covert policing tactics, such as passively deceptive surveillance, or the police adoption of the role of a victim rather than that of a fellow criminal. (12) Excluded too are instances where police may cross ethical boundaries but not legal ones, such as when undercover investigators stage homicides or other fictitious violent crimes in hopes of building credibility. (13) In Part I, I further situate authorized criminality in the context of covert policing, by discussing how undercover operations differ and why undercover police participate in crimes. While empirical data is limited, the available evidence shows that authorized criminality is a widely used aspect of undercover work.

In Part II, I argue that, despite its widespread use in covert operations, authorized criminality is the subject of little regulation or guidance. In the vast majority of situations, the police are immune from prosecution, so long as their actions lie within the scope of their official undercover role. A legal justification called the "public authority defense" shields these activities from criminal liability. (And the defense is rarely needed because police are very seldom prosecuted. (14)) Other potential sources of regulation, including the entrapment and due process defenses that can be raised by defendants targeted in covert operations, are equally unlikely to regulate authorized criminality in day-to-day practice.

The absence of any meaningful regulation is remarkable because, as I argue in Part III, authorized criminality implicates some of the most fundamental questions regarding the role of police in a democratic society, questions that have captivated legal scholars of the police for the past fifty years. (15) Transparency and rulemaking counterbalance the pervasive and necessary use of police discretion. Yet secrecy and untrammeled discretion characterize the participation of covert police in criminal activity. This has important practical and normative consequences. We do not know much of what covert police do or how they decide to do it. What is known-- that the police may in some circumstances act "above the law"--puts the police in a position of moral ambiguity. Enforcement tactics trump concerns about the moral standing of the state. (16)

With these harms in mind, I offer three proposals in Part IV. First, regular public reporting on the frequency and nature of authorized criminality would increase accountability. We know too little about how often and in what circumstances covert police are permitted to participate in crime. The absence of publicly available information about authorized criminality is especially troubling in light of its lax regulation, its consequences, and its increasing importance in terrorism investigations. (17) Greater transparency increases accountability, and can provide us with a basis for determining when participation in crime is not worth its benefits.

Second, the use of administrative guidelines within police departments would curb unnecessarily free discretion when police engage in authorized criminality. Courts and legislatures have expressed little interest in regulating undercover work. And though a few legal doctrines exist to limit police behavior, undercover investigators are too rarely the subject of criminal prosecution for these doctrines to provide meaningful restraint. Courts overwhelmingly deny legal challenges to undercover tactics, albeit with a discomfort exemplified in comments of one federal appellate court: "Undercover police work in general ... is an unattractive business, but that is the nature of the beast...." (18) But this ill-defined notion of necessity usually doesn't involve any consideration of competing concerns, and thus doesn't help regulate authorized criminality in any way. Administrative guidelines, by contrast, can both guide and restrain the police when difficult judgments must be made in the field.

Finally, the scholarly agenda regarding the regulation of the police must venture beyond the confines of the United States Supreme Court's concerns. Legal commentary focuses primarily on constitutional criminal procedure. (19) While undercover policing has long engaged the attention of sociologists, psychologists, and screenwriters, (20) it has failed to capture the sustained interest of legal scholars to the same degree other police practices have. (21) Undercover policing is a marginal legal academic interest. (22) Yet covert policing is rife with "complexity and paradox"; (23) so too is the particular practice of "state sanctioned lawlessness" (24) that takes the form of undercover participation in crime. One explanation for this neglect may be the "pull" of criminal procedure. To the extent that the United States Supreme Court has addressed undercover policing in the investigative stage, (25) it has found the practice to lie outside of the Fourth Amendment's protections. (26) This focus has meant that those police practices left mostly untouched by federal constitutional law lie beyond the focus of the legal academy as well. It isn't obvious, however, that authorized criminality is any less challenging to notions of democratic policing than is racial profiling or excessive force, to take two examples of extensive critical and popular interest.

I. UNDERCOVER PARTICIPATION IN CRIME: AN OVERVIEW

What is the role of authorized criminality in undercover work, and how is the latter to be distinguished from ordinary street policing? Scholars have identified several analytically useful ways of categorizing undercover work. This Part uses these categories to provide an introduction to undercover policing and the place of authorized criminality in it.

A. The Difference Between Undercover and Conventional Policing

At first glance, it may seem that the key distinction between undercover work and all other kinds of policing is deception. Deception is used, however, in many aspects of policing. (27) The detective may lie to the defendant in order to gain a confession. A uniformed officer might con an armed and barricaded suspect into providing entry by promising no arrest. And so the fact is that petty deceptions pervade the craft of effective policing. (28) The difference between these deceptions and those of undercover work may be a matter of a degree, but it is a significant one. A detective may lie in the interrogation room about the status of a case to encourage a confession: a deception of purpose. In undercover work, suspects are unaware of both the purpose and the identity of the police. (29) Indeed, the objective of undercover policing is to capture criminals in their "natural" state, although of course the irony is that the observers are duplicitous, or, in the cases of bait-sales and street crime decoys, (30) are part of the circumstances of the crime.

B. The Contemporary Significance of Undercover Policing

Investigative deception is a firmly entrenched aspect of contemporary American policing. Even critics of undercover work generally acknowledge that its elimination is neither feasible nor desirable. (31)

And two related historical developments suggest continued, if not greater, reliance upon undercover policing. First, the increasing complexity of the United States Supreme Court's criminal procedure cases in the post-Warren Court era (32) exerts a "hydraulic pressure" on the police to use techniques that the Court has chosen not to regulate as heavily as it has with regard to searches and seizures of homes, cars, and people. (33) Nowhere is this more explicit than in the Court's creation of the third-party doctrine. In a series of cases, the Court has emphatically denied Fourth Amendment protection to those who, while under police investigation, have disclosed information to third parties, whether that third party is a true criminal associate, a police informant, or an undercover investigator. (34) Criminals assume a risk that their friends are not allies at all, and the police retain a powerful investigative technique where no warrant or any other prior justification is necessary. In addition, the Court has held the Miranda warnings inapplicable in the context of undercover interrogations. (35)

Second, over the past fifty years, the police have gradually deemphasized physically coercive techniques in favor of others that emphasize psychological coercion or deception. Evidence once obtained by the "third degree" or other similarly brutal tactics is neither tolerated by legal constraints nor social mores. (36) Deception, whether in an investigation or the interrogation room, is one of the tools the police have come to rely upon in the place of brute force.

C. Types of Undercover Policing

Unlike an impulsive or opportunistic crime, some crimes involve secretive, complex, and consensual activities. The manufacture of methamphetamine, (37) the bribery of local officials, (38) food stamp fraud, (39) prostitution, (40) dogfighting rings, (41) and, at one time, homosexuality, (42) are examples of such offenses, and they are difficult, if not impossible, to investigate if the police must wait for victim complaints, witness statements, or physical evidence. (43) If these crimes are to be prosecuted successfully, then the police must infiltrate criminal ranks or play willing victims.

Such undercover operations are not the specialty of a few departments, but are instead used widely among police departments of varied sizes. Likewise, undercover operations are usually used as an initial course of action rather than as a means used when others have failed. (44) A leading scholar of undercover policing, sociologist Gary Marx, identifies three different types of undercover investigations, distinguished by their varying objectives: (1) surveillance or intelligence operations, which are the most passive activities, followed by (2) preventive operations, which take a more active approach, and (3) facilitative operations, which require the most active involvement of the police. (45)

1. Surveillance

Surveillance operations use deceptive techniques to gather information about completed, ongoing, or planned crimes. The undercover agent's primary role is to gather information, rather than to influence events. Most surveillance operations are anticipatory rather than postliminary. (46) Thus, while some undercover investigations seek missing persons or goods (i.e., crimes that have already taken place), most target crimes that have not yet occurred. Undercover agents may be sent into various settings--prisons, schools, bars, or other institutions where malfeasance is suspected-- and be instructed to look out for suspicious activity. (47) Given the limited ambition of the operation, the possibilities for impermissible police encouragement--entrapment--of targets is less likely in these investigations than they are in facilitative operations. (48)

2. Prevention

Requiring more action than surveillance investigations, preventive undercover activities seek to stop an offense from taking place at all, or at the very least, make its commission much more difficult. Prevention may take the form of weakening or diverting the suspect: an undercover agent planted in a political demonstration advocating violence may try to defuse the crowd by arguing for nonviolence. (49) Alternatively, the operation may focus on strengthening victims ("target hardening"): a law enforcement agency may advertise "get rich quick" schemes to lure unsuspecting customers for the purpose of providing them with warnings and advice against future fraud. (50)

3. Facilitation

In contrast to preventive operations, facilitative ones attempt to encourage the commission of an offense, either through strengthening suspects or by weakening potential victims. This may be done by the provision of aid, encouragement, goods, resources, or markets for the suspect. The role that undercover agents play in facilitative operations depends on whether they are posing as accomplices or as easy victims. In the former case, cops play the willing car thief, fence, hit man, or corrupt politician. (51) In the latter, police may pose individually as decoys for assaults or pickpocketing, or in more complex investigations agents may set up a house of prostitution or a business ripe for extortion. (52)

The nature of facilitative operations has changed over time. While traditional covert investigations involve targeted policing based upon intelligence, covert policing has expanded to include more diffuse and open-ended investigations premised on probabilities and temptations, and thus without specific suspicions, complaints, or suspects. (53) Today, not only are facilitative operations aimed at traditional vice crimes such as narcotics use and prostitution, they have also expanded into areas such as the "integrity testing" of public officials. (54)

Of the three types of covert policing outlined here, facilitative operations are the most controversial. The possibility of police entrapment is most likely in a scenario where the police are actively encouraging crime. And whether or not a particular investigation meets the high hurdle of legal entrapment, (55) the conscious decision on the part of the police to create "opportunity structures" for the commission of crimes leaves many uneasy. Police may pose as motorists to catch extortionist traffic police, as small business owners vulnerable to shakedowns by health inspectors, and as corrupt politicians agreeable to influence. (56) While surveillance and preventive operations have analogues in conventional policing, facilitative operations attempt to maintain a fine balance of creating criminal opportunities in order to impose crime control. (57) From the police perspective, facilitative operations use fewer resources and produce the necessary evidence and arrests more quickly than a surveillance operation can.

Facilitative operations also raise the serious issue of crime amplification: the possibility that the very undercover investigation meant to catch criminals in the act may actually produce more crime. (58) Crime amplification can refer to the crime targeted by the investigation; would it have occurred but for the existence of the investigation itself The concerns of crime amplification can, however, extend much more broadly: what unintended criminal consequences did the facilitation produce? In the latter category, facilitative operations may generate the following effects: the production of black markets that generate funds for more crimes; the introduction of ideas, motives, and confidence for further offenses; and the presentation of attractive temptations to those not specifically targeted by the investigation but who nevertheless take advantage of the opportunity created by the police. (59)

D. Participation in Crime

Undercover officers participate in authorized crimes for a number of different reasons. Two of the most important are: (1) to provide opportunities for the suspects to engage in the target crime, and (2) to maintain a false identity or to facilitate access to the suspect. These needs are at their greatest in facilitative operations, when police must both maintain their covert identities as well as encourage the commission of crime (short of entrapment). As discussed in Part II, the police may legally participate in crime so long as the conduct furthers legitimate objectives. When undercover officers stray from crime control objectives and participate in crime, however, these "rogue cops" leave the bounds of authorized criminality and become mere criminals themselves.

1. Providing opportunities

In facilitative operations, the police furnish a simulated environment (60) that can be as elaborate as the establishment of a false business or as simple as the presentation of a false identity as an especially vulnerable victim. (61) Many of these facilitative activities would constitute crimes had the police agents not been given the authorization to commit them.

In the most commonplace stings, the police may pretend to be drug users or illegal gun buyers looking for a willing seller. (62) In variations of "reverse stings," undercover officers may provide the illegal drugs themselves, the chemicals necessary for drug manufacture, or the "buy" money to the suspects. In United States v. Russell, for example, the United States Supreme Court upheld the government's supply of a chemical (phenyl-2propanone) to the defendant so that he could use it to manufacture methamphetamine. The Court observed that "the infiltration of drug rings and a limited participation in their unlawful ... practices" is a "recognized and permissible means of investigation...." (63)

2. Maintaining cover and access

Police participation in crime can also play an important part in maintaining an officer's covert status. (64) Criminals try to flush out suspected undercover investigators by testing their willingness to engage in crime. (65) A reluctance to participate on the part of an apparent criminal associate can "jinx a deal and arouse suspicion" in a covert investigation. (66) Without the police playing their fictitious roles as closely as possible, criminals could easily exclude those suspected of infiltrating their ranks simply by refusing to tolerate passive behavior. (67) The need for such participation is well recognized. For instance, in affirming the conviction of a defendant over his objections to an undercover officer's participation in drug use, an Ohio appellate court stated that "an undercover agent engaged in the business of trying to stamp out the illicit drug traffic may smoke marijuana in order to give the appearance of validity to his conduct." (68)

This participation in crime may not always dampen suspicions. A suspicious drug dealer may pride himself upon identifying the signs of a "narc": a disheveled appearance that nevertheless looks staged, a physical bearing that betrays the quasi-militaristic culture of the police, and eyes that look "alive" and untouched by real addiction. (69) Authorized criminality is just one of the dramaturgical tools needed by the undercover officer for maintaining the deception. (70)

And participation in crime may not always be triggered by suspicion. The police may decide that participation in offenses increases access to a target, even if an agent's false identity is not in question. Thus, for example, a deep cover operative in a criminal organization may deem it necessary to participate in crimes in order to rise in the hierarchy and gain access to the organization's upper echelons. Or, undercover officers may conduct buy and busts in order to "flip and roll" drug dealers, i.e., turn them into informants. (71)

3. Rogue cops

Finally, the isolation, stress, and psychological toll of undercover work (72) sometimes lead undercover investigators to exceed the bounds of authorized criminality altogether, and participate in offenses as ordinary criminals. It is not entirely uncommon for undercover cops to "go native" and believe in the truth of their own fictive identities. (73)

The practice of authorized criminality may contribute directly to this problem. The conceptual line between authorized and unauthorized criminality is clear: unauthorized crimes further no law enforcement purpose. In the trenches, however, the difference between pretending to use drugs to maintain cover and using drugs to socialize with "friends" in the criminal underworld may be a difficult distinction to draw, particularly for those investigators who are asked to assume "deep cover" roles in which true identities must remain deeply suppressed for long periods of time. (74) In these situations, the costs and visibility of unauthorized criminal participation are low, while opportunities are pervasive. (75)

II. RULES FOR BREAKING RULES

Although courts and commentators have acknowledged that the practice of authorized criminality is troubling but necessary, the conditions under which undercover police officers may participate in crime have seldom been the subject of regulatory oversight. (76) Instead, what exists is a patchwork of applicable state and federal constitutional law restraints that loosely regulates undercover operations and generally accepts that undercover officers "violate the letter of the law in order to catch criminals." (77) This Part describes the relevant doctrines--the direct criminal liability of police officers engaged in authorized criminality, limitations on the prosecution of targets caught in undercover operations, and administrative guidelines within police departments--and concludes with a brief discussion of the experiences of other countries.

A. Direct Liability

Instances in which undercover police officers have faced prosecution are rare. (78) Nevertheless, it is possible that a police officer who participates in criminal activity during an undercover investigation might be prosecuted. If such a prosecution arises, mental state requirements and the public authority defense are likely to shield the officer from criminal liability.

1. Mental state requirements

In a number of instances, an undercover officer who participates in criminal activity will lack the mental state of an applicable crime, and so risks no criminal liability. (79) The traditional distinction between general and specific intent crimes illustrates the problem. For example, many (though not all) drug possession offenses require a specific intent to sell or distribute. (80) An undercover officer who only pretends to be a drug seller will lack any such specific intent; the mental state of the offense required for criminal liability does not exist.

2. The public authority defense

In other instances, the police participation will appear to meet the substantive definition of a crime. In the unlikely event that an undercover officer were prosecuted for his participation in crime, the public authority defense, recognized in every American jurisdiction, (81) would justify his actions and relieve him of criminal responsibility. Not limited to the undercover context, the affirmative defense, also known as the law enforcement authority defense, justifies otherwise-criminal conduct when that action is taken by a police officer (or a private person under the direction of a police officer) in order to effectuate an arrest, to stop a fleeing criminal, or to prevent a crime. (82) The defense exists so that the threat of criminal prosecution will not hamper police objectives, but it, like other defenses, has important limitations. The police conduct must be authorized, (83) and the means used by the police must be necessary. (84) Some jurisdictions may also impose an additional proportionality limitation. (85) Thus, for example, a police officer cannot resort to physical force if psychological coercion (such as a "command voice") would suffice; (86) nor could a police officer shoot (i.e., use deadly force against) a fleeing pickpocket. (87)

Since the public authority defense permits the police to engage in otherwise illegal conduct for legitimate law enforcement purposes, then it certainly should apply to the undercover context. (88) This "wholesale" immunity is not limited to the commission of particular crimes, nor is it limited to special categories of police personnel. (89)

As with self-defense and other criminal law justifications, the law enforcement defense exists to justify conduct that otherwise meets the elements of a criminal offense because of an overriding principle. Necessity and proportionality may be readily determined in the use of force by the police, but in the undercover context such determinations are more difficult. How, for instance, should we make a necessity determination when the police participate in a money laundering scheme and the reason for such participation is the success of a long-term undercover operation whose exact parameters have not yet been determined? Not every use of covert policing exhibits these ambiguities, but they do exist in long-term, facilitative, and open-ended investigations, where concerns about police use of authorized criminality are greatest. (90)

Whatever its conceptual underpinnings, the limits of the public authority defense have not been rigorously tested. Instances in which undercover police have used this defense are rare because they are seldom, if ever, prosecuted. (91) Prosecutorial discretion thus bolsters the "blanket" immunity of undercover investigators. (92) Most undercover police can be confident that they will not be prosecuted, and may indeed receive explicit assurances from the local prosecutor before the operation even begins. (93) For practical purposes, then, the use of the defense for authorized criminality largely exists as a scholarly curiosity. (94)

B. The Prosecution of Targets

Police engage in authorized criminality to obtain the necessary evidence for the successful prosecution of their targets. The entrapment and due process defenses, however, provide limitations on what the police may do. A successful defense raised by the target will bar prosecution. Courts have not interpreted these defenses very strictly, however. In addition, the trend of modem substantive criminal law has been to encourage undercover activity and discourage claims by defendants that they have committed no offense.

1. Defenses raised by targets

a. The entrapment defense

In cases where the target of the investigation claims that he was illegally induced by the police into committing a crime, the target can raise an entrapment defense to his prosecution. Raising the entrapment defense is a claim that one has, for instance, been bullied by an undercover agent into selling thousands of pseudoephedrine pills, (95) encouraged to solicit sex from an apparently underage girl on the Internet, (96) or cajoled into providing liquor to an undercover officer during Prohibition. (97)

The doctrine of entrapment is really a means to identify those facilitative investigations (98) that have crossed a line between the permissible and impermissible police encouragement of crime. (99) The judicially created doctrine imposes a limitation of reasonableness on the use of undercover techniques so that otherwise innocent persons are not unfairly selected and then pressured into committing a crime. (100) In the so-called "subjective" approach to entrapment that is used in a majority of jurisdictions, the police cannot induce a target who was otherwise not personally disposed to commit the offense. (101)

But the entrapment defense poorly regulates authorized criminality. A successful entrapment defense immunizes a criminal defendant from prosecution, (102) and so puts the police on notice as to what conduct will thwart a successful prosecution in the future. (103) But because the entrapment defense focuses primarily on the defendant's predisposition to criminality rather than the level or degree of police encouragement, the doctrine has not prompted courts to devise a "meaningful definition of what constitute[s] impermissible participation in the offense" (104) by the police. Most instances of police participation will not constitute entrapment (105) so long as the defendant was a ready and willing criminal. (106) The police may also deliberately thwart an anticipated defense. For instance, an undercover officer may act specifically with the intent to undermine an anticipated entrapment defense by, for instance, developing conversations with the target that demonstrate very explicitly the target's personal motivations for committing a crime. (107) In sum, because successful entrapment defenses are relatively rare, (108) they pose an impractical source of regulating police behavior. (109)

b. Due process limits

Even in cases where the defendant has failed to prove entrapment (because of his predisposition to commit the offense), (110) the conduct of the police may nevertheless in some cases violate due process rights. (111) The standard used in the due process analysis varies, (112) but the basic principle underlying the claim in successful cases is that the police conduct has violated basic principles of justice and fairness. (113)

One example: Two undercover officers repeatedly tried but failed to obtain cocaine from their targets, Stanley Robinson and Bobby Shine. Robinson, tired of being badgered at his local bar, sold the officers a bag of sugar. Enraged by the deception, the undercover officers, after drinking for several hours, entered Robinson's home in the middle of the night with a brandished weapon and a demand for drugs or money. Searches of Robinson and Shine at gunpoint yielded two bags of cocaine. In reversing Shine's conviction, the state appeals court noted that this was "one of those rare cases" where police conduct constituted a denial of due process. (114)

But such a case is exceptional. In the undercover context, such claims of outrageous government conduct rarely succeed. (115) Generally, judges are reluctant to impose restrictions on the lengths the police may go in undercover operations by participating in authorized crimes. Some judges have expressed the view that there is, in theory, a limit to what the police can do, but few, if any, cases are found to cross that line. (116) Even when they do, the due process standard doesn't guide future police action particularly well. If the police may not manufacture crack cocaine for use in reverse stings because it is "outrageous," (117) why does the sale of "ordinary" cocaine in a reverse sting pass muster? (118) No clear standard defines acceptable from unacceptable police conduct.

The due process defense is unlikely, then, to regulate authorized criminality in any effective way. Like the entrapment defense, a successful due process defense immunizes the defendant from criminal liability, rather than sanctioning the police officer directly. As for the police whose conduct is considered so outrageous that it violates due process, the due process defense doesn't add more regulatory oversight than that provided by the public authority defense. Presumably, undercover officers engaging in outrageous conduct are not acting in an "authorized" manner, (119) and consequently face criminal liability through direct prosecution. (120)

2. Eliminating barriers to conviction

As the previous sections show, a defendant can rarely raise an entrapment or due process defense with success. Moreover, the trend of American criminal law has been one of removing barriers to conviction in the undercover context. The Model Penal Code's reform approach to inchoate crimes reflects this view. (121)

At common law, the defense of "legal impossibility"--but not "factual impossibility"--permits a defendant charged with attempt to avoid criminal responsibility. (122) Thus a person could not be guilty of attempting to shoot a stuffed deer out of deer season in the belief that it was alive--a case of legal impossibility--but could be guilty of attempted murder by shooting into the empty bed of his victim--a case of factual impossibility. (123) Under the traditional approach, an undercover sting might prevent the conviction of the defendant for attempt, as in the famous case of Booth v. State. There, the defendant successfully raised a legal impossibility defense in his prosecution for an attempt to receive stolen property; the police interception of the coat before it reached Booth's hands had rid the coat of its "stolen" character. (124) The Model Penal Code's elimination of any impossibility defense resolves the difficulty many jurisdictions faced in distinguishing between the two categories. (125) Booth would have been guilty under the Code. (126)

This is also the case with the crime of conspiracy. The bilateral requirement of common law conspiracy means that there must be at least two people who agree to conspire, thus barring conviction where the target "conspires" with an undercover officer. (127) As with attempt, the Model Penal Code facilitates convictions in these situations by eliminating the bilateral requirement. (128)

In these two respects, the Code, a reform project of the American Law Institute, (129) embodies an approach seeking to make apprehension and prosecution of persons through undercover operations easier. And the approach is consistent with the Code's general aim to punish those who have demonstrated an antisocial mental state. (130)

These developments in substantive criminal law, along with the relatively infrequent use of criminal prosecutions for police, reflect a permissive attitude and "largely instrumental focus" (131) in American law regarding undercover policing and authorized criminality in particular. Neither legislatures nor courts have shown any enthusiasm for regulating authorized criminality in any significant way.

C. Internal Guidelines

Internal departmental or agency guidelines provide another source of potential control over authorized criminality in undercover operations. (132) At the federal level, the Department of Justice refers to the Attorney General's Guidelines on Federal Bureau of Investigation Undercover Operations, (133) most recently revised in 2002. (134) "Ordinary" undercover operations require prior approval by the Special Agent in Charge of each FBI office, based on a written determination that the proposed investigation will be effective and that it will be conducted in a minimally intrusive way. (135) When especially sensitive circumstances exist, such as the proposed investigation of public officials, media organizations, or an alleged terrorist organization, an Undercover Review Committee consisting of Department of Justice and FBI officials must approve the proposed undercover operation. (136) Ordinarily, an authorized undercover operation may last up to six months, subject to a six-month renewal, and involve expenditures of no more than $100,000. (137)

The Guidelines also explicitly consider the involvement of FBI agents in illegal activity during the course of an undercover operation, referred to as "otherwise illegal activity": "any activity that would constitute a violation of Federal, state, or local law if engaged in by a private person acting without authorization." (138) In an ordinary undercover operation, the Guidelines explicitly forbid undercover officials from participating in violent acts except as a matter of self defense, encouraging criminal activity in a manner that would constitute legal entrapment, (139) and using illegal investigative techniques such as illegal wiretapping. (140)

The Special Agent in Charge may, however, authorize undercover FBI agents to participate in certain offenses such as the payment of bribes, the purchase of stolen or contraband goods, money laundering (though not more than five transactions not to exceed $1 million), the controlled delivery of drugs (so long as they do not enter commerce), and the making of false representations to third parties. (141) Any official providing authorization for illegal activity must consider that illegal activity is justified only if it is needed to obtain evidence that is not otherwise "reasonably available," to establish or maintain a secret identity, or to prevent death or serious bodily injury. (142) Felonies not specified in the Guidelines are considered sensitive circumstances that must be approved by the Undercover Review Committee as well as the FBI Director, Assistant Director, Deputy Director, or Executive Assistant Director, depending on the circumstances. (143) In all cases, the Guidelines mandate that all "reasonable steps" be taken to minimize the participation by FBI agents in illegal activity. (144)

There is, however, one important limitation to the Guidelines: they are non-binding. (145) The Guidelines, meant for "internal DOJ guidance" only, state that they

> are not intended to, do not, and may not be relied upon to create any rights, substantive or procedural, enforceable by law by any party in any matter, civil or criminal, nor do they place any limitations on otherwise lawful investigative or litigative prerogatives of the Department of Justice. (146)

Thus while a violation of the Guidelines may reflect a breach of agency policy, the Guidelines lack the regulatory teeth of a statute or judicially created doctrine that might impose sanctions on the police or provide a defense to a target of an undercover investigation.

Internal guidelines at the federal level, moreover, do not provide a representative picture of administrative rulemaking over covert policing. American policing takes place primarily at the local, and not the national level. According to recent figures, local and state police agencies employ about 770,000 police officers, (147) compared to, for instance, only 12,242 FBI officers. (148)

At the state and local level, the use of guidelines for undercover operations varies greatly; no systematic collection or review of such guidelines exists. A 1994 survey of eighty-nine police departments around the country yielded varied results. (149) While all the departments surveyed conducted undercover operations, only a subset--sixty-two of them--had written guidelines. Of those with guidelines for undercover work, more than half emphasized procedural rules (such as steps for checking out equipment and the proper method of filling out forms (150)) rather than authorization issues (such as when or why operations should be initiated (151)). In their conclusion, the study authors expressed "surprise[] to learn that 23 large municipal police agencies using undercover police work did not have written guidelines" at all. (152)

D. Authorized Criminality in Comparative Perspective

American law is aimed at responding to abuses in undercover policing, but not at regulating ordinary practices. (153) But not all democratic societies provide such "wholesale" immunity for undercover policing. (154) Consider two sources of comparison:

Italian law begins with the presumption that the practice of authorized criminality is illegal. (155) Rather than provide a wholesale form of immunity for authorized criminality in covert investigations, Italian law provides for statutory exemptions that shield Italian police from criminal liability on a crime-by-crime basis. (156) Unlike their American counterparts, then, Italian undercover investigators face a real risk of prosecution if their participation in crime is not expressly authorized by statute, even if the police conduct is meant to further a law enforcement objective. (157) For instance, a specific statute insulates undercover police from criminal liability for participating in drug buys. (158) A reluctance to provide undercover police broader immunity for illegal acts reflects a concern that to do so would "corrode the rule of law." (159)

In Canada, the Parliament addressed authorized criminality directly in response to a 1999 decision of its supreme court, R. v. Campbell. (160) The disputed police activity in Campbell was a garden-variety reverse sting: federal police officers offered to sell a large quantity of hashish to the defendants. (161) The Canadian Supreme Court held that absent direct Parliamentary exemption, police were not clearly immune from criminal prosecution for actions that would be otherwise illegal. (162) While the Canadian Narcotic Control Act explicitly permitted officers to possess illegal drugs in covert operations, no such provision existed for their sale. As a direct result of the Campbell decision, some covert operations were suspended or closed to avoid the potential prosecution of officers in covert operations. (163)

In 2001, the Canadian Parliament enacted a law enforcement justification defense to clarify the status of authorized criminality and to set limits upon its use. 164 Section 25 of the Canadian Criminal Code provides for a justification for otherwise illegal acts committed by the police in the course of an investigation. A police officer may commit an action that is otherwise considered illegal so long as it is "reasonable and proportional in the circumstances." This assessment should take into account factors such as the nature of the authorized criminality, the nature of the operation, and the "reasonable availability of other means for carrying out the public officer's law enforcement duties." (165) While the defense is not limited to specified offenses, excluded from its application are those actions taken by the police which result in "death or bodily harm," constitute a violation of the "sexual integrity of an individual," or a "willful attempt" to obstruct justice. (166) In addition, the statute requires police departments to publish annual reports providing details on the frequency and nature of the acts covered by the defense. (167)

III. THE HARMS OF POLICE PARTICIPATION IN CRIMINAL ACTIVITY

While police, prosecutors, and judges may view authorized criminality in undercover policing as a sometimes unpleasant but practical necessity, the tactic exacts its costs. Some commentators have pointed out that undercover policing by its very nature risks significant social harms because it necessarily involves deception and secrecy. (168) The practice of authorized criminality raises even more serious problems because it adds the perception of criminality to an investigative technique that is already secretive and deceptive. We can't consider the real merits of authorized criminality without weighing the crime control benefits against the harms it visits upon the police and the public's perception of them.

This Part considers three different kinds of harms posed by authorized criminality: the lack of transparency about basic information regarding authorized criminality, the exercise of unfettered police discretion, and the moral ambiguity that arises when police engage in criminal activity in order to pursue criminals.

A. Transparency and Police Action

Police decisions about authorized criminality in undercover operations lack basic accountability because of their largely secret nature. There are no widespread norms regarding systematic data collection on undercover policing generally or with regard to the nature and extent of authorized criminality specifically. (169)

Indeed, those seeking detailed official information on authorized criminality are likely to encounter difficulty. The exemption of federal law enforcement procedures and techniques from the Freedom of Information Act (FOIA) requirements is illustrative. (170) The FOIA provides a person with a legally enforceable fight to obtain access to federal agency records, provided that the information does not fall within one of nine exemptions. (171) Among the Act's nine categorical exemptions is Exemption 7(E), which permits nondisclosure of law enforcement information where it "would disclose techniques and procedures for law enforcement investigations or prosecutions, or would disclose guidelines for law enforcement investigations or prosecutions if such disclosure could reasonably be expected to risk circumventions of the law." (172) The exemption consists of two separate clauses, both of which have been construed broadly by courts to permit non-disclosure of law enforcement procedures, policies, and records.

(173) While the second clause ("circumventions of the law") permits withholding of information based on an assessment of harm to law enforcement interests, the first clause is even more expansive, permitting nondisclosure of a law enforcement procedure without any demonstration of a harmed interest.

While the "techniques and procedures" that fall under the scope of Exemption 7(E) have been interpreted as those not generally available to the public, even commonly known techniques have been protected as exempt from FOIA requests when "the circumstances of their usefulness.., may not be widely known." (174) Thus, while undercover policing is a widely known investigative technique, courts have upheld the non-disclosure of information pertaining to specific undercover practices, on the grounds that disclosure of particular techniques would reduce their effectiveness. (175) In fact, nondisclosure has been justified as especially warranted when the technique itself--whether the use of polygraph examinations, (176) bait money, (177) or undercover policing--is meant to operate with some secrecy. (178)

The absence of systematic and specific information is not limited to the undercover context. Although publicly available data is used to monitor many types of executive decision making in modem government, such transparency is often absent in the exercise of police authority. (179) Erik Luna has forcefully argued that a democratic conception of police discretion necessitates the "systemic visibility" of official police actions and justifications. (180) Hiding police decisions from public view, whether or not those decisions are legal or publicly supported, is never benign. (181)

The simple absence of transparency in police decisionmaking can be destructive, both in its potential to breed police abuse as well as to foment public distrust. There is little available public knowledge about the frequency, nature, and conditions of authorized criminality in undercover work. Yet the practice suggests a normative paradox: here the state permits the police to act seemingly "above the law" as they enforce the law. Rather than allay concerns about authorized criminality by holding it up to public scrutiny, the reality is that it is itself a practice under cover. Secrecy suggests that there may be illegitimate reasons to hide the decision making process in this area. Moreover, the potential for abuse is greater when little or no public oversight is available to weigh in upon police decision making.

Finally, cordoning off police decisions from public scrutiny encourages public distrust of the police. As a number of studies of public attitudes toward policing have shown, trust is much more effective as a foundation for public compliance with the law than the threat of punishment or reliance upon personal morality. (182) Public distrust not only conflicts with democratic norms, but a public wary of the police is much less likely to be a legally compliant or cooperative one. (183)

B. Unfettered Discretion

In many instances, undercover officers (and their departments) who participate in authorized crimes also lack significant constraints on their discretion, a situation that lies in tension with basic principles of democratic law enforcement as well as the historical concern about placing restraints on police discretion.

1. Police discretion and democratic policing

The "discovery" of police discretion in the 1950s by police researchers introduced a topic of study and a set of issues that continue to occupy scholars and judges to this day. (184) By itself the concept is uncontroversial; discretion exists whenever two or more choices are available to the decision maker. (185) The police exercise discretion out of necessity. While they may be entitled to exercise their legal authority in many situations, factors that are both practical and symbolic influence what they decide to do in practice. Budgetary concerns can serve as practical constraints, and the attitudes of the community policed can also influence priorities of enforcement. (186) Finally, the culture of the police themselves--a distinct world view emphasizing danger and authority--heavily influences the kinds of persons who are targeted for police interest. (187)

Yet discretion is especially problematic for the police in a democratic society. (188) We ask the police to assume the primary role in enforcing the law and imposing public order, while armed-- quite literally--with the ability to rely upon the state's monopoly over legitimate force. (189) At the same time, we expect the police, within the framework of their legal, practical, and symbolic constraints, to exercise their authority fairly. (190)

A great deal of scholarly and practical attention on the police has focused on restricting and guiding this police discretion. Indeed, "police discretion" simpliciter is something of a dirty word, evoking less the motorist let off with a warning than the minority-race motorist stopped for a legally adequate but ethically suspect reason.

Although many of the criminal procedure cases reaching the United States Supreme Court have raised issues of police discretion, the Court has been reluctant to restrict police in their ability to make a variety of decisions in the investigative process. Thus, for instance, the police may: conduct an inventory search of a defendant's car so long as the search is exercised according to some minimal criteria; (191) stop a motorist for a legally adequate reason even if it is not the actual reason for the detention; (192) and arrest someone for a very minor crime if the applicable law permits arrest, even if most police officers would issue only a citation. (193) One area where the Court has reined in discretion is in vagrancy laws so vaguely written that they provide the police with broad license to detain anyone they wish. In its most recent decision of this kind, the Court struck down a Chicago anti-gang ordinance that permitted the police to arrest those on the streets without any apparent purpose. (194)

Ironically enough, the Court's striking down of the Chicago law prompted a robust advocacy of decreased judicial control over police discretion regarding "quality of life" offenses. This policing approach, focusing on the enforcement of minor crimes such as littering and open container laws, (195) has been used on the ground with success in New York and elsewhere. (196) The scholarly debate does not so much focus on the desirability of the "broken windows" approach as question whether a traditional reliance on constitutional void-for-vagueness concerns or a community oversight model should serve as the primary source of constraint over police discretion. (197)

The dominant theme regarding discretion is apparent: we begin with the assumption that wholly unfettered police discretion is undesirable and probably harmful, not just to the individuals who are on the wrong end of unwise exercises of discretion, but also to the public whose support for the police in a democratic society is essential.

2. Discretion and authorized criminality

When should undercover police participate in crimes? Which crimes should they participate in? How many times and for how long should this participation last? Few legal restrictions constrain undercover police regarding the scope of their permissible conduct in the case of authorized criminality as a practical matter. (198) These critical questions are left to individual agencies and departments to decide. (199) The police have considerable latitude over undercover operations, which can range from a straightforward "buy and bust" to a deep undercover operation that may last years (200) and require significant psychological and social adjustments for the officers involved. (201) The applicable legal doctrines--the defenses of public authority, entrapment, and denial of due process--are invoked so infrequently, let alone successfully, in cases of authorized criminality, that as limits they are more theoretical than practical. (202)

Instead, courts often justify authorized criminality by a vaguely defined principle of necessity. For example, if necessity requires a balancing of costs and benefits, few courts consider the potential harms when undercover investigators participate in crime. Typically, courts take the view that "criminal proceedings are not designed to establish the relative equities among police and defendants." (203) While a few opinions have expressed ambivalence about the "unattractive business" (204) of investigative deception while affirming a target's conviction, courts tend not to delve too deeply into the issues raised by undercover policing that have been discussed here. Instead, they frequently find it sufficient to declare that authorized criminality is a necessary though unpleasant evil.

In United States v. Murphy, for instance, the Seventh Circuit considered a prosecution obtained as a result of "Operation Greylord," a complex undercover operation aimed at targeting fixed cases in Cook County, Illinois. The FBI contrived an elaborate undercover operation in which agents staged fictitious cases in the Cook County Courts by posing as defendants and lawyers. In upholding the conviction of John Murphy, a former state judge, the Seventh Circuit rejected his contention that the government's fake cases prohibited them from pursuing crooked judges:

> Murphy's complaint is a more traditional objection to creative acts by prosecutors.... In Operation Greylord agents of the FBI took the stand in the Circuit Court of Cook County and lied about their made-up cases. Perjury is a crime, and Murphy tells us that those who commit crimes themselves cannot prosecute others' crimes.... Bribery ... is a secret act. Because the crime leaves no complaining witness, active participation by the agents may be necessary to establish an effective case. (205)

Ultimately, the Court's refusal to disapprove of the police tactics in Operation Greylord rests on the view that even if the police tactics appear unpalatable, social disgust is not the appropriate measure: "In the pursuit of crime the Government is not confined to behavior suitable for the drawing room." (206) Other courts have made similar observations. (207)

Likewise, police and prosecutors have deemed it an essential tool for investigation and in some cases superior to the available alternatives, such as exclusive reliance upon confidential informants.

(208) This has been a view held even in times when intense public scrutiny has been directed at undercover tactics. In the late 1970s, the FBI initiated an undercover investigation, later known as ABSCAM, in which covert agents and con-man-turned-informant, Melvin Weinberg, posed as representatives of a fictitious sheik seeking favors from public officials--including members of Congress--in exchange for money. (209) Although the investigation eventually resulted in a number of convictions, the FBI's tactics drew controversy and eventually the attention of Congress, which held a series of hearings to examine FBI undercover techniques. (210) In its final report issued in 1982, the Senate Select Committee to Study Undercover Activities, while concerned about the "serious risks to citizens' property, privacy, and civil liberties," as well as to "law enforcement itself" posed by undercover investigations, nevertheless stated that "some use of the undercover technique is indispensable to the achievement of effective law enforcement." (211)

The problem with these justifications, however, is that they extend too broadly. Shielded by an expansive view of necessity, undercover policing enjoys little in the way of searching judicial or legislative scrutiny. Limiting discretion in covert policing is not a priority.

C. Moral Ambiguity

Moral ambiguity is a third significant consequence imposed by the participation of undercover officers in authorized crimes. Those harmed by this moral ambiguity include not only the participating police but also the larger community.

1. Moral uncertainty and the undercover officer

a. The stress of deception
Undercover work exacts many personal costs from individual investigators. Occupational hazards are legion. Not only must the undercover officer present and maintain a credible false identity in a criminal milieu, often he must also gain the confidence of his criminal associates. Accidental disclosure can result in violence against the agent, or, at the very least, the abrupt end of the investigation. These tasks and decisions take place in isolation from other police officers, with the more difficult "deep cover" assignments assumed with even less oversight and less frequent regular supervisory contact. (212) In addition to these risk factors, some departments prefer to use young recruits or relatively inexperienced officers as undercover agents, in part because they pose a smaller risk of recognition by targets. (213) A young detective

plucked directly from the police academy and assigned to a two-year
deep cover role to investigate Islamic extremists in Brooklyn
received no undercover training prior to assignment and remained in
contact only with his supervisor, at first only by email. (214)

And the more time spent as an undercover agent, the greater
the risk that personal problems will appear. A number of studies have
documented the harms visited upon undercover officers: corruption,
disciplinary problems, alcohol and drug abuse, (215) interpersonal
problems, (216) a "loss of self," and paranoia. (217) In extreme
cases, the agents "go native" and become indistinguishable from their
targets. (218)

Some of the unique risks and harms to the individual officer
can be attributed to the paradoxical nature of the job itself. (219)
Because undercover work requires the presentation of a false identity,
deception and secrecy are essential skills to the job. Important too is
the ability to adapt to the changing demands of the criminal
underworld. Thus, successful undercover investigators tend to be
those who are especially adept at dissimulation and risk-taking. (220)
One undercover officer told a researcher that in deep-cover work in
particular the agent "'must have the ability to improvise' because
'there are no rules' to deep-cover work and the person must be
'basically deceitful.'" (221) These same officers, however, are also
expected to maintain high standards of professional integrity and to
avoid temptations to delve into unauthorized activity in the midst of a
social setting where the normal constraints of social convention are
loosened or wholly absent. (222)

And the irony of this pretense is that it may become reality.
Undercover officers can feel torn between actual camaraderie that
develops between them and their targets, and the larger purpose for
which they have been assigned. (223) Similarly, undercover agents
can develop romantic relationships with targets that muddy their
priorities. (224) Along with these changed loyalties there may
emerge altered attitudes and beliefs, including changed beliefs about
the propriety of law itself. (225)

b. The harm of engaging in authorized crime
Permitting agents to participate in crimes adds yet another layer of
strain to this tangle of conflicting demands and loyalties by
heightening role confusion. Maintaining a dual identity is by itself a
difficult task. When the agent is permitted in his official capacity to
participate in crime, this may be justifiable and non-criminal as a
legal matter, (226) but to the agent, this authorized criminality is, in
psychological terms, not a mere simulation. (227) There is

56

camaraderie in a band of thieves; participating in the same crimes as those being investigated increases the risk of over-identification with targets.

Authorized criminality may also contribute to the "moral corrosion" of the undercover agent who is immersed in a world where ethics have already been compromised. (228)

And while the line between authorized and unauthorized crimes may be clear to supervisors, prosecutors, and judges, that is less likely to be the case for undercover agents. To the undercover agent, there may be few sharp distinctions between engaging in crimes to maintain one's cover and those that are simply for self-gain. The temptations to join one's criminal associates are numerous. Working in isolation and secrecy provides opportunities to take shortcuts. The success and thrill of deception can augment a sense of bravado, as well as sow a note of confusion for the agent as to who he "really" is. (229)

While most undercover agents may not deviate from their assigned roles, the dangers are there. These are risks that are inherent to the job of undercover work itself, and authorized criminality exacerbates the problem. Aping the argot, garb, and conventions of crooks already introduces strain to the agent's perspective; to then ask the agent to engage in the criminal acts challenges the agent to ask: who am I?

2. Moral authority and the community

If authorized criminality can unmoor the agent from his moral compass, it may also undermine the moral authority of the police in their relationship with the public. When the police engage not only in investigative deception, but in acts that would otherwise be criminal in the name of crime control, is the "moral tattiness" insufficient to outweigh the benefits of a potentially successful investigation? (230) If, in general, undercover work undermines "the social convention that there is a sharp difference between evil-doers and the righteous," (231) then the particular practice of authorized criminality strains this distinction even further.

Whether or not the action is justified as a matter of legal doctrine, the knowledge that the police are permitted to participate in crime, even for justifiable ends, erodes public trust in the police. (232) To the extent that people react to law in terms of its didactic and expressive functions, authorized criminality transmits a contradictory message. Official police participation in crime, even if to catch criminals, suggests that the state punishes without being

what Justice Brandeis called the "potent" and "omnipresent teacher."
(233)

And these harms may well outweigh the value of the cases
won through undercover means. Public trust and moral authority are
essential for the police in a democratic society. Yet the practice of
authorized criminality reflects undesirable expressive legal norms.
(234) It suggests that criminal wrongdoing is relative or situational,
depending on the identity of the perpetrator. It also promotes police
behavior that is free of the basic rule-of-law principles that are
thought to be basic to democratic policing: public accountability and
constrained discretion.

IV. ADDRESSING THE CHALLENGE OF AUTHORIZED CRIMINALITY

By itself, covert policing raises a host of problems about the optimal
mix of effective enforcement tactics and ethical police behavior. The
participation in crime by undercover police is a little known and
secretive practice that by its very nature challenges core
presumptions about democratic policing. When police are permitted
to take the additional step of behaving as if they were in fact
criminals but for doctrines justifying their conduct, they pose a host
of potential harms to themselves, the public trust, and the stability of
what it means to enforce the law.

At least three implications follow from this more complete
portrait of authorized criminality. First, we should permit much
broader public access than is now available to basic information on
undercover work, including the use of authorized criminality.
Second, one step towards guided discretion would be the use of
administrative guidelines. Third, legal scholars of the police must
extend their agendas beyond those concerns identified by the
Supreme Court, thus drawing attention to neglected subjects like
authorized criminality.

A. Increasing Transparency for Undercover Operations

We have greater routine and systematic collection of data on the
police today than we did a half-century ago. The federal government
collects annual data on arrests, clearance rates, and other police
activities from around the country. (235) Yet, as previously
discussed, we know little by comparison on undercover activity.
(236) There is no systematic collection of data on undercover
investigations made publicly available, (237) and in fact much

information is deliberately withheld from public view. (238) Instead, researchers must rely upon media coverage, reported cases, the occasional release of official information from government reports and agency press releases, and often sensationalized memoirs from former undercover investigators. (239)

This inattention is unwarranted. Police participation in authorized criminality raises troubling issues of secrecy, unfettered discretion, and moral uncertainty. These are matters no less pressing than racial prejudice, police corruption, excessive force, and other matters that regularly draw public and scholarly attention to the police. The absence of transparency increases the likelihood of public mistrust, hides potential police abuses, and expresses undesirable norms about the moral standing of the police as those entrusted to enforce the law.

The reluctance on the part of the police to disclose such information is understandable. By its very nature, undercover policing tends to draw suspicion. To release details of fictitious identities, police-run brothels and fencing businesses, false intimacies with criminals, and similar sordid details is unlikely to win favor with the public, even if in the legitimate pursuit of criminal activity.

Yet without basic knowledge about the nature and extent of authorized criminality, there is no empirical basis upon which sensible constraints or clear objectives can be crafted. What is the focus of any department's undercover efforts? What is the frequency of and basis for engaging in authorized criminality? Are the police spending the bulk of their time fencing stolen televisions, tendering bribes to public officials, or buying narcotics off the street? One might imagine limiting authorized criminality to certain offenses, or to limiting its use to certain kinds of investigations, but these kinds of street-level decisions should not be made in the abstract. Without knowing basic facts about undercover participation in crime, it is impractical to make substantive decisions about, for instance, which crimes may or may not merit this kind of deceptive practice when balanced against potential harms.

And the need for transparency can accommodate concerns about compromising policing techniques and interfering with pending criminal investigations and prosecutions. Take the example of arrest data once again: we collect a number of details about police arrests, make it publicly available, and do not undermine individual cases or police efficacy as a result. (240) There are good reasons to be more sensitive about undercover work, of course, because it may indeed compromise investigations to divulge very specific information, but these are matters that can be remedied without justifying a wholesale blackout on the collection and publication of less specific information. (241)

Moreover, greater transparency can provide the basis from which regulation can arise. It may be that undercover policing is deemed necessary for the investigation of many crimes, but perhaps not as many as police departments and executive agencies now claim. Even when some crimes may not be as effectively investigated without the ability of police to engage in authorized criminality, a clear understanding of the factual circumstances, including the costs to officers and the kinds of crimes under investigation, may counsel the prohibition of some authorized criminality in light of the potential harms. Transparency fuels informed decision making, which in turn can curb discretion as well as address concerns about public trust.

B. Limiting Policing Discretion in Undercover Work

Undercover police have few restraints on the exercise of their discretion when invited to participate in crime during an investigation. Perhaps the lack of significant curbs on discretion can be attributed to characteristics inherent to undercover policing. Undercover operations can be unpredictable and an investigator may be faced with a sudden invitation to participate in crime. More importantly, though, the legal framework that tells the police what they may and may not do when participating in crime in an undercover capacity isn't particularly useful in the day-to-day operations of the police.

Doctrines like the due process defense and entrapment serve to delineate the outer limits of acceptable undercover police work, but the truly difficult questions have to do with the ordinary situations that police will encounter repeatedly in undercover investigations. We can probably all agree that an undercover police officer cannot participate in murder, but there are a great many other less serious but nevertheless important crimes that the police sometimes do participate in; the due process and entrapment defenses don't particularly help here. Likewise, the public authority defense is no significant curb on discretion; the doctrine doesn't answer the thorniest questions about authorized criminality. Just because undercover officers obtain supervisory authorization to engage in drug sales, forgery, and prostitution does not necessarily mean they have appropriate guidelines in knowing when, how, and to what extent to participate.

60

The lack of interest shown by the judicial and legislative branches might reflect a concern that neither possesses sufficient expertise to regulate undercover policing. Indeed, George Dix, lamenting the dearth of legal regulation over undercover policing more than thirty years ago, suggested that the "law's failure" to control this investigative technique could be attributed in part to the conscious reluctance of courts and legislatures to delve into matters in which the practical understanding necessary for careful guidance was lacking. (242) But the fear of undue judicial interference has not stopped courts from regulating the police in interrogations, searches, and seizures. In the absence of judicial and legislative intervention, what else might regulate undercover police participation in crime?

Internal departmental guidelines may serve as a starting point. The FBI guidelines are a helpful model; they explicitly acknowledge the practice of authorized criminality and place limits on its use. (243) By requiring explicit authorization in most instances, minimization of police participation in crime, and justification in only limited circumstances, the federal guidelines provide guidance to the FBI prior to any involvement in authorized criminality. Model guidelines might be developed along these lines and provide more guidance than the FBI guidelines do, such as specifying what considerations must be balanced in the extent, degree, and duration of authorized criminality in a given operation.

Not only would guidelines have instrumental value, they would serve symbolic functions as well. Most police officers, when asked about their craft, are unable to justify their actions in terms more precise than "common sense" or "proper action." (244) Regardless of the actual skill involved in police work, such justifications of police work are inadequate in a democratic society. Clear guidelines on police discretion can both dispel some of the morally ambiguous nature of police work as well as assure the public that common problems of police work--which are usually morally and legally complex as well--have been addressed explicitly by the department as a formal matter. (245)

There are good reasons, however, to maintain a healthy skepticism about the likelihood of police-initiated rulemaking in this area. (246) As a practical matter, some have argued that guidelines can be unintentionally helpful to would-be criminals trying to identify police infiltration. (247) Such concerns may justify withholding some information from public view, but not a failure to provide formal guidance over discretion at all.

As a historical matter, police departments have been reluctant to assume the task of internal rulemaking on discretion. While administrative rulemaking was widely embraced in the 1960s and 1970s by reformers and academics alike as a source of control over police discretion, in practice the reaction of police departments has been mixed. (248) Despite the urgings of academics, public policy figures, and some reform-minded police chiefs, rank and file officers often balked at what they perceived to be control by outsiders. (249) For most police departments today, guidelines that do exist tend to focus on internal administrative issues, rather than the problems faced in ordinary police work. (250) When they have been implemented, guidelines have tended to be "crisis-driven" rather than the product of considered reflection. (251) Those institutions in a position to require police rulemaking--the legislatures and the courts--have not used their authority to any significant degree. (252)

C. Expanding the Research Agenda Beyond Criminal Procedure

The lack of substantial data and the reluctant engagement of courts explain a little, but not much, of the curious lack of interest in undercover policing by legal academics who study the police. (253) As a general matter, the police generate a seemingly limitless body of commentary by legal academics. Why has undercover policing and its reliance upon authorized criminality been neglected if, as I have argued, such practices contradict or undermine basic premises of democratic policing?

Part of the answer may lie in the pull of the Court's criminal procedure jurisprudence, and its considerable influence over the research agenda of legal academics. The Supreme Court has played a central role in regulating police investigation through its decisions on the Fourth and Fifth Amendments, which concern searches, seizures, and interrogations of suspects. This regulation has been so considerable that constitutional law, rather than federal or state lawmaking, is the primary source of regulation in these areas. (254)

The central role of the Court in regulating police procedure has had a number of undesirable consequences. As William Stuntz has argued, the aggressive constitutional regulation of procedure has made it more costly for legislatures to regulate policing, and thus they have turned their attention to areas left largely untouched by the Court: substantive criminal law and noncapital sentencing. (255) Yet if criminal justice is to be "representation-reinforcing," that structure is illogical. (256) The Court regulates in areas where legislatures are likely to be most responsive and democratic, and leaves beyond the

scope of constitutional law matters such as crime definition and
police discretion where concerns about discrimination on the basis of
race or wealth are especially high. (257) This distorting effect has
led, in Stuntz's view, to skewed legislative attention (and spending)
on those areas left largely unregulated by the Court, which in turn has
led to over-criminalization and ever harsher sentencing policies.
(258)

This too may be the case with the legal scholars of the police
and their research agendas. Taking its cue from the Court, legal
scholarship has taken up many thorny issues of policing left open,
unresolved, or problematic by the Court's Fourth and Fifth
Amendment cases. These questions deserve the attention legal
scholars of the police have paid them, but that attention has come at
the cost of scholarly attention to areas where the Court has paid very
little attention: undercover policing, police discretion, and police
corruption, to name a few. (259)

Legal scholars of policing experience a pull from
constitutional criminal procedure that obscures or overshadows other
areas of policing that raise not only doctrinal problems but also
fundamental, rule-of-law type concerns as compelling as those
addressed in the context of police seizures or interrogations. A
roughly comparable dilemma in law and society scholarship is
instructive. In a seminal article, Austin Sarat and Susan Silbey
warned that an uncritical attempt to address the "pull of the policy
audience" tended to distort scholarship. (260) By addressing
problems primarily in the "scientific" perspective and terms
demanded by the policy audience, law and society scholarship is
diminished and critical opportunities are lost. (261) Scholarship
exclusively shaped by the policy audience encourages an uncritical
acceptance of questions, premises, and objectives of the
policymakers. (262)

This problem is a species of agency capture, and criminal
procedure scholarship isn't beholden to the Supreme Court in quite
the same way. But Sarat and Silbey offer a larger insight about
scholarly attention with application here. Taking cues from the Court
about the key issues in police regulation tends to reinforce the idea
that these are the issues to be addressed as a matter of scholarly
interest. Matters left unregulated by the Court are left to the periphery
by scholars as well.

But legal scholars of the police should not be constrained by
the pull of constitutional criminal procedure. Searches and seizures
by beat cops and interrogations by detectives, while important, do not

represent the entire spectrum of police behavior. Renewed scholarly attention can raise fresh insights about police problems outside of the dominance of constitutional criminal procedure. Undercover policing, unregulated by constitutional criminal procedure, ignored by legislatures, and marginalized by academics, has been a victim of this neglect.

CONCLUSION

Investigative techniques can't be measured by their ability to secure convictions alone. Covert operations are an important tool of the police, but the unrestrained use of deceptive practices should make us as concerned as a proposal for total and pervasive surveillance would. The participation of undercover officers in criminal activity should give us pause. Even the appearance that the police are in some instances above the law is troubling. Over time, we have decided that some police tactics cannot be countenanced in a democratic society, whatever their instrumental value. It may not be possible to eliminate authorized criminality, but we should remain alert to its potential for harm.

NOTES DELETED

Elizabeth E. Joh, Visiting Professor of Law, Stanford Law School; Professor of Law, University of California, at Davis (eejoh@ucdavis.edu). Thanks to Mariano-Florentino Cuellar, Floyd Feeney, George Fisher, Gary Marx, Charles Reichmann, Robert Weisberg, the participants in the 2008 Hixon-Riggs Forum for Science and Technology, the U.C. Davis Law Faculty Workshop and the Stanford Law Faculty Workshop for their helpful comments and conversations; to the staff of the Stanford Law Review for their editorial assistance; to the staff of the Mabie Law Library at U.C. Davis School of Law, Erin Murphy, Jacob Storms, and Andrew Zee for their research assistance; to former Dean Rex Perschbacher and current Dean Kevin Johnson of the U.C. Davis School of Law for their support.

8

Corruption Cases Tainted Philadelphia Police in 2010

Troy Graham

In 2010, Philadelphia police officers made some spectacularly bad headlines for acts of corruption, prompting Police Commissioner Charles H. Ramsey to warn that "it could get worse before it gets better."

That trend will continue into the new year, with several more corruption cases "coming to a head in 2011," Ramsey said in an interview this week. "Irrespective of the embarrassment it may cause, it's worth it if we can get rid of people," he said. "In the long term, we'll be a much better, much stronger department." Ramsey did not elaborate on the ongoing investigations, but at least two officers in the 25th District are suspected of working with drug dealers and robbing the dealers' rivals. Those officers were the targets of an October sting operation that eventually netted two other 25th District officers, Sean Alivera and Christopher Luciano, now accused of helping to rob a drug dealer of marijuana and cash. Three other officers -- two from the 39th District and one from the 25th District -- were nabbed in a separate federal investigation in July for allegedly planning the theft and resale of 300 grams of heroin from an alleged drug supplier.

Two other officers were charged in 2010 with murder after off-duty shootings, and others faced charges for thefts and assaults. The year was capped by the federal extortion indictment of Inspector Daniel Castro, one of the department's rising stars, who was once considered a future candidate for commissioner. Castro, a 25-year veteran who was head of the Traffic Division, was accused of

Graham, T. Corruption cases tainted Philadelphia police in 2010. Philadelphia Inquirer (Philadelphia, PA), Dec 30, 2010.

seeking to hire an enforcer to recoup money he had lost in a real estate investment.

"For every person who commits a corrupt act, it overshadows literally hundreds of cases where police officers did the job appropriately," Ramsey said this week. "It's just a shame." As the year of bad news unfolded, Ramsey focused more and more on corruption and talked of making the department a more professional organization. He sent several messages through the ranks and, in August, produced an eight-page report on preventing corruption. This month, Ramsey achieved one of the signature elements of that report when the Civil Service Commission approved changes he had sought in hiring standards. Previously, academy recruits needed to be 19 and have a high school diploma or GED. Under the new standards, a recruit must be 21 and have 60 semester hours of college credit or two years of military service. Recruits also must have three years of driving experience. Ramsey also has beefed up Internal Affairs and assigned a team to work with the FBI to investigate corruption. The department launched a hotline and e-mail address to log public complaints, and officers are receiving more ethics training more often. "We're putting the resources in," he said earlier this year. "We're going to fix this problem."

9

Problems, Sure. Broken? Not These Everyday Heroes.

DEBATE: How Should the Indianapolis Metropolitan Police Department Be Fixed

Bill Owensby

When i was asked to write a response to the question for this column, I wanted to scream, "IT'S NOT BROKEN?"

Okay, I will admit to a little bias. I've spent my adult life working for IPD and IMPD as a civilian and a sworn officer. I've bled for this community, cried for peers and friends as they are laid to rest, and endured the rough spots we have gone through as a department.

I'm not alone by a long shot. Every day, there are stories that aren't told about the heroism our men and women display, and the unselfish acts they perform for our community. I know them; you may not.

That may lead to a perception that seems prominent in the last few months that we are a broken department full of bad officers and that we are in desperate need of a savior. Nothing could be further from the truth.

Owensby, B. Problems, sure. Broken? Not these everyday heroes. DEBATE: HOW SHOULD THE Indianapolis Metropolitan Police department be fixed. Indianapolis Business Journal, Dec 27, 2010 v31 i44 p6B(1). Reprinted by permission of author.

68

Let's get the big elephant out of the room first. Do we have discipline issues? Darn right, we do. Find me an organization of 1,700 men and women that doesn't. You won't find a profession that doesn't have a few bad apples. I guess that would beg the question, "Well then, what do you do with them when you find them?"

I can tell you this, and I can prove it--in IMPD, when we encounter an officer who makes an overt decision to commit a felony, we prosecute them, fire them or both.

As spokesperson for the organization representing nearly all of Marion County's law enforcement community, I wholeheartedly support that position. I've said it many times: No one wants a bad officer in their ranks--not the community, and not the officers who work alongside them.

I've looked at discipline administered or requested from 30 days' suspension to termination since the merger of the Indianapolis Police Department and the Marion County Sheriff's Office in 2007. Here are the results:

In 2007, there were six cases of discipline on record, with one resulting in termination and the others resulting in various amounts of suspension without pay.

In 2008, there were 13 cases of discipline on record, nine of which resulted in termination or resignation, and several pending criminal cases.

In 2009, there were 11 cases of discipline on record, with three resulting in termination, resignation or retirement.

In 2010, there have been eight cases of discipline on record, with the results pending for many of those. There have been four cases resulting in termination or resignation.

Granted, when you have a high-profile case like we have had this year, the magnifying glass is on you, which in my opinion leads to the misconception that we are broken.

We are doing many things right. In 2007, a program was developed by then-Chief Michael Spears and Lt. Rick Snyder that was dubbed Career and Leadership Development. The philosophy of the program in the simplest terms is to build leaders, not just supervisors.

In three years, the program has gained international recognition for its advanced "next practices" training. The program also has dealt with the promotional process and performance management, and developed a master patrolman/master detective designation.

IMPD is also developing another trailblazing approach to excellence. Capt. Brian Nanavaty has developed a program designed to examine officers who have experienced more than one or two minor rules violations and work one-on-one with them in a mentoring capacity to make them productive employees again. He deals with root issues, ethics, and rules and regulations, and concentrates on the real meaning of discipline, which is not to punish, but to correct behavior.

We are doing things right, and doing the right things. The FOP stands ready to move forward, and improve on what is a fine, professional organization. What's our next step? Renewed dialogue with the mayor.

* Owensby is president of the Fraternal Order of Police Lodge 86 in Indianapolis, and has worked the mayor's security detail, among other positions. Send comments on this column to ibjedit.com.

10

City's Integrity Squad Disbanded

Ex-Chief Says it Was Effective

Bobby Kerlik

A decade ago, a $5 dollar bill left on a table in the Hill District police station could sit untouched for a week because officers feared it was an internal sting. Word had spread among Pittsburgh police officers that such tests were the work of then-Chief Robert W. McNeilly Jr.'s Office of Special Investigations, an internal affairs unit known as the "Integrity Squad." "It helped weed out a lot of officers who shouldn't be there," McNeilly said. The small unit didn't actually run such random integrity tests, acting more on tips from within officers' ranks about dirty fellow cops. The arrests last month of city Officers Ken Simon and Anthony Scarpine on corruption charges reignited a debate about how effective the squads are. The city axed the squad about five years ago as part of budget cuts when the state declared Pittsburgh financially distressed under Act 47, according to Deputy Chief Paul Donaldson. The city had the civilian-run Office of Municipal Investigations, which investigates all city employees, including citizens' complaints of police misconduct. "Currently, integrity checks are routinely undertaken, or they are triggered by an allegation or suspicion of police misconduct," Donaldson said in a prepared statement. "The investigation is performed by OMI, or in some instances by the FBI. Our present methods are sufficient, and both agencies are thorough and professional." A sergeant and five officers are assigned to OMI along with civilian investigators. McNeilly, who served as Pittsburgh chief from 1996-2006 and is the chief in Elizabeth Township, said

Kerlik, B. City's Integrity Squad disbanded; ex-chief says it was effective. The Pittsburgh Tribune-Review (Pittsburgh, PA), Dec 6, 2010.

the Integrity Squad was far more effective in combating corruption. "There were a lot of things the Integrity Squad was able to investigate that OMI couldn't," he said. McNeilly says pressure from the police union ultimately was responsible for the squad's demise. Fraternal Order of Police Fort Pitt Lodge No. 1 attorney Bryan Campbell denied the union had a hand in disbanding it, and union Vice President Chuck Hanlon blasted the idea of starting another one. "(Simon and Scarpine) haven't even been convicted, and here we are again. We're already cash-strapped and low on manpower. If you want (crime) to get out of control, keep stripping the streets of officers," Hanlon said. "If you start an Integrity Squad, it'll be guys sitting on their hands. There's nothing wrong with the department." Simon, 49, and Scarpine, 58, are accused of fabricating charges and wrongfully arresting two men during a July drug bust in the North Side. Prosecutors charged the officers after video surveillance contradicted the officers' account of what happened, authorities said. Lawyers for the pair say the officers stand by the arrests. Larger departments such as those in New York, Los Angeles and New Orleans have integrity units that help deter corruption, experts said. "It's a matter of resources. Obviously, departments cannot ignore the complaints of citizens, but to test how officers respond in certain situations costs money. Five or six detectives costs a few hundred thousand dollars a year," said Maki Haberfield, a professor who specializes in police ethics at the John Jay College of Criminal Justice in New York. "The pros are that it keeps officers on their toes, but on the other side, it's sort of demoralizing. It's effective if you have a department with extensive corruption." Steve Rothlein, a retired deputy chief and 30-year veteran of Miami-Dade police who works as a police training consultant, oversaw an internal affairs unit in Miami that did targeted stings. "(Integrity units) can be effective in those departments that have a big problem," Rothlein said. "But in most departments 99 percent of the officers are honest. Why run around and test honest officers?" Mona Wallace, who retired from Pittsburgh police last year, worked on McNeilly's squad. She said 70 percent of the cases the squad worked came from other officers.

"The rumor was that we did random integrity tests, but we never did that. The people we did test, there was a reason to do it," Wallace said. Wallace said the squad was effective with its four or five investigators. "They knew we were out there and that we were proactive. Truthfully, if it made somebody think twice, it was effective."

Use of Force

11

Force Data Show Taser Becoming Most Used

A Eugene Police Report Finds that the Use of Pepper Spray is Falling

Jack Moran

Eugene police Lt. Doug Mozan said the city's police oversight system "is more robust than (in) most places." That quotation, included in a story that appeared in Wednesday's A section, incorrectly indicated that Mozan was referring only to the police auditor's participation in internal affairs cases, rather than the entire oversight system's functions.

A new report shows that Tasers have replaced pepper spray as the weapon that Eugene police officers are most likely to turn to when confronting resistant people.

Forty patrol officers began carrying the controversial stun guns in early 2008. During the next two years, police used Tasers to subdue people in 49 separate cases - 25 in 2008 and 24 in 2009.

In that same two-year period, Eugene police fired pepper spray at people in 43 total instances - 25 in 2008 and 18 last year.

That's a substantial decrease from 2007 - the year before officers began using Tasers. That year, police used pepper spray during 57 encounters, according to the report released this week that details Eugene police force statistics between 2007 and 2009.

Moran, J., Force data show Taser becoming most used. City/Region A Eugene police report finds that the use of pepper spray is falling. The Register-Guard (Eugene, OR), April 7, 2010.

Police Taser use in Eugene could increase further if the department purchases 60 more stun guns for its officers. That plan is on hold until after police Chief Pete Kerns signs off on changes to a Taser use policy that the city police commission is now considering.

While the new report shows no significant change in the number of injuries suffered by people subjected to police force since Eugene officers began carrying Tasers, officials would expect a drop if the department purchases additional stun guns.

"I think you probably would see a reduction in both officer injuries and suspect injuries," police Lt. Doug Mozan said.

That result has been reported by officials in several other cities in which police carry Tasers.

Also included in the report are statistics showing that in 2009, Eugene police used weapons - ranging from guns to Tasers to pepper spray - in 48 cases, a seven-year low. That's despite evidence that more people in recent years carried guns and knives during incidents that resulted in police force, according to the report.

The report indicates that police issued Taser warnings but did not discharge the stun gun 54 times in 2009 and 92 times in 2008.

Police officials say it's not uncommon for a potentially combative subject to comply with an officer's commands after being threatened with a Taser. But it's unclear if that's why overall police use of weapons decreased last year, officials said.

The report also points out that drunk and drugged people are the ones who typically end up injured after resisting Eugene police officers' efforts to control them.

Statistics show that about 71 percent of people subjected to police force in the city between 2007 and 2008 were under the influence of alcohol or drugs. That's on par with the city's long-term average, but significantly higher than police agencies in other parts of the country have indicated in similar reports, police service improvement analyst Terry Smith said.

"I think it's clear that we do have an alcohol and drug problem in this area," Smith said.

Also, the report notes that while the number of force complaints filed against Eugene police is about average in comparison to other cities, the percentage of those complaints that are ultimately upheld by the police chief is significantly lower in Eugene than elsewhere.

Just four of 141 complaints alleging excessive police force were upheld as valid between 2007 and 2009. Nine of the 48 complaints filed against Eugene officers last year remain under investigation, according to the report.

Mozan said each force complaint is investigated thoroughly with participation from a voter-approved police auditor. The auditor's participation in internal affairs cases "is more robust than (in) most places," Mozan said.

Police Use Force

Since 40 Eugene police officers began carrying Tasers in early 2008, other types of police force have decreased.

Eugene Police Use of Force

Since 40 Eugene officers began carrying Tasers in early 2008, other types of force have decreased.

2007 2008 2009

Control holds 34 25 15

Takedowns 63 39 38

Pepper spray 57 25 18

Hand or fist strike 24 14 17

Elbow, knee or foot strike 23 8 12

Tasers n/a 25 24

Other less-lethal weapons 10 11 5

Other 7 7 3

TOTAL NUMBER INCIDENTS 107 88 94

Note: Force used by type exceeds total number of incidents because more than one tactic was used in most incidents. Less-lethal weapons include rubber bullets, beanbag rounds, billy clubs.

12

Police Investigations of the Use of Deadly Force Can Influence Perceptions and Outcomes

Shannon Bohrer and Robert Chaney

B asic law enforcement training covers using force, including deadly force, and investigating crimes, even those involving assaults and shootings by police. The relationship between these two events--the use of force and the police investigation of this use of force--can have far-reaching consequences, both good and bad, for the public, the department, and the officers involved. (2)

The law enforcement profession spends considerable time and resources training officers to use firearms and other weapons and to understand the constitutional standards and agency policies concerning when they can employ such force. Society expects this effort because of the possible consequences of officers not having the skills they need if and when they become involved in a critical incident.

In addition to receiving instruction about the use of force, officers are taught investigative techniques. They must reconstruct the incident, find the facts, and gather evidence to prosecute the offenders. And, historically, they have done this extremely well. But, is the same amount of attention paid to examining the investigative process of the use of deadly force and how this can affect what occurs after such an event? Are there any reasons why the police

Bohrer, S., & Chaney, R. Police investigations of the use of deadly force can influence perceptions and outcomes. The FBI Law Enforcement Bulletin, Jan 2010 v79 i1 p1(7)

should approach the investigation of an officer-involved shooting differently? To help answer these questions, the authors present an overview of perceptions about these events and some elements that law enforcement agencies can incorporate into investigations of officer-involved shootings that can help ensure fair and judicious outcomes.

PERCEPTIONS OF DEADLY FORCE

All law enforcement training is based on the two elements of criticality and frequency. Skills that officers need and are required to have to perform their duties fall into both: 1) how often they use them and 2) how crucial it is to have them. Training officers to handle potentially lethal incidents, by nature, is vitally important. Investigating officer-involved shootings constitutes a critical function, but, for most departments, it does not occur that frequently. Only examining training needs from the perspective of preparation for the event does not necessarily take into account what can occur afterward. Just because the officer had the right to shoot and the evidence supports the officer's actions may not guarantee a positive, or even a neutral, reception from the public.

In addition, who the police shoot seems to mold some perceptions. For example, a bank robber armed with a shotgun presents a different connotation than a 14-year-old thief wielding a knife. (3) Sometimes, it is who the police shoot that also can set the tone for the direction of the investigation surrounding the incident.

The Officer's Perception

Interviews conducted with officers who have been involved in shootings have revealed that while many were well trained for the event, they often were not prepared for the investigation afterward. (4) Some believed that these investigations centered on finding something that officers did wrong so they could be charged with a crime or a violation of departmental policy. (5) Others felt that the investigations were for the protection of the agency and not necessarily the officers involved. (6)

Officers can have broad perceptions that often depend upon their experiences of being involved in a critical incident or knowledge of what has happened to other officers. A trooper with the Arizona Department of Public Safety commented, "I did not choose to take that man's life. ... He chose to die when he drew a gun on an officer. It was not my choice; it was his." (7)

The Public's Perception

Perceptions by the public of officer-involved shootings usually are as wide and diverse as the population, often driven by media coverage, and sometimes influenced by a long-standing bias and mistrust of government. (8) Documented cases of riots, property damage, and loss of life have occurred in communities where residents have perceived a police shooting as unjustified. Some members of the public seem to automatically assume that the officer did something wrong before any investigation into the incident begins. Conversely, others believe that if the police shot somebody, the individual must not have given the officer any choice.

The Department's Perception

Departmental perceptions can prove diverse and difficult to express. For example, when interviewed, one chief of police advised that "it is sometimes easier to go through an officer being killed in the line of duty than a questionable police shooting." (9) The chief was referring to the public's response, including civil unrest, to what was perceived as an unjustified police shooting. At various levels, however, administrators may feel that a full and fair investigation will clear up any negative perceptions by the public. While not all-inclusive, departmental perceptions include many instances when an officer-involved shooting was viewed with clear and objective clarity before, during, and after the investigation. (10)

ELEMENTS OF THE INVESTIGATION

Few events in law enforcement attract the attention of the media, the political establishment, and the police administration more than an officer-involved shooting. In some instances, such intense interest can affect the investigation. Is this scrutiny related to the incident, the investigation, or both? Docs it affect the focus and outcome of the investigation? And, conversely, can the investigative process influence this close observation of the incident? (11)

With these issues in mind, the authors offer six elements for investigating officer-involved shootings. While they are not meant to be all-inclusive or broad enough to cover every conceivable situation, they can be useful as a guide.

The Investigators

The first element involves investigators who have correct and neutral attitudes. Not all officers are suited to conducting police-shooting

82

investigations. Examining such incidents requires open-minded, experienced investigators who have empathy toward the involved officers and members of the general public. Starting with the right investigators will ensure that the process has a solid foundation.

If possible, at least two primary investigators should oversee the case from the beginning until the end. They should be responsible for such activities as supervising the crime scene investigation, reviewing witness statements and evidence and laboratory reports, and coordinating with the criminal justice system. They should not be heavily involved in the initial routine investigation except for handling the interaction with the involved officers, including taking statements.

The Crime Scene

The second element entails the appropriate response to and protection of the crime scene. Homicide or criminal investigators should protect the site. They need to take their time and broaden the protected area, possibly adding a safety zone beyond the immediate vicinity. They should establish a press area with a public information officer available to respond to media inquiries.

Before inspecting the crime scene, the investigators should videotape it and the surroundings and then periodically videotape the area, along with any crowds and parked vehicles, during the course of the examination. Such information may prove valuable later in locating additional witnesses. They should use up-to-date technology and evidence-gathering methods, calling on experts as needed.

Before releasing the crime scene, the investigators should consult with the criminal justice officials who will be responsible for the case. It can be easier to explain the circumstances of the incident while still in control of the location where it occurred. (12)

The Involved Officers

Removing the involved officers from the scene as soon as possible and taking them to a secure location away from other witnesses and media personnel constitute the third element. The investigators need to explain to the officers that these actions will help maintain the integrity of the case. They also should invite the officers to stay within a protected area to participate in the follow-up investigation. When possible, they should only take statements from the involved officers once they clearly understand all of the facts and crime scene information. Moreover, in the initial and early stages of the investigation, authorities never should release the names or any personal information of the involved officers. (13)

Sometimes, it is beneficial for involved officers to revisit the crime scene later to help them recall events. If at all possible, the investigators should accompany them.

It is important to keep the involved officers informed. Someone should contact them on a regular basis. In many agencies, the officers have advocates, including peer support, union representation, and legal aid. Keeping the officers advised may require the investigators to go through the advocate. (14)

The Civilian Witnesses

The fourth element highlights the importance of investigators gaining the confidence and respect of civilian witnesses. After all, they need their assistance. In most cases, investigators should handle them the same way as involved officers.

Before interviewing the witnesses, investigators should have a full understanding of the crime scene and the facts of the shooting. If any statements conflict with the crime scene examination or information from other people who observed the incident, investigators should have the witnesses view a crime scene videotape or take them back to the site to help them recall events. They may wish to consult with the criminal justice investigating authority beforehand to ensure that the revisit does not invade the privacy or cause harm to the witnesses. And, of course, investigating authorities never should release any information concerning the witnesses.

The Criminal Justice Authorities

The fifth element, the need to have these cases vetted through the criminal justice process as soon as possible, proves critical to the involved officers, their families, and their employing agencies. Sometimes, backlogs may delay report completion but should not hinder clearance procedures. (15) Close consultation with the appropriate criminal justice authority may alleviate the need for a completed formal report if a written statement for the proper authority confirms the facts. For example, medical examiners and ballistic experts can provide their findings to investigators with formal reports to follow.

Presentations of the investigation should include all videotapes, photographs, and copies of all statements, investigative reports, and other necessary documents. Throughout the criminal

84

justice proceedings, investigators should update the involved officers and their departments about the progress of the case.

The Media

As the final element, the department's public information officer should contact the media before their representatives approach the agency. (16) In the early stages of the investigation, the department should demonstrate that it wants to cooperate with the media. By informing the public through press releases and interviews, the agency shows that it is investigating the incident and that as information can be released, it will be. Departments should remember that the proverbial "no comment" often gives the impression that the police are hiding something.

Without a positive relationship with the media, poor communication between the public and the police can develop, creating a lack of faith in the management and operations of the department and mistrust from all parties. The time to prepare press releases for officer-involved shootings is before one occurs.

In addition, agencies should encourage the media to print and air stories on the responsibilities of officers and the training conducted to enhance their abilities. General information on past shootings, simulator experiences, and the perspective of the reasonable objective officer can help develop a cooperative association. (17) Such a collaborative effort between the police and the media is not a magic pill and will not alleviate all of the public misperceptions and problems. However, it may reduce or prevent false perceptions, especially with officer-involved shootings. (18)

Finally, investigators should review all of the related printed materials and media interviews to identify further witnesses and, if needed, interview them as soon as possible. Sometimes, these individuals may not understand why the police would want to interview them after they have talked to the media, so a diplomatic approach can prove helpful. This highlights the importance of a positive working relationship that often can result in shared information between the media and the police.

CONCLUSION

Often, it is not a law enforcement shooting that generates negative consequences, but, rather, it is how the involved agency handles the incident that can foster and feed misperceptions. As a Santa Monica, California, police officer pointed out, "No one knows about the

hundreds of instances when a police officer decides not to shoot. Perhaps, no one cares. After all, people say we're trained to handle such things, as if training somehow removes or dilutes our humanity." (19)

While the six elements presented in this article may not be all-inclusive, they offer an outline that may reduce the negative events that sometimes occur in these situations. Having the appropriate investigators and a positive working relationship with the media constitute the bookends of an effective process. After all, the right investigators are the foundation for a thorough investigation, and a cooperative connection with the media forms the basis of public understanding. Joining together and sharing information can help both the police and the media deal with officer-involved shootings in a fair and judicious manner.

ENDNOTES DELETED

The FBI Law Enforcement Bulletin has been available to our readers online since March 1990. With the August 2009 issue, we began sending our readers e-mails announcing the latest edition and providing a direct link to the FBI Law Enforcement Bulletin on http://www.fbi.gov. There, you will be able to find the current edition, as well as previous issues of the FBI Law Enforcement Bulletin going back 10 years.

To receive these e-mails each month, please access http://www.fbi.gov and click on "Get FBI Alerts" at the upper right-hand corner of the FBI home page. Enter your e-mail address and select any monthly alerts you are interested in receiving, including the FBI Law Enforcement Bulletin. Once you have registered your e-mail address at http://www.fbi.gov, please contact us at lebonline@fbiacademy.edu with your name, position, organization, and e-mail address, as well as any thoughts you might have on the magazine or this online e-mail announcement system. If you encounter any difficulties, please let us know by e-mailing us at lebonline@fbiacademy.edu.

We look forward to hearing from you at lebonline@fbiacademy.edu. Please continue to send comments, questions, or suggestions regarding articles to the FBI Law Enforcement Bulletin editors at leb@fbiacademy.edu.

Editor

FBI Law Enforcement Bulletin

"When a police officer kills someone in the line of duty--or is killed--it sets in motion a series of internal and external reviews and public debate that normally does not end until several years later when the civil and criminal court trials are over." (1)

13

Teaching Police When to Use Deadly Force

Nick Sambides Jr.

I n more than 25 years of teaching police how to use deadly force properly, Urey W. Patrick has heard all kinds of questions. Most, he said, come from people who don't know what the law and training require of those charged with keeping the peace.

One question that often arises when police kill someone is: Why didn't they shoot to wound?

"Most people seem to have an understanding of the issue based largely on movies and TV. They see people fast-draw, snap-shoot and think that you can always react fast enough to stop the other guy," said Patrick, a retired FBI supervisory special agent.

"None of that is real. That is sort of the special-effects version of a police shooting," said Patrick, whose book "In Defense of Self and Others ... Issues, Facts & Fallacies -- The Realities of Law Enforcement's Use of Deadly Force" is available through Carolina Academic Press.

POPKOWSKI INVESTIGATION

The reality of police shootings might become more apparent when the Maine Attorney General's Office releases its findings on the death of retired U.S. Marine Corps Lt. James Popkowski near the Togus VA Medical Center campus on July 8.

A veteran forced to retire by a rare form of cancer, Popkowski, 37, of Grindstone was hit in the throat by one round as he turned, rifle in hand, slightly toward two officers during a confrontation that

Sambides, N. Teaching police when to use DEADLY FORCE. Bangor Daily News (Bangor, ME), Nov 6, 2010.

88

followed by as many as 45 minutes reports of a shot or shots striking the hospital, officials have said.

Witnesses reported that several shots, as many as a dozen, were fired at Popkowski, who suffered from depression caused by his illness or medications. In the hours before he went to the VA, where he had been a patient, Popkowski put a sign in his yard indicating he believed doctors were killing him by denying him stem-cell medicine, neighbors have said.

Paul Stevens of Belgrade, who claimed to have witnessed the shooting of Popkowski and recorded it with his cell phone camera, said "there was nothing in his demeanor that showed aggression whatsoever."

Attorney General's Office spokeswoman Nicole Sacre said this week that the investigation is continuing and she declined to speculate when the report will be released. But officials said last week that the officers who shot at Popkowski, Veterans Affairs police Officer Thomas Park and Maine Warden Service Sgt. Ron Dunham, are back at work. Park is on desk duty and Dunham on full duty. Game Warden Joey Lefebvre, who was at the scene but did not fire his weapon, is also back on the job, officials said. The wardens and Park had been on paid administrative leave, per standard procedure.

The Popkowski shooting was the second this year in which Maine officers used deadly force. On July 28, Attorney General Janet T. Mills ruled that Maine State Police Trooper Robert Flynn and U.S. Border Patrol Agent Robert Kipler were legally justified in killing 54-year-old Cyr Plantation resident Neil Begin inside his home on April 23.

The officers had repeatedly ordered Begin to drop his rifle and shot him when they saw him moving his left hand to the rifle and leveling it toward the officers, Mills said.

Begin's sister, Nancy Martin of Van Buren, said in late July that many members of her family felt that the officers involved in the incident resorted to lethal force too quickly.

"This definitely could have been handled a lot differently," said Martin. "Usually if the police find that someone is armed, they wait outside if there's no one else in harm's way. Instead, they ran in there and shot. It was unbelievable."

According to statistics provided by the attorney general's office, Maine police have used deadly force 82 times in the last 20 years, including the Popkowski case. In 44 situations, the use of force resulted in death. In no case was the use ruled not justified. No national statistics on the number of police deadly force cases in which officers were judged to have responded incorrectly appear to be available.

EACH CASE IS DIFFERENT

Patrick declined to comment on the Popkowski case, but the 63-year-old Winterport man -- now a firearms and deadly force training consultant, including for Maine police -- said he wasn't surprised that so many Maine police officers had been cleared over the years.

"You have to take police shootings individually, one at a time, because any use of deadly force is a discretionary, personal decision made subject to a person's training, education, experience and the totality of the situation they find themselves in," Patrick said.

"If you get to the end of the line and you have that many shootings over 10 or 20 years in which an officer is cleared, that doesn't mean that something's fishy. I think it's a testament to the training and proficiency in Maine law enforcement. As a general perception, I would say Maine law enforcement is really, really good," he added.

Under U.S. Supreme Court rulings that act as a universal guide to American law enforcers, police can use deadly force to prevent the escape of dangerous people, stop an attempt at serious injury, or to avert the threat of it, Patrick said.

The first and perhaps most elusive aspect of deadly force usage, Patrick said, is that police must prevent, not react to, imminent risk of serious injury to themselves or others as they perceive it in the moment it occurs.

Another is that police are trained to treat armed and noncompliant individuals in their proximity, usually within 30 feet, as automatic, imminent risks of serious injury, he said.

"Police can't read minds. They can only react to what a person does," Patrick said. "If there is somebody standing there with a gun in his hand and he does something consistent with bringing that gun into use, [the officer] doesn't have to wait to see what's next." Nor does it matter under the law if events prove an officer wrong -- for example, that what was thought to be a gun was actually a toy -- or reveal other options for eliminating the threat, Patrick said.

Police must also recognize and plan for the universal limits of physiology. It takes a second for a person to process and react to stimuli, Patrick noted. Tunnel vision, loss of fine motor control, extreme adrenaline flow and the "fight or flight" response are among the reactions they must endure.

"If that person standing there has a gun down at his side, there is already imminent risk of serious injury, simply because of the reaction time," Patrick said. "Even if you have your weapon drawn, you cannot react fast enough to stop somebody from quickly firing a shot at you. It's just impossible."

Yet for all that, most police avoid deadly force. In 2009, 57,268 officers were assaulted on duty in the U.S. Of them, 26.2 percent, or about 15,000, received injuries requiring hospitalization -- incidents involving at least a risk of serious injury, Patrick said.

But U.S. Justice Department statistics show that about 360 people are killed annually in justified police shootings -- which tells Patrick that police take on risk beyond what the law and proper training advise. "An awful lot of people don't get shot that could," he said.

No statistics are available on the number of people police wound or miss.

BREADTH OF EXPERIENCE

Patrick has studied tens of thousands of use-of-force incidents throughout his FBI career and as a private consultant. John B. Rogers, director of the Maine Criminal Justice Academy in Vassalboro, said Patrick teaches all of the academy's firearms instructor development courses, serves as chairman of the academy's tactical team advisory board and is a good all-around adviser to instructors and cadets because of his great breadth of experience as an instructor and agent.

"He is the content expert," Rogers said Thursday. Even in retirement, he still goes "all over the country ... to talk firearm shoots and use-of-force-type training." Academy instructors "are going to see mistakes by cadets and get all kinds of what-ifs from them, and we want instructors to be able to answer those questions in terms of their legal authority and justification," Rogers said. "There has got to be a single opinion that everything flows from, and Urey is [the] guy who can bring that to people.

"He has the ability to get through to people and make them understand what their legal authority is and how to use [different] force options," Rogers said. He has the ability to "make people understand, and that's what I like about Urey."

The goal of deadly force is not to kill, Patrick said, but to immediately incapacitate a person threatening serious injury. Bullets don't always do that. One lethal force failure allowed bank robbers William Russell Matix and Michael Lee Platt to kill two FBI agents and wound five others in Miami in 1986. Matix suffered six wounds and Platt 12 during the five-minute incident.

Miami's coroner said Platt took a terminal hit, a shot through an armpit and lung, in the first 30 seconds but kept shooting, according to Patrick.

"Most people give up because a gun is pointed at them, a shot fired, or because they realize they have been wounded. For whatever reason, they stop, but it's nothing you can count on," Patrick said. Deadly force incidents are often wrenching for officers due not to any regrets they might have, Patrick said, but because a community's reaction is often negative, even when force is justified. Besides the negativity, the ambivalence of their superiors, the chill of the investigative process and the likelihood of civil lawsuits leave "a bitter taste in an officer's mouth."

"He did something very hard, made a difficult decision, and that is pretty much overlooked given the treatment he gets," Patrick said, referring to an officer who has to use deadly force.

Patrick, who said he has never been involved in a deadly force shooting himself, recalled visiting a U.S. Border Patrol office long after an officer there had killed someone in the line of duty.

"I told this agent, 'I want you to know that you didn't do anything wrong. You did what you had to do,'" Patrick said. "He started crying and said, 'You know, you are [only] the second person in five years to tell me that.'"

The lack of support, Patrick said, "is the circumstance that ruins a police officer."

Emerging Technologies

14

Weber State Developing Blimp for Police

Jessica Miller

O gden may soon have extra eyes in the sky. City officials have been talking with the Utah Center for Aeronautical Innovation and Design at Weber State University about the development of a blimp equipped with a night-vision camera that would travel overhead at night.

"It's really an extra patrolman in the sky," said Bradley Stringer, director of UCAID. Mayor Matthew Godfrey said during the city council meeting Tuesday that the Ogden Police Department intends to buy the unmanned blimp, which can be controlled with a remote control and can also fly autonomously in an auto-pilot type feature. Though plans have been worked on for several months, Stringer said, there has not been any official contract or timeline set on the project yet. "Everything has been oral at this point," he said. Police Chief Jon Greiner said the blimp was "one of many options" the police department has considered. He said the plans are still in the preliminary stages, adding that he hasn't made any presentations or had discussions with the city council about the possibility of adding a blimp to the city's police force. He said he has been researching systems like this for the last two years. Stringer said the blimp will be shaped like a cigar, 52 feet long and four feet in diameter. The night-vision video can be viewed in real-time at ground level, and the blimp can be moved if an area needs extra patrol or video surveillance. "It would be unmanned, which is far less expensive than manned," he said. "It's a low-cost way to supplement patrolmen and other cameras." The city already has several cameras throughout the area, Stringer said, but because they are stationary, they are not as beneficial as a blimp, which can be moved to any area that needs it. Stringer said it is difficult to estimate how much the system would

Miller, J. Weber State developing blimp for police. Standard-Examiner (Ogden, UT), Jan 13, 2011.

cost, because they still have not finalized exactly what kind of technology the police department would need to equip the blimp. While this is not WSU's first video surveillance system -- they have created both fixed wing and rotary wing machines for clients in and out of state -- this will be the first time they are developing a lighter-than-air blimp surveillance model.

15

Tapping In to Tablets

Knox County Sheriff's Detectives Find iPads Helpful with Investigations

Don Jacobs

C ops used to say the bad guys can't outrun the police radio. Now, crooks in Knox County have to worry about the digital power of the iPad. In November 2010, 16 members of the Knox County Sheriff's Office Major Crimes and Family Crisis units began using the Apple iPad. Now detectives walk around with the 1.5-pound device rather than be shackled to a desk computer or a laptop installed in their cars.

Detectives use the $600 devices to make audio recordings of witness statements, share photos of suspects, call up an in-house crime map to detect patterns or send a case file to prosecutors to determine the proper charge to file against a suspect. "The iPad is all about convenience," said KCSO Detective Aaron Yarnell, who was the first to propose widespread use of the new technology. "With this, I've got everything in my hand and I don't have to wait for it to boot up. Anything others can do from their desk computer, I can do from the field." Yarnell introduced the devices to co-workers when he bought one for himself in April 2010, as the iPads hit the market. He found that he was regularly using the device for work. One day at roll call, Yarnell spoke to Lt. Bobby Hubbs, who commands the KCSO information technology unit, about the virtues of the iPad. An excited Hubbs then took the concept to Knox County Sheriff Jimmy "J.J." Jones. "He's very progressive in that way," Hubbs said of the sheriff. "He's opened the door for all this technology." Hubbs said the department first bought a couple of iPads in July to see how well the

Jacobs, D. Tapping in to tablets: Knox County Sheriff's detectives find iPads helpful with investigations. Knoxville News-Sentinel (Knoxville, TN), Jan 7, 2011.

technology meshed with detectives' daily needs. "Security and connectivity were the biggest concerns," Hubbs said. "Anyone can get on the Internet, but we had to have security." Once those issues were resolved, Jones approved the purchase of 16 of the iPads. Hubbs said he removed the $850 laptop computers in detectives' cars and gave them to the patrol division. Detectives got the iPads. "So patrol and detectives benefited," Hubbs said. The iPads also provide monthly savings. While the laptop computers required a $40 monthly air card to provide Internet access, the iPads offer the same connectivity for $25 a month. While the relatively young Yarnell readily embraces new technology, even the veteran detectives are warming to the devices. "This is much easier to learn than anything else I've seen," said 23-year veteran Lt. Clyde Cowan. "It's a lot more user-friendly. No one is showing any resistance. They (veteran detectives) are going to the young guys and saying, 'Show me how to do that.' " Yarnell said he recently used his iPad to audio tape statements from crime victims in a hospital room. He was able set the device to the side and got a high-quality recording he shared with other detectives in seconds. "It's real intimidating when you lay a tape recorder down in from of them," Cowan said. "With these, you set it off to the side and they know they're being recorded, but it's easier for them to talk." With the Internet access provided by the iPad, Yarnell said he can use the devices to get more accurate details from witnesses. If someone describes a car used in a robbery, Yarnell can call up a car site to make sure it matches the one described by the witness. Yarnell recently used his iPad to share the picture of a robbery suspect with other detectives and patrol officers. Yarnell said he took a picture with his cell phone from the store's surveillance video, loaded the picture from his phone onto his iPad and sent the images out to co-workers' computers. "So the patrol officer was looking at three possible suspects and was able to see if they look like the picture and eliminated them as suspects," Yarnell said.

The iPad also has an automatic GPS system that allows detectives to pinpoint their location. The device provides officers access to the in-house crime map that shows reported crimes and the location of sex offenders. "So if I've got a missing child, the first place I'm going is to the nearest sex offender's house," Yarnell said.

By taking field notes on his iPad, Yarnell is able to share the raw data with others. "If I take notes on a piece of paper, I have to make copies to share with other detectives," Yarnell said. "With this, I take notes and hit the e-mail icon and it goes out to everyone."

Cowan said the iPad is so versatile, he finds it easier to type on the device than with a standard computer keyboard. Yarnell said he can send his entire case file by e-mail to the Knox County district attorney general from the field "to see what charges we can bring, within minutes." Because the Sheriff's Office is the first law-enforcement agency in the area to use the iPads, Hubbs said he intends to write a report for the National Institute of Justice describing how detectives use the devices and how the agency overcame the security and connectivity issues. Federal funding through a Justice Assistance Grant paid for the iPads. Meanwhile, Yarnell is developing other applications he can add to the iPad, including a blood splatter program to help officers better understand the hidden meanings that blood drop patterns can convey to the trained eye. "It's enforcement through communications," Yarnell said. "I feel strongly about that." He also feels strongly about staying one step ahead of criminals. "We have to stay ahead of the curve," he said. "If we don't have it, the bad guys will. They watch television, so they know the technology that's out there."

16

Memphis Police Department Reduces Crime Rates with IBM Predictive Analytics Software

Gains Ability to Identify and Map Crime "Hot Spots," Reduces Serious Crime by More Than 30 Percent

I BM (NYSE: IBM) today announced that Memphis Police Department (MPD) has enhanced its crime fighting techniques with IBM predictive analytics software and reduced serious crime by more than 30 percent, including a 15 percent reduction in violent crimes since 2006. MPD is now able to evaluate incident patterns throughout the city and forecast criminal "hot spots" to proactively allocate resources and deploy personnel, resulting in improved force effectiveness and increased public safety.

Leading law enforcement agencies like MDP are using IBM analytics software to predict trends, allocate resources and identify "hot spots" to reduce crime rates - including directed patrol, targeted traffic enforcement, task forces, operations, high-visibility patrol and targeted investigations.

The FBI's Uniform Crime Reporting Program mirrored what the city of Memphis was seeing on the municipal level: crime,

Memphis Police Department Reduces Crime Rates with IBM Predictive Analytics Software. PR Newswire, July 21, 2010.

noticeably violent crime, was on the rise. Aware that traditional policing approaches were becoming less effective, MPD created Blue CRUSH(TM) , or **C** riminal **R** eduction **U** tilizing **S** tatistical **H** istory, an innovative, evidence-based approach using IBM predictive analytics software, built in partnership with the University of Memphis' Department of Criminology and Criminal Justice .

IBM predictive analytics software compiles volumes of crime records in seconds, including incoming data sources from patrols, pertaining to type of criminal offense, time of day, day of week or various victim/offender characteristics. MPD can now better guide daily decisions that address criminal activity and place officers in a better strategic position to respond to an unfolding crime. For instance, in January 2010, targeted police operations in Memphis' Hollywood-Springdale neighborhood resulted in more than 50 arrests of drug dealers; and, the area has witnessed a 36.8 percent reduction in crime.

"As crime becomes more sophisticated, law enforcement must become even smarter by adopting advanced crime prevention tactics made possible with IBM predictive analytics software. Memphis Police Department now has the invaluable insight all of our staff can use - from the commanders to the patrolling officers - to specifically focus investigative and patrol resources with the goal of preventing crime and making our neighborhoods safer," said Colonel James Harvey, commander, Ridgeway Station, at MPD. "IBM's comprehensive set of capabilities for data access, data preparation, analysis and reporting allow us to get the most value from our analytical resources, empowering every officer on the force to take a proactive role in the city's ongoing commitment to crime prevention and public safety."

To listen to Colonel James Harvey discuss the importance of IBM predictive analytics software in Memphis Police Department's Blue CRUSH program, click here. [http://www.spss.com/10/memphis-police/]

Blue CRUSH uses software to analyze past and present information and create multi-layer maps of crime "hot spots" based on various arrests and incidents. MPD is able to evaluate incident patterns throughout the city and connect the dots - such as outside of concert venues; or crime trends, such as increased car burglary on rainy nights. The software enables Blue CRUSH to analyze an array of data in areas as wide as the city's entire nine precincts or narrowed down to a single block.

Blue CRUSH has greatly expanded over the years and now works in tandem with MPD's Real Time Crime Center (RTCC), a $3 million state-of-the-art crime monitoring and analysis hub that opened in June 2008. This unique approach to fighting crime earned IBM and Memphis Police Department a 2010 Technology ROI Award from independent analyst firm Nucleus Research . MPD recorded an 863 percent ROI in just 2.7 months, an average annual benefit of $7,205,501. Download the full case study here . [http://nucleusresearch.com/research/roi-case-studies/roi-case-study-ibm-spss-memphis-police-department/]

"The Memphis Police Department is changing the face of law enforcement. By analyzing past criminal behavior patterns and then mapping their anticipated future occurrence, police departments are able to deliver critical real-time information to the field, allowing for appropriate deployment of forces. In becoming smarter through its use predictive analytics, Memphis is now a safer community and better addresses the needs of its citizens," said Anne Altman, general manager, Public Sector, IBM.

In the last four years, IBM has invested $11 billion to build its business analytics portfolio, dedicated 5,000 services consultants and made 19 acquisitions. Today, IBM is working with more than 250,000 clients worldwide on predictive analytics, including 22 of the top 24 global commercial banks, 18 of the world's top 22 telecommunication carriers and 11 of the top 12 U.S. specialty retailers.

17

City of Gary Expands ShotSpotter Gunshot Location System

The City of Gary and the Gary Police Department announced the expansion of its ShotSpotter Gunshot Location System - Stationary Array (GLS-SA).

According to ShotSputter, the latest expansion was funded using $630,000 in COPS Technology Grant Funds through the Department of Justice. The system now covers an 8.5 mile area and includes the addition of a mobile software client which will allow the technology to be used directly by both 9-1-1 dispatch and patrol officers. Since its initial installation in 2005, the Gary Police Department has attributed dozens of apprehensions, weapon confiscations and arrests directly to the ShotSpotter GLS.

The system is used to detect, locate, alert and track gunfire and other explosive events in near real-time. Each event is logged into a historical database for strategic and tactical crime analysis that reveals crime trends, patterns, and hot spots within a coverage area. ShotSpotter GLS data has also been used to corroborate and refute eye witness testimony, establish a timeline of events, and aid in crime scene reconstruction.

"Building on the initial success of the system, the ShotSpotter GLS will provide us with critical actionable intelligence and more complete data on gun crime within the community," said Police Chief Gary Carter. "Using system data, we will be able to enhance anti-crime strategies that are already in place and further reduce gun violence within the community."

"This technology is a vital tool in our arsenal and will play a valuable role in our efforts to combat Gary's gun crime," said Mayor

City of Gary Expands ShotSpotter Gunshot Location System. Wireless News, July 15, 2010.

Rudy Clay. "The end result will be improved safety for responding officers and the citizens of Gary."

"The Gary Police Department has continued to rely on the ShotSpotter GLS to give them previously unavailable gun crime intelligence," said Gregg Rowland, senior VP of ShotSpotter. "Their continuing commitment to deriving benefit from the system has allowed officers to better analyze, monitor and respond to gun-crime trends and build more targeted crime prevention strategies. The result has been safer neighborhoods and improved quality of life within the City of Gary."

Over 50 cities and counties around the world use ShotSpotter GLS data and analytics capabilities to drive intelligence-led policing and targeted anti-crime programs. Agencies using the ShotSpotter GLS report reductions in violent crime rates by at least 30 percent and gunfire rate reductions by as much as 60 to 80 percent after the first year of operation.

Evidence-Based Policing

18

GIS Prevalent at the Stockholm Criminology Symposium

Nigel Waters

The importance of geography and, subsequently, GIS in explaining the occurrence of crime is well established, so it's not a surprise that GIS-based research again was evident at this year's Stockholm Criminology Symposium held June 14-16, 2010.

The symposium, held on an annual basis since 2006, was a notable success due to the remarkable organizational skills of Jan Andersson and Anna Cory and their team from the Swedish National Council for Crime Prevention. The symposium attracts the best criminologists in the world, and this year was no different, with more than 200 speakers and 600 delegates from more than 30 different countries.

The conference had two distinct tracks: one concerned with policing matters and the other with the analysis of crime patterns. The two tracks frequently coalesced in those presentations that sought to use new policing strategies and the results of crime analysis to reduce the level of crime.

THE STOCKHOLM PRIZE IN CRIMINOLOGY

Since 2006, the Stockholm Prize in Criminology has been awarded annually at the symposium. The prize, of at least 1 million Swedish Kroner and under the auspices of the Swedish Ministry of Justice, seeks to recognize contributions to the field of criminology that

Waters, N. GIS prevalent at the Stockholm Criminology Symposium. GEO World, August 2010 v23 i8 p14(2).

include "greater knowledge of alternative crime prevention strategies inside and outside the judicial system."

This year, the prize was awarded by a distinguished jury of 11 academics and practitioners to David Weisburd, a professor of criminology cross appointed at the Hebrew University of Jerusalem and George Mason University, where he is the director of the Center for Evidence-Based Crime Policy.

Weisburd won the prize primarily for his almost two decades of research focusing on the analysis of crime "hotspots." He received the citation from the Swedish Minister of Justice, Beatrice Ask, in the Stockholm City Hall, the home of the Nobel Prizes (see accompanying figure on page 15).

In a series of GIS-based studies in Jersey City, N.J., and Seattle, Weisburd was able to demonstrate, using randomized control trials (RCTs), that by greatly increasing police patrols in areas of exceptionally high crime rates (including robbery, prostitution and illegal drug markets), crime could be reduced dramatically. Contrary to conventional wisdom, increased police presence in these areas didn't lead to the expected displacement of crime to surrounding neighborhoods; there was instead a "diffusion of benefits" resulting from the heightened police presence in the area adjacent to the hotspot.

A DISSENTING VOICE

Although RCTs are viewed as the "gold standard" of evidentiary criminology, such approaches have limitations. Todd Clear (2010), in his presidential address to the American Society of Criminology (ASC), observed that every RCT study takes place within a specific context, selects certain target groups, and uses research and policing teams that may or may not be typical.

This isn't an indictment of RCTs, but rather a plea to have more of them, so their conclusions can be applied in varying contexts to different crimes and jurisdictions over longer time intervals. It indicates that we don't yet have sufficient RCT-based evidence for unequivocal policy decisions to reduce all crimes in all places.

Clear argues for more meta-analyses, where the results of similar studies are aggregated to determine a consensus. But if there are too few RCTs, this likely will be uninformative. Clear suggests that other types of non-experimental evidence are needed and shouldn't be disparaged.

RCTS PROS AND CONS

One of the most detailed expositions (and ostensibly successful applications) of the experimental method to crime control is the work of Weisburd, Anthony Braga and their colleagues (1999), who routinely use GIS in their research. In a study in Jersey City, they selected 12 control sites and 12 intervention sites for their RCT experiments into the effectiveness of problem-oriented policing (POP) in violent-crime hotspots. The POP interventions resulted in crime reductions relative to the control areas.

The researchers also examined areas surrounding the intervention sites and were able to show that, contrary to expectations, there was no displacement of crime, but rather a displacement of the benefits of increased enforcement. Surprisingly, they deliberately didn't look at what was happening in the rest of the city outside the areas set aside for the experiment.

Although these experiments in reducing violent crime at hotspots are universally acclaimed, Weisburd and his colleagues would, I believe, be the first to urge researchers to improve on the method of RCTs. They wouldn't want themselves or others to rest on their laurels.

HOW TO IMPROVE RCTS

1. Crime research needs to determine which policing tactics work best in which places. Braga and colleagues state that their "specific tactics ... [and interventions used] varied from place to place" and included increased patrols, dispersion of loiterers, increased summons, and stop-and-frisk actions against suspicious persons.

This POP approach produced a statistically significant reduction in citizen calls for emergency service, a measure of criminal behavior that, according to criminologists, is a more reliable indicator of criminal activity than police-reported incident and arrest data. If the research is to be more widely deployed, other police departments will have to replicate the POP approach, but the RCTs weren't able to determine if one tactic worked better than another.

2. Crime research must consider what's happening across the city. Braga et al's "evaluation design did not focus on whether violent crime decreased across Jersey City." Determining what is happening "across the city" should simply involve accessing the GIS that most large police departments use routinely.

Ignoring this information, even if it's not part of the RCT experiment, isn't a good research strategy. Politicians and citizens will want to know whether the extra policing in the crime hotspots led to increased crime anywhere in the city. Have response times and other measures of police service been adversely affected? Extra policing in the hotspots might lead to reduced service (in some locales) or the need for higher taxes or both.

Examining the whole city would have been useful for detecting crime that had been displaced more than the two blocks considered in the researchers' displacement buffer.

3. The confounding effects and interactions of other variables should be considered, and criminologists need to develop the methodology of RCTs so that police departments can determine optimal levels of policing at all locations.

4. Calls to service were used to determine the success of the POP approach to hotspot crime reduction, and this has been argued by criminologists as the best surrogate for crime levels that are hard to specify directly because of the police's discretionary powers in reporting incidents and making arrests. Further research is needed to see how calls to service correlate with actual crime levels as well as determine if elected officials and citizens find this a convincing measure.

5. What's the cost of the new program, will a benefit-cost analysis yield a favorable ratio, and how does the new program compare to other interventions? Criminologists routinely cite the success of the RCT approach in medical research, but even there its efficacy doesn't go unchallenged.

One study citing more than 50,000 RCTs published between 1966 and 1988 noted that only 0.2 percent included an economic analysis, but this was still 121 studies--more than all the RCTs ever conducted in place-based crime research (see www.jstor.org/pss/3766218). Crime research has much to learn from the medical literature.

6. How long will the effects of the crime intervention last? Some studies, such as the Kansas City Crack House Raids Experiment, reported effects that were modest and decayed rapidly. But a subsequent study on drug dealing that involved contact with landlords in the crime areas demonstrated that benefits of police interventions could be sustained (Weisburd et al, 2010).

7. It was argued at the symposium that RCTs can't be used to compare different policies at the international level, such as how countries deal with sentencing strategies and their resulting impact on incarceration rates. Thus, crime researchers would have us believe that their gold standard can provide no advice on how Americans can reduce their horrific incarceration rates that are approximately 15 times higher than in Sweden. Again, crime research has much to learn from the use of RCTs in medical research, where such inter-country comparisons are routine (see www3.interscience.wiley.com/journal/118709077/abstract).

REFERENCES

Braga, A.A., Weisburd, D. et al. 1999. "Problem Oriented Policing in Violent Crime Places: A Randomized Control Experiment." Criminology, 37, 3, 541-580.

Clear, T.R. 2010. "Policy and Evidence: The Challenge to the American Society of Criminology: 2009 Presidential Address." Criminology, 48, 1-25.

Weisburd, D., Telep, C.W. and Braga, A.A. 2010. "The Importance of Place in Policing: Empirical Evidence and Policy Recommendations." Swedish National Council for Crime Prevention, Stockholm, Sweden.

Nigel Waters is professor of geography and director for the Center of Excellence for Geographic Information Science, George Mason University; e-mail: nwaters@gmu.edu.

19

My Search as a Cop for Justice in a Flawed Criminal System

Sunil Dutta

Thirteen years ago, in a fit of idealism, I left my comfortable career as a scientist and joined the Los Angeles Police Department.

Like most of the academics, I believed that the police were corrupt. I wanted to learn the reality of policing and to serve as a model for positive change. When I started, major scandals in the LAPD were breaking out. Officers were allegedly involved in the murder of rapper Notorious B.I.G., providing protection to criminal rap artists, and the Rampart scandal had tarnished the image of the world-famous police agency once again.

The LAPD was in transformation. Chief Bernard Parks had terrified the entire LAPD with his heavy-handed disciplinary system; cops were leaving the department in droves.

Though suspicious, I found that the majority of officers were professional and honorable. True criminal cops, like Rafael Perez and David Mack, were the rarity. More prevalent was misconduct that was based on laziness and cutting corners, not with a criminal intent, but with a "the ends justify the means" mentality.

The major shortcoming in policing was something far more dangerous and something that has not been addressed seriously by our criminal justice system. Major harm could result from our reliance on two very fallible tools: eyewitnesses and shoddy forensic science.

Dutta, S. My search as a cop for justice in a flawed criminal system. The Christian Science Monitor, Oct 28, 2009 p9. Reprinted by permission of the author.

Consider a recent example: On Feb. 17, 2004, Texas executed Cameron Todd Willingham for the arson deaths of his three daughters. In September, an investigative article in The New Yorker revealed that Mr. Willingham was innocent. It sparked a series of investigations that found he was the victim of shoddy crime scene investigation and outdated theories.

The tragic miscarriage of justice in Willingham's case is not isolated. Many harrowing tales exist: Frank Lee Smith spent 14 years on Florida's death row and was exonerated as a result of DNA testing 10 months after he died awaiting execution.

The number of postconviction DNA exonerations in the US is more than 200. Since 1973, the US has released 135 people from death row due to DNA exonerations. Some were convicted due to mistaken eyewitnesses, others due to police and prosecutorial zeal and misconduct.

People, especially in law enforcement, have a hard time comprehending such stories. Don't we live in a free society where criminals have too many rights and the police's hands are tied up by too many regulations? Every cop knows at least a few criminals who walk around free because we can't charge or convict them.

Yet innocent people are railroaded through our "justice" system, all the way to lethal injections and the electric chair. Why?

The answer lies both in our human and institutional natures. As humans, we tend to believe whatever fits our self-interest, discarding facts that tend to challenge our hypotheses. The errors of deduction can therefore multiply in an investigation when shoddy science is applied or where we rely solely on eyewitnesses. As Willingham's case demonstrates, the combination can be fatal.

Early in my career, my training officer and I responded to an attempted murder investigation. The victim was shot from close range. Thankfully the shooter missed the intended target's vitals and only managed to hit the victim's biceps.

Within moments, my partner had stopped three kids who he believed had shot the victim. Our victim emphatically stated that these suspects were not the shooters. The victim's cousin, who was present during the shooting, insisted that the three were the shooters. Whom could we believe? Absent a video or other clinching evidence, how could we be certain that we were making the right decision?

Another example: A victim of an assault with a deadly weapon in my division identified the criminal. When my officers and sergeants went to arrest the suspect, he, in common with almost everyone, proclaimed his innocence. My officers spent considerable time checking the alibi of the suspect and finally determined that a video at his work established that he was indeed innocent. What if there had been no video to confirm his alibi?

Our criminal justice system would fail without eyewitness assistance to try and convict criminals. Yet numerous scientific studies have shown that even the most well-intentioned eyewitnesses can identify the wrong person or fail to identify the perpetrator of a crime.

Aside from the fallibility of eyewitnesses, our political model of control over the police can lead to inadvertent mistakes. Municipal police departments dance to the tune of their political masters who thrive on the constant drumbeat of "tough on crime" rhetoric. The only evidence that police can measure to tout our tough-on-crime rhetoric is increasing the number of arrests and reducing crime rates.

This pressure to be productive, the lack of personnel and time, and the desire to wrap up an incident, combined with the unreliability of eyewitnesses, increases the odds that an innocent person may be arrested, or worse, convicted. Add to this our system that rates prosecutorial performance on conviction rates and we are on a slippery slope. And when corrupt prosecutors who present false evidence, even in death penalty cases, such as the now disbarred Arizona prosecutor Kenneth Peasley, enter the mix, only God can save the innocent.

As the Texas father's case proves, sometimes what amounts to voodoo passes for scientific analysis of crime scenes. That the agencies which take part in prosecution and conviction (police, fire, district attorneys) consider anything less than scientific analysis should be considered malpractice.

Police departments across the country need to establish standardized tough, scientifically accurate procedures for evidence collection and analysis. Without that, innocent individuals will continue to be wrongly jailed because of an unwitting and erroneous eyewitness or an overzealous but scientifically illiterate investigator. As error-prone humans, we can't guarantee a fail-safe criminal justice system; therefore, to be truly just we must abolish capital punishment.

We need to move away from number-based evaluation of police departments' productivity and increasing reliance on crime statistics to measure police success.

It should also be mandated that all police contacts be recorded on video. And when a case for prosecution is built solely on eyewitnesses or informants, it should go through enhanced scrutiny by the judicial branch. The benchmark should be a nationwide standardization of policies on evidence collection and analysis.

The success of police agencies should be evaluated based upon satisfaction of the communities they serve. Such satisfaction surveys should be conducted by independent external entities. As procedures for police training and evidence collection and analysis already exist and only need to be streamlined and improved, none of the proposed solutions entail major financial expenditure or rely on political process, ensuring a quicker implementation. This will help create a truly just criminal justice system in our country.

Sunil Dutta, PhD, is a lieutenant in the Los Angeles Police Department. The views expressed here are his own.

20

On the Block

A Pilot Program in Oakland, California, Combines Community Policing With Social Services and Gets At-Risk Young Men Off the Street

Chris Smith

It's been raining and the San Francisco Giants are on TV, so the streets are quiet. We're cruising through East Oakland, one of the most violent parts of a violent city. A knot of drug dealers loiters in front of a housing project, and crackheads sit in folding chairs on the sidewalk. Two teenagers in hoodies saunter by; another weaves back and forth on a small bike. Anthony DelToro gestures toward them: "When you see youngsters like that, all in black, the majority of the damn time they got guns." He pauses. "This is Oakland--everybody got a gun."

DelToro, a 24-year-old East Oaklander who wears an extra-large white T-shirt and a Giants baseball hat, knows of what he speaks. He grew up in a Norteno gang neighborhood, sold coke, heroin, and weed and served stints totaling two-and-a-half years in county jails. He now leads a Street Outreach team of locals in their 20s to 40s--some are ex-gang members and drug dealers, some have lost loved ones to violence. The common denominator is that they all command respect on the street.

They don white jackets (inscribed with the words "For a Safer Oakland") and walk through rough neighborhoods four nights a

Reprinted with permission from Chris Smith, "On the Block," The American Prospect: January/February 2011. Volume 22, Issue 1. http://www.prospect.org. The American Prospect, 1710 Rhode Island Avenue, NW, 12th Floor, Washington, DC 20036. All rights reserved.

week. Crime drops when they're on the job: from 20 percent in an East Oakland hotspot to 32 percent in West Oakland, according to a study done for the city by an independent auditor. Statistics, however, don't measure everything the outreach workers do. They negotiate truces, act as mentors, and offer criminals a future--that doesn't involve prison or death--through jobs, counseling, or a face-saving way to return to school. "We may not have the answer," DelToro says, "but we can lead them to the people who do."

There are only a dozen Street Outreach workers, but they play an outsize role in the city's fight against crime. They're not cops--far from it. Still, they are an integral part of Oakland's Lifeline program, the local iteration of an innovative alternative-policing strategy that has cut down on arrests and decreased homicides by up to 50 percent in cities nationwide by combining iron-fisted law enforcement with old-school "root causes" measures such as wraparound social services.

As it turns out, in the most troubled neighborhoods, neither approach works well in isolation. Aggressive policing alienates the communities it aims to help, and the sheer level of dysfunction in places like East Oakland can frustrate even the best social programs. The success of Lifeline is that it joins these elements and ensures that each of the main actors (cops, community leaders, and service providers) reads from the same script. As Kevin Grant, an elder street statesman who spent over a decade in a federal prison for selling drugs and now coordinates the city's violence-prevention network, puts it, "It's a tag-team effort."

The model was test run in Boston in 1996, at the tail end of the nation's crack epidemic. David Kennedy, then a researcher at Harvard and now a professor at John Jay College of Criminal Justice, and two colleagues noticed that less than 1 percent of the population was responsible for the majority of violence in most cities. They decided to concentrate on these high-volume criminals, many of whom were gang members. They designed a program in which a coalition of authorities, both legal and moral, told these apparent incorrigibles to quit killing and offered immediate job training and counseling if they did. If they refused to quit, the law came down on them--hard.

Operation Ceasefire, as it is known, was startlingly successful. Boston saw a 50 percent drop in murders. As Ceasefire spread to other cities, it became obvious that Boston wasn't a fluke. In Cincinnati, gang-related murders fell by half. In Stockton, California, a working-class city about 75 miles east of Oakland, gang-related youth homicides fell from 18 in 1997 to just one in 1998.

While the model focuses on curbing violence, it also tries to ensure its social-services work takes hold. (Outreach teams aren't used everywhere, but some cities have found them highly effective at both reducing violence and convincing offenders to accept help.) Kennedy now co-chairs the National Network for Safe Communities, of which Oakland and cities like Los Angeles and Chicago are a part.

Kennedy, who first published his ideas in this magazine (see "Can We Keep Guns Away from Kids?" Summer 1994), co-founded the network to help cities adapt the Ceasefire model to their needs by offering technical assistance, research, and specialists to aid in the rollout. In Oakland, the NNSC is beginning to fine-tune the city's violence-prevention strategies and to research their effectiveness. These measures are essential for securing the necessary funding and institutional support to entrench the programs as official policy. Kennedy's intention is to "reset" the relationships between law enforcement and offenders by implementing the program everywhere it is needed. If that happens, he estimates, "it'll cut the homicide rate by half nationwide, maybe more."

Oakland certainly needs help. In 2009 it was ranked the nation's third most violent city, according to the publisher CQ Press, which analyzes the FBI's annual crime numbers and assigns an overall score for almost 400 cities. Oakland is a divided city, split between affluent hilltop neighborhoods and flatlands in which the poor scrape by, their streets patrolled by a police force often seen as an occupying army.

The city has experimented with what has become known as community policing. In criminal justice, that's often shorthand for an alternative enforcement strategy that puts police in close contact with the communities they serve, collaborating to prevent crime instead of reacting to it. Of course, as implemented across hundreds of jurisdictions, community policing has meant different things depending on the locale.

In Oakland, a dedicated beat officer works proactively with neighborhood crime-prevention groups on local concerns like prostitution and drug-dealing to ensure that each community has a fixed point of contact with the police. The policy has seen a number of false starts (one past police chief, for instance, didn't like the idea of his officers "going native"), but crime has dropped over the last few years.

Faced with a budget deficit of $30.5 million last summer, however, Oakland laid off 80 cops and more than half of its neighborhood service coordinators and reassigned its community-policing officers to patrol. More budget cuts and layoffs are likely to happen by the end of this year. The Oakland Police Department insists that community policing will continue, but it is unclear what it will look like.

Howard Jordan, Oakland's assistant chief of police, says that the department has trained its officers in preventive- and community-oriented policing, and that patrol officers will continue to tackle neighborhood problems when they have the time. "Our ideal is to make everyone a community-policing officer," he says. "It just depends on your definition of community policing."

Lifeline, which plans to hire more outreach workers, promises to fill some of the gaps in police presence. While Lifeline's work isn't community policing, it serves many of the same ends. Lifeline doesn't ask cops to become social workers, as the cliche goes; it just asks them to enforce the law more selectively to avoid the indiscriminate crackdowns that anger communities, which frees police to concentrate on the worst offenders. The outreach workers help tamp down violence in the city's most volatile areas and connect young guys on the corners with the social services that provide a path out of the thug life. When all the parts work together, communities can reclaim their neighborhoods. So far, Lifeline's approach appears to be working.

LAST SPRING, A POLICE OFFICER hand-delivered a letter to Erik Agreda, a 28-year-old repeat offender who lives in West Oakland, demanding he attend a meeting for habitual offenders at City Hall. This is known as the "call in," Lifeline's police-run component. Call-in participants are either on probation or on parole and possess lengthy rap sheets. Agreda was no exception. He had just finished his latest stint, 11 months for crack possession, in November 2009.

Agreda and 10 other men were summoned to a municipal conference room where they stared down a crowd of cops, U.S. attorneys, FBI agents, and neighborhood community leaders. Each speaker came at the subject from a different angle. The cops threatened prison time; the community leaders, which included relatives of crime victims, struck a more conciliatory tone. Their message was unmistakable: Stop the violence.

Agreda says he wasn't impressed by the tough talk: "I thought it was bullshit. They tried to scare us, saying they were going to hand our files to the feds."

Afterward, an outreach manager asked Agreda if he needed help with anything. Agreda was unemployed and shot back sarcastically, "Yeah, can you find me a job?"

"I meant it as a bluff," Agreda says. He probably would have forgotten about the offer of help, but the case manager followed up a few days later with an opening for a temporary position. Soon Agreda was sorting trash and recycling and loading trucks and building furniture for Pottery Barn and West Elm.

Agreda is trying to make the change stick. He's been out of prison for a year-his longest period of being a free adult--and trying to get off probation for the first time in seven years. "I've been in trouble most of my life," he says. "Usually it's seven months and I'm back in again. It's time to grow up."

Little hard data exists yet on Lifeline's effectiveness, but the preliminary evidence is encouraging. There have been 11 call-ins with 80 habitual offenders since November 2009. (Another meeting was scheduled for November 2010.) Oakland's unemployment rate is 17 percent, and these men rank among the city's least employable, but nearly 30 percent have already found work. Close to 20 percent, meanwhile, are back in school. While 19 of the men have violated their parole or probation, only eight have committed new offenses, a 10 percent recidivism rate compared to the county-wide recidivism rate of 39 percent within the first year. Plus, only a handful of the new violations were violent, a minor miracle considering the group's history.

A similar trend has played out in Ghost Town, a mostly African American neighborhood in West Oakland. This pocket of empty storefronts and rundown bungalows has seen 149 shootings and killings since 2007, the third-highest total in the city. Before Lifeline became involved, the police regularly swept the neighborhood and made many arrests, but it wasn't enough. "Traditional police work hadn't done the job," Jordan says.

In 2008, the outreach teams began their work. The following year, police started the call-ins, zeroing in on the worst offenders. The violence has dropped sharply: Only nine of those 149 shoot rags and homicides occurred in the first seven months of 2010. "When we started this process, there were bodies on the streets," says Don Link, a former member of the city's Community Policing Advisory Board who chairs a neighborhood crime-prevention group. "Now shootings are the exception rather than the rule."

FOR ALL ITS PROMISE, Lifeline is still evolving, and its future is uncertain. Oakland's politics are defined by fiefdoms that rarely agree on criminal-justice issues, and programs come and go with terrifying speed. There's no guarantee, for instance, that the next mayor, who takes office in January, will continue to support Lifeline. Grant, the violence-prevention coordinator, has seen this process up close over the years. "You can have a perfect program," he says, "and it's working, but in two years they'll say, 'Oh, it's over with. There's a new mayor in town, and that was married to the old mayor so wipe it from the table.'" It can be frustrating, but he says he hopes the new administration, seeing Lifeline's success, will allow the program to grow.

Beyond crime statistics, Lifeline already has accomplished things that many Oaklanders would have thought unlikely, if not impossible. In its small-bore way the program is helping to bridge the divide between police and communities. Jordan was skeptical at first of working with ex-felons, but he's a believer now: "The outreach workers reach the hearts and minds of people who would never listen to us."

Back in West Oakland, Agreda says he's doing well, managing his family's gift store and raising his 3-year-old son. He remains skeptical about the call-in but admits that it pushed him in the right direction: "In a weird way, it served its purpose."

Chris Smith is a writer and photographer who has worked in Africa, the Middle East, and at home in the Bay Area. His work has been published in Afar, California, and on MotherJones.com.

21

How to Fix America's Broken Criminal Justice System

Sunil Dutta

America's criminal justice system is deeply flawed. Beyond the harsh sentences and wrongful convictions (including innocents on death row), the system we've created fails to support victims or reform criminals. Furthermore, the entire system is rooted in a punitive approach to crime.

America, the land of the free, has the world's largest prison population (2.3 million) and its highest incarceration rate. And our overcrowded prisons are disproportionately filled with blacks and Hispanics, causing many urban communities to lose trust in a system they consider biased and racist.

In short, our criminal justice system is providing neither justice nor security.

These fundamental flaws have been ignored for years, but the staggering cost of fighting crime at a time when cities and states are going broke is forcing taxpayers to pay attention. People are right to ask: Why continue to perpetuate a disastrously expensive and largely ineffective approach to public safety? Isn't there a better way?

There is. But we have to be willing to dismantle our current piece-meal measures and replace them with an integrated model: a single Public Safety Agency (PSA) at the local level.

Dutta, S. How to fix America's broken criminal justice system. The Christian Science Monitor, Dec 30, 2010. Reprinted by permission of the author.

Current System: A Heavy Burden on Taxpayers

Crime - and fighting it - is expensive. Taxpayers bear a heavy burden to fund the police and related emergency services (911, medical response, trauma centers), the courts, the correctional system, probation and parole agents, and social service agencies.

The costs of these services is exacerbated due to the system's built-in inefficiencies such as redundancies, turf battles, compartmentalization, lack of cooperation, and lack of integration. The relationship among various components - for example, between parole agents and social service agencies - is often adversarial. This undermines effectiveness and leaves those most in need of help caught in the middle.

Finally, the political incentives that pervade the system lead to a focus on superficial metrics achieved (arrests, convictions) - not lives changed. This focuses the system in a wrong direction and also neglects the prevention of crime because prevention cannot be quantified.

The net result is that victims and their traumatized families rarely receive adequate financial or psychological help. And criminals rarely get rehabilitated; instead they go to prisons that serve as virtual graduate schools for criminality. As a lieutenant in the Los Angeles Police Department, I have lost count of how many times I've seen repeat criminals on the road to jail again. Society ends up paying economically and morally.

A Bold, New Approach

PSAs would be a paradigm shift.

It would make law officers true servants of the public, enhance transparency in law enforcement operations, and provide proper support to the victims, law violators, and their families.

The PSA would prevent first-time offenders from getting hardened and hardened criminals from getting worse. It would break the cycle of crime. Additionally, the system would provide far superior services at a fraction of the cost of the present system. The PSA would represent a complete transformation in how government provides justice and safety to communities across America. In essence, it would be a person-centered, not crime-centered approach to law enforcement.

The PSA would be a comprehensive collaboration of all public-safety personnel. Sworn officers, prosecuting and defense attorneys, emergency response teams, child and family services, social-welfare agents, community-service specialists, rehabilitation, job training, drug- and alcohol-abuse counselors, negotiators, psychological counselors, and probation and parole agents would all work together in the same building with the same mission.

They would work seamlessly and transparently with a goal of preventing crime and rehabilitating criminals. Consolidation of numerous entities would cut the cost of operations instantly by perhaps two-thirds, saving taxpayers billions. Cross-training officers of the new agency would create well-rounded public servants. Increased transparency and focus on rehabilitation would bridge the chasm that exists between the police and the public, enhancing cooperation that would lead to true community policing.

Coordinated Response to a Crime

Any time a crime occurs, sworn PSA agents would respond. Depending on the incident, prosecutors, public defenders, and appropriate family service agents might accompany them. As soon as the crime scene was stabilized, supporting agents would assist both the victim and the alleged law violator.

A coordinated response would bring greatly needed checks and balances, ensuring that officers properly enforce the law and that the prosecutors and public defenders uphold the rights of the accused. Additionally, family services and psychological counselors would assist the victims and provide support in coping with traumatic incidents.

Justice and Security Through Rehabilitation

A key distinction of these new PSAs would be their focus on rehabilitation. The person arrested would receive instant attention from counselors, and efforts to reform and reintegrate the law violator would continue until true rehabilitation has been demonstrated.

The criminal's family would be enlisted to create an environment that promotes rehabilitation. The collaborative efforts of PSA agents specializing in probation, parole, social services, education, job-training and counseling would combine to turn a law violator into a law-abiding citizen. Constant monitoring and support makes all the difference between a mere ex-con (who may well end up back in jail) and a productive member of society.

Additionally, the PSA would work to stop crime before it starts. Professional mediators would patrol high-stress communities, helping to resolve neighborhood disputes before they escalate into gang violence.

Proven method

The PSA's integrated approach has been tried on a smaller scale. In the early 1990s, the Los Angeles Police Department tried a program called the Domestic Abuse Response Team (DART), which paired civilian counselors with police officers. In case of any crime involving domestic violence, after the uniformed officers declared the area safe, the DART personnel (plainclothes officers accompanying civilian case workers) responded and took care of the victim and victim's family.

They provided aid, counseling, information, and helped find shelter for the victim. Their approach directly contributed to breaking the circle of violence in domestic situations. This was a very successful program. The only component missing was that the suspect was not provided counseling on how to control his behavior and thus break the cycle of violence. Unfortunately, due to lack of resources and funding, the program could not be implemented department-wide.

Case studies suggest the PSA approach is promising. In one of the rare consolidation studies conducted, public safety lieutenant Vinicio Mata compared three consolidated public safety agencies (in Sunnyvale Calif., San Diego, and White Plains, N.Y.). Mr. Mata concluded that consolidation is beneficial compared to historical stand-alone entities that managed emergencies via specialization and fragmentary response.

Further evidence that a PSA system should be embraced across America comes from the effective collaboration and efficient sharing of information in smaller cities where several components of the criminal justice system are housed in the same building, such as the city hall.

In these times of tight budgets and diminishing resources, we can reduce spending on policing, transform the structure and functioning of law enforcement, make it more accountable to the public, and make it work to prevent crime and rehabilitate law-breakers by consolidating our disparate criminal-justice system resources into a unified agency that puts people first.

Sunil Dutta is patrol watch commander at Foothill Division for the Los Angeles Police Department. The views expressed here are his own.

22

Violent Crime Cut 40 Percent in Lopezville Area

Jared Taylor

S enior Deputy Marcos Garcia sits and waits.

The warrant officer at the Hidalgo County Sheriff's Office primarily crisscrosses the county, looking for suspects wanted for arrest.

But on this afternoon, Garcia has shifted gears. He's watching for suspicious vehicles -- anyone who breaks a traffic law and looks out of sorts. "You never know what you'll come across," says Garcia, an eight-year veteran of the office. Right on cue, a white Cadillac Escalade with a small assault rifle sticker on the back rolls through a stop sign. Garcia flips on his siren. After meeting with the driver, Garcia writes him a ticket for a suspended license. During traffic stops, Garcia and his fellow deputies have arrested 25 suspects with outstanding warrants. Hidalgo County sheriff's deputies normally leave enforcing traffic law to local and state agencies in their rural jurisdiction. That, along with greater visibility and specialized deputies patrolling the area, has helped cut the violent crime rate in the Lopezville area by 40 percent in six months, statistics show. Hidalgo County Sheriff Lupe Trevino calls the initiative Operation A.P.E. -- Awareness, Prevention and Enforcement -- an effort at community-oriented policing that seems to have shown some results in what was the county's district with the highest crime rate. HOW IT WORKS The sheriff launched A.P.E. in March by sending deputy cadets to more than 8,600 homes and businesses in Hidalgo Country east district 5 -- the area that encompasses Lopezville and San Carlos, east of Edinburg -- to give each resident a bilingual flyer about the new initiative. Deputies worked with homeowners and business owners on how to prevent property crime and domestic

Taylor, J. Violent Crime Cut 40 percent in Lopezville area. Monitor (McAllen, TX), Oct 10, 2010

130

violence. That meant holding community meetings and talking with people, telling them where and what criminals have been targeting and how to cope with it. Sometimes, that was a simple as turning on porch lights or hiding barbecue grills in the back yard, rather than out in the open. Deputies from eight specialized units -- gang, narcotics, tactical patrol, warrants and others -- work together while patrolling the district, using their training to gather intelligence about crime in the area. Normally, each unit would operate separately.

"We organized an alliance of separate units with one objective in mind while executing their specialty," Trevino said. On a recent weekday while Garcia was out serving arrest warrants, he was flanked by two gang investigators. While looking for fugitives, the gang investigators worked to identify gang members through interviews and by taking photos of their tattoos and faces. Several Loco 13 gang members were identified, but no fugitives were found. "Sometimes, they're needles in haystacks," Garcia said. "Sometimes they're out barbecuing." RESULTS Under Operation A.P.E., the district saw violent crime drop by 41 percent in five months, when comparing the same period in 2009. Forcible rape and robberies both dropped by half. Aggravated assaults fell

40 percent. Only the rate of murder, a crime law enforcement leaders say is most difficult to prevent, increased -- from one to two. But property crime was mixed under the operation. Property theft is down about 6 percent. Burglaries are practically the same. And vehicle thefts are up 26 percent. "This is where we failed," Trevino said.

Despite the mixed property crime results, the sheriff said the significant drop in violent crime makes the operation a victory.

"I have to say for now, it's a success," he said. "I think it would be more significant what happens in the next six months."

LOOKING AHEAD

Operation A.P.E. will not replace the way deputies investigate crime in most of Hidalgo County, the sheriff said. Rather, it will be a way to bring down crime in the county's most dangerous patrol districts. Ultimately, the sheriff wants to hire 20 additional deputies to devote to A.P.E., targeting the unit on other high crime districts in the county. The sheriff's office recently won a federal community oriented policing grant to hire 13 deputies who already graduated from the training academy, boosting the number of deputies that can be devoted to programs like A.P.E. "We catch up, lower crime to a manageable level and maintain it," Trevino said. "This is not an overnight success story."

-- Jared Taylor covers courts, law enforcement and general assignments for The Monitor. You can reach him at (956) 683-4439.

Section III

COURTS AND THE ADJUDICATION SYSTEM

A contemporary issue related to the courtroom workgroup is the legitimacy of the system. In other words, is this branch of the criminal justice system honest and ethical in all of the proceedings and decision making, is justice truly blind? In the first part of this section you will read two very contrasting pieces. The first article addresses coercive actions by judges and prosecutors in recommending guilty pleas from criminal defendants. If you were to place yourself in the position of these defendants, would you make the same decisions? What would you base your decision on? The second article tells the story of a federal prosecutor under investigation for alleged unethical behavior. After reading this article do you think the prosecutor was truly involved in unethical behavior or was he a victim of political influence?

In Part 2 of this section, the readings address sentencing strategies. In the first articles a SCRAM alcohol monitoring program is discussed for use in probation matters. In the second article, sentencing guidelines are addressed. Do you feel sentencing guidelines are a good idea?

Part 3 addresses the Miranda rule. The first article explains the recent rulings of the United States Supreme Court related to the original Miranda ruling (Miranda v. Arizona 384 U.S. 436, 1966) regarding admissions and confessions. The next two articles address specific cases that apply to admissions and confessions. Do any of the recent findings of the United States Supreme Court apply in either of these instances?

In Part 4, the wide variety of alternative or specialty courts is presented. The purpose of these courts is to address a specific type of offender with unique needs and treatments. Proponents of alternative courts argue that offenders who are the subject of these courts are more likely to be successful and less likely to recidivate. As you read about these specialty courts, think about what other alternative courts could be developed. What is your opinion on the effectiveness of these alternative courts? Should we allow extra expenditures for these types of courts?

Ethical Behavior of Judges and Prosecutors

23

When Defendants Are Threatened to Plead Guilty

Joel Cohen

Anyone who has seen even a few "Law & Order" episodes knows the time-tested, formulaic players in the TV justice system. That is, a smarmy, unctuous defense lawyer with a dismissal motion lodged in his hip pocket ("I'll see you in court!"); a wisecracking arraignment judge who has never been to the law library and who, given the opportunity, might remand Mother Teresa herself ("Bail? You've got quite a sense of humor, counselor. Next case."); and an over-the-edge, sanctimonious prosecutor who would prosecute his own grandmother for driving without a seatbelt, as a felony ("No one—no one—is above the law!").

Now, anyone even mildly familiar with the actual criminal justice system knows that it never happens this way in the real world. Indeed, it is the rare defendant who will sit with his lawyer in the prosecutor's office or in an interview room at Rikers Island and dramatically overrule his lawyer in order to directly confess his crime to the prosecutor. The confession, of course, is the prelude to a guilty plea designed to gain a lower sentence, as happens in nearly every episode.

In the real world, prosecutors and judges sometimes cajole or even threaten defendants directly, or far more cautiously, through their lawyers—that if they don't plead guilty, "things will go a lot worse at sentence." (Going through the lawyer makes sense, of course, since a fellow member of the legal fraternity is far less likely

Cohen, J. When defendants are threatened to plead guilty. New York Law Journal, Oct 12, 2010.

138

to go under oath to repeat the potential abuse of a defendant's rights
by a judge in the robing room, although it does happen.)

It is true that things should and do go "a lot better" if a
defendant effectively shows remorse and saves the state and victims
the cost, monetary and emotional, of a full-blown trial. Word also
quickly gets around that pleading guilty before a particular judge can
go a long way. However, in a justice system so reliant on guilty
pleas, a defendant facing a potential plea is often moved to action by
the implied or explicit consequences of hanging tough when the
moment of decision is at hand. Sometimes, the communication
emanating from the prosecutor or judge is not at all subtle.

'FRIEDMAN V. REHAL'

What are the ethical and legal consequences when prosecutors and
judges push the envelope on this score? Interestingly, the "threat"
phenomenon is a far more pervasive issue in the case of threats by
judges rather than prosecutors, and it arose recently in a notorious
case in Nassau County, culminating in the Second Circuit's
affirmance of the District Court's denial of federal habeas relief.
Specifically, Friedman v. Rehal1 addressed the conviction of Jesse
Friedman, the 19-year-old son of Arnold Friedman, both charged
with multiple counts of felony child abuse.2

While the U.S. Court of Appeals for the Second Circuit dealt
with many issues raised by Friedman not pertinent here, we focus on
Mr. Friedman's claim that (1) the prosecutor pressured him to plead
guilty by threatening him with indictment on many more charges not
previously indicted and (2) the trial judge for whom "[t]here was
never a doubt in [her] mind" about the guilt of Mr. Friedman (who
protested his innocence) allegedly told Mr. Friedman's attorney that
"if [Friedman] went to trial, she intended to sentence him
consecutively on every count."3 Specifically because of the judge's
threat, Mr. Friedman told his attorney that he wanted to plead guilty
"because he believed that if he went to trial he would be found guilty
and would spend almost the remainder of his life in jail."4

While the Second Circuit denied relief, the court noted that the
trial judge's threat to Mr. Friedman "would be sufficient by itself to
sustain a challenge to the plea if [his attorney's] affidavit is credited,"
essentially establishing a per se violation of the defendant's Sixth
Amendment right to trial—which, under the circuit's case law, would
actually have required a resentence before a different judge had the

defendant rejected the pressure and proceeded to a trial and been convicted.

PROSECUTOR THREATS

Interestingly, the court, for habeas procedural reasons, felt compelled to let the conviction and sentence stand (even though it also raised serious questions about the police and prosecutorial conduct in the cases involving Brady claims). And while it challenged the judge's conduct in threatening a harsher sentence if Mr. Friedman chose to proceed to trial (even though the threat was not made directly to Mr. Friedman, but to his lawyer), the court did not challenge the prosecutor's threat to pile on additional charges in order to result in a harsher sentence.

Why? Notably, the U.S. Supreme Court in its seminal decision in Bordenkircher v. Hayes,5 in 1978, held that there is absolutely nothing wrong with a prosecutor carrying through on his threat to bring additional charges to raise the potential sentence when a defendant refuses to plead guilty. Indeed, actual vindictiveness on the part of the prosecutor is even permissible.6

> While confronting a defendant with the risk of more severe punishment may clearly have a "discouraging effect on the defendant's assertion of his trial rights, the imposition of these difficult choices [is] an inevitable"—and permissible—attribute of any legitimate system which tolerates and encourages the negotiation of pleas…It follows that, by tolerating the negotiation of pleas, this Court has necessarily accepted as constitutionally legitimate the simple reality that the prosecutor's interest at the bargaining table is to persuade the defendant to forego his right to plead not guilty.7

Still, judges stand in different shoes at the bargaining table. The ethics rule that applies to judges, ABA Model Rule of Judicial Conduct 2.6(B), says: "A judge may encourage parties to a proceeding and their lawyers to settle matters in dispute but shall not act in a manner that coerces any party into settlement"—although the case law that deals with the problem doesn't typically cite the ethical proscription when dealing with the issue.8

The Federal Rules actually forbid a judge from even participating in the plea bargaining process,9 the only exception being one that allows judges to accept or reject a plea package presented to the court after it has been negotiated and signed by the parties and presented to the court under Fed.

R. Crim. Pro. 11(c)(3)(A). Accordingly, unless the federal judge completely ignores the federal rules and tells the defendant or his lawyer specifically what the lay of the land will be in a plea resolution versus trial, a federal judge will not run afoul of the "threat" problem.10

JUDGE THREATS

For state judges, the law is fairly clear that they may not "threaten" a tougher sentence after trial,11 but is that rule actually true in practice? In People v. Stevens,12 the Appellate Division, First Department, was confronted with the following facts: during the plea negotiations, the trial judge told the defendant: "Mr. Stevens, I repeat, once we go forward, there will be no turning back. If you're convicted after trial, given the circumstances of this [burglary] case under which you were apprehended, and the nature of your record, 25 to life, that's what you're going to get."13 Presumably based on that "threat" the defendant pleaded guilty with a sentence promise of 12 years to life that was imposed.

The Appellate Division, faced with defendant's effort to undo the plea, found that "this statement was more than a description of the full range of possible sentences," as the District Attorney had argued in defense of the conviction, and citing a number of cases said that "[i]t was the type of outright coercion that has repeatedly been held to be impermissible." Rather than "impart[ing] a reasonable assessment of the sentencing prospects in the event of a conviction," the judge's comments:

> unequivocally stated that upon conviction, the maximum sentence would be imposed. Then, as defendant discussed the offer with his legal advisor, the court reminded the defendant that if he was convicted after trial, the 'perimeters' would 'double' since he would 'literally' get a life sentence.14

Obviously, a judge can't more directly instill fear into a defendant to plead guilty and cut his losses than as happened in Stevens—although, obviously, it would be worse if the judge, adding to the threat, overstates during plea negotiations what the maximum sentence could be under law.15

WHAT IS A THREAT?

But how tightly are the judge's hands tied in according a defendant the knowledge he must have about the judge's "sentencing philosophy" in order to make an informed decision? In People v. Villone,16 for example, the trial judge told the defendant during plea negotiations the possible sentences that could be imposed if he were convicted of the charges in the indictment. In rejecting his claim that "coercion" by the judge led Richard Villone to plead guilty, the Appellate Division, Fourth Department, said that the trial judge's remarks simply served to:

> impress[] upon the defendant the strength of the People's case, the potential sentence to which the defendant was exposed under the indictment, and the favorableness of the plea bargain (citing People v. Campbell, 236 A.D.2d 877, 878, 653 N.Y.S.2d 758, 758 (4th Dept. 1997). The fact that the defendant may have pleaded guilty to avoid receiving a harsher sentence does not render his plea coerced.17

While this author was not present to see the interaction with the court, the Fourth Department analysis seems correct. A defendant must be informed about what he exposes himself to by insisting on a trial. And, obviously, there's nothing wrong, in that context, with a judge telling a defendant that even though the potential maximum sentence is X, "I'm going to extend you the leniency of Y if you save the court and the victim the need for a trial and thereby show remorse in that process."

The problem here is precisely what the defendant "hears" at this very vulnerable moment in his life, particularly if his lawyer, who appears before this judge week in and week out, knows the judge's reputation as being "Maximum Joe," or the like. Clearly, that lawyer should, indeed, be telling his client the judge's reputation for maximum sentences after trial—whether the judge's protocol is intended to obtain pleas from defendants who should plead guilty, or simply to manage his docket—and she fails her client miserably if she withholds that critical information.

But what does that defendant "hear" when the judge, even if appropriately so, tells the defendant the maximum sentence imposable after trial? Is there a meaningful distinction between a judge telling a defendant, "I will accord you leniency if you accept the prosecutor's [or my] plea offer to you" or instead uttering the legally verboten threat of a maximum sentence after trial? And what if the judge candidly communicates his belief that the prosecutor's plea/sentence offer is far too lenient (meaning, given his druthers he would insist on a much tougher sentence), but nonetheless the judge intends to honor the plea offer? Fortunately for those reading this column (and myself), we haven't faced having to decipher what the judge is truly saying to us while we stand before him as a defendant.

Remember Learned Hand's famous articulation in another context, "Words are chameleons which reflect the color of their environment."18 Needless to say, given Hand's reality, judges need to be cautious in how they communicate even what a defendant needs to know to make an informed decision on whether to risk trial. The judge, and even the defendant's lawyer, may see what the judge is saying as having a pink hue, whereas the defendant who occupies the environment of a shackled or even non-shackled man awaiting trial may perceive the judge's words in blinding red. Caution and sensitivity are the order of the day.

24

Casualties of Justice

Jeffrey Toobin

B
y the conventional standards of Washington scandals, the prosecution of Senator Ted Stevens flashed only briefly across the national consciousness. Stevens was a major figure in Alaska history, and was serving his sixth full term in office when he was indicted, in 2008. He was charged with failing to report gifts, principally in the form of renovations to a small house he owned. Stevens was convicted in October of that year and, two weeks later, narrowly lost his race for reelection. Before he was sentenced, his attorneys, led by Brendan V. Sullivan, charged that the verdict was tainted by government lawyers' misconduct in the case. In April, 2009, Eric H. Holder, who had just become Attorney General, came to agree with that claim. Holder asked that Stevens's conviction be vacated and the indictment against him dismissed. This past August, when Stevens was killed in a private-plane crash, he was mourned across the state as a hero. His funeral drew three thousand people, including Vice-President Joseph Biden, a longtime colleague in the Senate, who said, "No state has ever had a more fierce defender of that state's way of life than Ted Stevens."

The matter of the botched prosecution faded from public view. Stevens, despite losing his Senate seat, had largely restored his good name; out-of-town guests at his funeral flew into Ted Stevens Anchorage International Airport. Brendan Sullivan and the federal trial judge in the case, Emmet Sullivan (no relation), moved on to other cases. There were two pending investigations of what went wrong in the Stevens prosecution, one by the Justice Department and the other by a Washington lawyer chosen by Judge Sullivan; neither has yet released its findings.

But the Stevens case was more than an unsuccessful prosecution. It was a profoundly unjust use of government power against an individual--a case flawed in both conception and

Toobin, J. Casualties of Justice. The New Yorker, Jan 3, 2011 v86 i42 p39. Reprinted by permission of the author.

144

execution. Holder asked that all charges against Stevens be dismissed because the prosecutors had failed to disclose to the defense critical exculpatory evidence--a fundamental breach of prosecutorial ethics. It remains unclear which of the several Justice Department lawyers on the case was primarily responsible for this failure; likewise, it's difficult to say if the prosecution team's errors were inadvertent or intentional. What's indisputable is that the government did not play fair with Ted Stevens.

Still, all the prosecutors in the case remain with the government, except one. Nicholas Marsh, as a relatively junior lawyer in the Justice Department, built the case against Stevens, and, working with F.B.I. agents and local prosecutors, coordinated a massive investigation of corruption in the state's politics. The efforts of Marsh and others resulted in nine convictions, including six guilty pleas, and culminated in the Stevens trial. But when that case fell apart Marsh suddenly found himself the subject of a criminal inquiry rather than the leader of one.

Marsh came to feel that this scrutiny was destroying his life. Against his will, he was transferred by Justice Department superiors out of the elite Public Integrity Section and into the relative backwater of the Office of International Affairs, which does not conduct prosecutions. Marsh awaited the results of the two investigations, but months, and then a year, passed without either one coming to a conclusion. His impatience gave way to despair. On September 26th, Marsh committed suicide. He was thirty-seven.

The F.B.I. dubbed the Alaska investigation "Operation Polar Pen," because it started when government officials uncovered corruption in plans to build a private prison in the state. In 2004, a former corrections commissioner agreed to cooperate with the authorities, and taped notable Alaska figures discussing bribes to public officials. This evidence helped prosecutors obtain court orders to place a bug and a hidden camera in Suite 604 of the Baranof Hotel, in Juneau, the state capital. During legislative sessions, the suite was reserved for the use of the Veco Corporation, a major oil-services firm, and its chief executive, Bill Allen.

The tapes from Suite 604, which became notorious in Alaska, revealed the operations of what was known as the Corrupt Bastards Club, a group of legislators who solicited and accepted bribes from Allen and others. For most of the politicians, the amounts of the bribes were no more than a few thousand dollars, but the atmosphere was one of brazenness. At the trial of Pete Kott, a former speaker of the Alaska House of Representatives, his girlfriend testified that she embroidered the letters "CBC" on about a hundred baseball caps. The Justice Department had sent Marsh from Washington to Anchorage, to run the investigation, along with a team from the local U.S. Attorney's office.

Marsh spent four years commuting to Alaska. "It was covert for a good chunk of the time he spent working on it," Ray Hulser, a supervisor in the Public Integrity Section, told me. "It was wiretaps and bugs in hotel rooms. Nick was the guy who was on it from the start, like no one else. He was the one people looked to on the team as having the most institutional knowledge. That's an unbelievable amount of pressure and scrutiny to go through." In time, Marsh negotiated plea bargains with some of the best defense lawyers in Alaska, and conducted two trials. "The lawyers in the U.S. Attorney's office were a couple of decades older than Nick, but there was no doubt that he was the top dog," Jeff Feldman, who represented an early target of Operation Polar Pen, said. "He was making the decisions."

The case came into public view in August, 2006, when F.B.I. agents executed search warrants at a number of legislative offices in Juneau. In 2007, Marsh moved into the courtroom to help make the case against Kott on charges of conspiracy, bribery, and extortion; Kott was convicted and sentenced to six years in prison.

In many respects, though, Marsh's most important task was negotiating a deal with Bill Allen, whose bribes fuelled so much corruption in the state. "I don't think I ever had a personal conversation with him," Robert Bundy, an Alaska lawyer who represented Allen, said of Marsh. "Nick was all business, all the time--always cordial, but very focussed on the cases." In the end, Allen pleaded guilty, on May 7, 2007, to charges of bribery and conspiracy for his dealings with four state legislators, including the state senator Ben Stevens, Ted's son. Most important, Allen agreed in his plea bargain to cooperate with the government in making more cases. (Allen is currently serving a sentence of thirty-six months.)

In practical terms, that meant Marsh and his colleagues had the elder Stevens in their sights--and Bill Allen was going to be the key witness against him. "Nick was obviously bright, hardworking, well educated, aggressive, but he seemed tightly wound," Feldman said. "To meet and engage him, he was the personification of the young prosecutor who had gone pretty far pretty fast, and I would have said, as an older person, that it might be good if he knew a little more about people and a little less about law."

The family of Linda DeVries, Marsh's mother, settled in Kentucky in the seventeenth century. "We are all devoted Kentuckians, and Nick bled Kentucky blue, especially for the basketball team," she told me. Nick was born on June 26, 1973, in Elizabethtown, a small city about forty miles from Louisville. "When Nick was three," DeVries told me, "we were at the grocery store one day and he asked me to hand him a box of cereal, which wasn't Apple Jacks, his favorite. I asked him why. He said, 'Well, Mom, I want to read if the surprise comes in the box or whether you have to mail away for it.' That's how precocious he was." His mother worked as a surgical nurse, and his father was an insurance agent. (They divorced when Nick was fifteen.) A much loved only child, Nick was raised to revere the Bluegrass State but also to excel on a bigger stage.

Schoolteachers pressed Nick's parents to let him skip grades in grammar school, but they preferred to keep him with friends his own age. He went to St. Xavier High School, a leading Catholic school in Louisville, and he did so well that he was offered full scholarships at several local colleges. (While Nick was in college, his mother was remarried, to William DeVries, a heart surgeon best known for implanting the first artificial heart.) But instead of going to school at the home of his beloved Wildcats, or elsewhere in Kentucky, Marsh went to Williams College, in Massachusetts. He was an immediate hit in New England. At six feet, with dark-brown hair, he had the soft accent and proper manners of the border South, and a taste for mint juleps. "Nick definitely had the polite thing going on," Victor Lopes, a classmate, recalled.

Marsh spent his junior year at Oxford, majored in philosophy, and hedged his bets on a career choice when he went to law school at Duke--where he also picked up a master's in literature. After earning his law degree, in 1998, he took a clerkship with Andrew J. Kleinfeld, a federal appeals-court judge in Fairbanks, Alaska. Marsh thrived, despite the harsh weather, and he steered away from academia and into law practice. "We had a twenty-three-day stretch when it didn't get above minus thirty, and it was dark all the time," Rob Maguire, his co-clerk, said. "If you were prone to depression, you'd get it there. But Nick loved doing his job. He wore the kind of charcoal pinstripe suit that you don't see in the West. He collected fountain pens. You could just see that this was a guy who was headed for the big time of New York or Washington."

After his clerkship, Marsh moved to New York and joined the firm of Sullivan & Cromwell, where he endured the frustrations common to junior lawyers at big firms. "Rote work, endless days reviewing documents--Nick longed for greater individual responsibility," his friend Josh Waxman, a colleague at the time, said. Three years later, Marsh joined the New York outpost of another large firm, which was then known as Hale & Dorr. Even though he quickly made junior partner, he sought work of larger meaning. A friend, Joshua Berman, had joined the Public Integrity Section, at the Justice Department, and Marsh sent him his resume. "He so wanted to be a prosecutor and public servant, and left pretty soon after becoming a partner," Berman said. This was around the time, his mother recalled, that Marsh decided that someday he wanted to be a judge.

The Public Integrity Section had about thirty lawyers, and Marsh flourished from his first day. "Nick was one of a couple of attorneys starting in the fall of 2003, and just showed tremendous promise as a prosecutor right away," Ray Hulser said. "Typically, our people work at the grand-jury and trial level, but the smartest folks are the ones who do the court-of-appeals work as well. It's sought-after work. He ended up arguing three cases in the circuit courts in his first year. That's uncommon. And he won them all, too." Marsh was sent to New Hampshire, for his first major trial, where he won a conviction against a Republican official who concocted a scheme to jam the phone lines of a Democratic get-out-the-vote operation in the 2002 election. (Because of a legal error by the judge, the conviction was later overturned.)

Marsh had been a federal prosecutor for only about a year when he was sent to Alaska on what became the Stevens investigation. The work was so secret and sensitive that he never contacted Judge Kleinfeld, for whom he had clerked, during his time in the state. On July 30, 2007, investigators obtained a warrant to search Stevens's home, in Girdwood, on Alaska's Pacific coast. A year later, a grand jury in Washington, D.C., indicted Stevens on seven felony counts of filing false financial disclosures. (Senators are required to disclose their income every year.) Stevens was charged with failing to disclose "things of value" that Bill Allen and his company, Veco, had provided to him.

The case against Stevens was dubious from the outset. He was not charged with bribery; there was no allegation that he provided any quid pro quo to Veco, even though the company was receiving more than a hundred and seventy million dollars a year in federal contracts. (Veco is now defunct.) Moreover, the worth of the "things of value" was not easily determined. In what became the heart of the case, the indictment claimed that Stevens failed to report that he had accepted "more than $250,000 in free labor, materials, and other things of value in connection with the substantial renovation, improvement, repair and maintenance" of his Girdwood home. But the indictment went on to say that Stevens had paid Veco for the renovations--just not enough to cover the true costs. For a senator renowned for controlling many billions of dollars of federal appropriations, the numbers in the case against him were rather small. And the Girdwood house, an ungainly A-frame perched on a dirt road, was a ramshackle affair, even post-renovation.

In white-collar-crime prosecutions, defense attorneys invariably seek to delay the trials of their clients. Memories fade; passions cool; evidence gets lost. The conventional wisdom is that the passage of time makes conviction less likely. But Ted Stevens had other motivations besides simply winning an acquittal. Just four months after his indictment, he would be facing Alaska's voters in his race for a seventh term, and he felt that he could win only if he had already beaten the case against him. So, in what must have been a major surprise to Marsh and his colleagues, Brendan Sullivan announced that he would demand a trial within seventy days of the indictment. This bold move by the defense had serious ramifications for the prosecution.

Although Marsh and Joseph Bottini, an Assistant U.S. Attorney in Alaska, had largely built the case, senior officials in the Justice Department decided that the trial team would be led by another lawyer--Brenda Morris, the principal deputy chief of the Public Integrity Section, who had been a prosecutor with the government since 1991. Morris is African-American, a fact that probably was not incidental in a case against a senior Republican in the District of Columbia. But Morris had only a short time to master the byzantine facts of the case and prepare for trial. With Bottini in Alaska, Marsh had to become Morris's tutor on the facts. That wasn't easy, either, because on May 24, 2008, Marsh had married Navis Bermudez, a congressional staffer on environmental issues, and gone on a two-week honeymoon in Turkey, returning shortly before the grand jury issued its indictment. Marsh's absence tightened an already rigorous schedule for the government.

The Stevens defense team filed a series of pretrial motions, which the prosecution had to respond to while also preparing for trial. In one, the defense asked that the trial be moved to Alaska, since most of the underlying events had taken place there, though the disclosure forms were filed in Washington. Both sides knew that Stevens would likely find a more sympathetic jury in his home state than in Washington. Marsh argued the issue against Brendan Sullivan, and Judge Sullivan decided to keep the trial in the District of Columbia--a victory that Marsh savored.

In many respects, though, the most contentious pretrial issue involved discovery--that is, the government's obligation to turn over its evidence to the defense. Some prosecutors adopt what's known as "open file" discovery, where they simply open all their files to the defense; in contrast, the Stevens prosecutors responded to the defense requests issue by issue, granting some and refusing others. The draining and time-consuming disputes about discovery, in an investigation that had generated thousands of documents and hundreds of hours of surveillance tapes, occupied much of the prosecutors' time.

The trial, scheduled to begin in late September, started on a sour note for Marsh. On September 12th, he e-mailed a friend, "Yesterday, the front office issued another fiat concerning the assignments for roles in the TS trial. Less than 2 weeks before trial, they countermanded my chief's staffing decision (which gave me a lot of responsibility, a lot of witnesses, the biggest cross, and the closing) and took away most of my responsibilities to give to Brenda. I now have 1/3 of the directs, 1/4 of the crosses, and no argument." This slight could have proved a blessing of sorts, because, once the trial started, Judge Sullivan found a great deal of fault with the prosecutors who were running the case.

In one matter, the prosecution introduced time sheets compiled by Veco of work done on the Girdwood house which turned out to be inaccurate; the records included workers who were not present in the area at the time. (Judge Sullivan excluded part of the records.) In another, both the prosecution and the defense had subpoenaed a witness named Rocky Williams, a Veco employee who had worked on the house. The government brought Williams to Washington to testify, but decided against using him, in part because he was in bad health, and sent him back to Alaska without telling the defense or the Judge. Brendan Sullivan claimed that the government was hiding Williams to prevent him from giving testimony helpful to the defense. Even though Marsh was not the lead counsel, Judge Sullivan scolded him in open court for the way he handled Williams. "I'm flabbergasted why you'd do this," the Judge said. "Why wasn't I consulted? I'm peeved now. It's a federal subpoena to appear in my court." (Williams died a few months after returning to Alaska.)

Most of these contretemps involved, in one way or another, discovery issues first raised in Brady v. Maryland, the 1963 Supreme Court case that established the principle that prosecutors have an obligation to produce exculpatory information and provide it to the defense. "The prosecution has an affirmative obligation to look through the files of everyone involved on its team to find whether there is any possible evidence that suggests that the defendant is not guilty or that there are credibility problems with the prosecution's witnesses," Stephen Trott, a federal appeals-court judge and former prosecutor who has lectured widely on prosecutorial ethics, told me.

Brady is one area of law that has become more pro-defendant in recent years, with prosecutors obligated to do more to ferret out exculpatory evidence. This change has transformed the way cases are both defended and prosecuted. "Defense attorneys have been waking up to the idea that the best defense is a good offense," Trott said. "Instead of only worrying about whether there's evidence to convict beyond a reasonable doubt, they focus on whether the government has complied with its duty to disclose. They think, How can I use Brady to knock the prosecutor and the government out. There's a lot of animosity out there."

No one has made this tactic more of a signature than Brendan Sullivan, who has long worked at the Washington firm of Williams & Connolly. Sullivan remains best known for his defense, in the nineteen-eighties, of Oliver North in the Iran-Contra scandal, in which he famously told the investigating congressional committee that he was not "a potted plant." (I first met Sullivan when I was a junior member of the prosecution team in North's criminal case; North was convicted of three counts, which were later overturned by an appeals court.) During the Stevens trial, Sullivan often mentioned a case that he had won in 1986, when charges against a corporate executive in Maryland were dismissed on the ground that the government had fabricated and altered documents turned over in discovery. This was the kind of misconduct that Sullivan was looking for in the Stevens case, especially when it came to the prosecution's handling of its star witness, Bill Allen.

Cooperating witnesses like Allen--who are also known as snitches, turncoats, flippers, and a variety of more colorful terms-- present daunting ethical problems for prosecutors. "Bad guys nowadays realize that the best way to get out of trouble is not to hire a great lawyer but to cut a deal," Trott said. "But they want to minimize what they do. They gild the lily. They are trying to get something by making themselves look better than they are. Prosecutors think they'll get a better deal if they get convictions in the cases where cooperators testify. They are motivated by terrible things. Young prosecutors aren't even close to being ready for this stuff. These cooperators are sociopaths."

In planning his cross-examination of Allen, Sullivan had one important asset: a note that Stevens had written to Allen while the renovations were under way. "Dear Bill," Stevens wrote. "Thanks for all the work on the chalet. You owe me a bill--remember Torricelli, my friend. Friendship is one thing--compliance with these ethics rules entirely different. I asked Bob P to talk to you about this so don't get P.O.'d at him--it just has to be done right." Bob Persons was a friend of Stevens's; Robert Torricelli was a New Jersey senator who had recently been forced out of office for accepting gifts from constituents. Sullivan built his defense around the Torricelli note. In his opening statement, Sullivan had said that the note "jumps off the page and grabs you by the throat to show you what the intent of Ted Stevens was."

But Sullivan received a surprise during Allen's direct testimony, which included the following exchange:

Q: Did you send Senator Stevens a bill or an invoice after you received this note from him?, A: No., Q: Mr. Allen, do you remember having a conversation with Mr. Persons after you got the note from Senator Stevens?, A: Yes., Q: What did Mr. Persons tell you?, A: He said oh, Bill, don't worry about getting a bill. He said, Ted is just covering his ass.,

This testimony turned Stevens's best evidence against him. It seemed to show that the Torricelli note was actually part of Stevens's cover-up rather than proof of his innocence. In cross-examination, Sullivan did his best to prove that the cover-his-ass testimony was just a recent fabrication on the part of Allen, but the jury apparently believed otherwise, and convicted Stevens on all counts.

Marsh and his colleagues did not have long to enjoy their triumph. In early December, five weeks after the verdict, in the waning days of the Bush Administration, Chad Joy, an F.B.I. agent involved in the case, filed a formal complaint against a fellow-agent, Mary Beth Kepner, and several prosecutors, saying that Kepner had behaved inappropriately during the investigation. He alleged that Kepner had had a flirtatious relationship with Bill Allen, suggesting that, as "a surprise/present," she had worn revealing clothes when Allen testified in court. More important, Joy said that the prosecutors had conspired to withhold exculpatory evidence. In particular, Joy said that even though Rocky Williams had been subpoenaed by both sides, Marsh sent him home to Alaska because he had fared poorly on a mock cross-examination, not because he was sick.

Judge Sullivan, who was already irritated with the prosecutors for their performance during the trial, was now outraged. He ordered them to turn over all internal communications regarding Joy's

152

allegations, and, on February 13, 2009, when they were slow to
respond, he found four of them in contempt of court--an
extraordinary sanction to impose on federal government lawyers, and
one that could, in theory, result in jail time. The four cited were
Morris; William Welch, the chief of the Public Integrity Section;
Patty Stemler, an appeals specialist; and Kevin Driscoll, a trial
lawyer who had just joined the prosecution team. (The Judge did not
sanction Marsh, who was not involved with researching the Joy
allegations.) The prosecution was a shambles, and Stevens hadn't
even been sentenced yet. Superiors in the Justice Department decided
to bring in a whole new team to try to salvage the conviction. After
four years of work, Marsh had been thrown off the case of his life.

In four decades as a criminal-defense attorney, Brendan
Sullivan had never had a prosecutor request permission to visit him
in his office. (Customarily, the defense goes to the government's
turf.) But on March 24, 2009, Paul O'Brien, the new Justice
Department prosecutor assigned to the Stevens case, asked to pay a
call on Sullivan and his partner Rob Cary, who was co-counsel
throughout the Stevens case, at the offices of Williams & Connolly.
O'Brien said that the new team had scoured all the records in the case
and found something that had not been disclosed before: an
undocumented interview with Bill Allen.

The session with Allen contained a bombshell. Stevens's
lawyers had turned over the Torricelli note to the prosecution early in
April, 2008, and the government lawyers brought Allen in to talk
about it on April 15th. For the meeting, Allen was in Alaska with
Bottini and James Goeke, another local Assistant U.S. Attorney, and
an F.B.I. agent; Marsh and Edward Sullivan (also no relation), a
junior member of the team, were on a speakerphone in Washington.
In the interview, Allen said that he remembered receiving the
Torricelli note but did not recall speaking to Persons about it. Allen
had not mentioned Persons's purportedly telling him that Stevens was
"covering his ass"--which became the most important evidence in the
trial. This previously undisclosed interview with Allen prompted
O'Brien's visit to Brendan Sullivan's office. Evidence of Allen's
initial failure to come up with the covering-his-ass story should have
been turned over to the defense months earlier. The interview
strongly supported the theme of Brendan Sullivan's cross-
examination of Allen--that the witness had fabricated the
conversation with Persons.

Sullivan made an appointment for 10 A.M. on April 1st to
visit O'Brien and argue that the newly disclosed information required
the government to dismiss the case against Stevens. An hour before

the meeting, O'Brien called Sullivan and told him that the meeting would not be necessary. Attorney General Holder had decided to drop the case. Six days later, Judge Sullivan brought the parties before him to make the end of the case official--and to excoriate Marsh and his colleagues. "In nearly twenty-five years on the bench, I've never seen anything approaching the mishandling and misconduct that I've seen in this case," Judge Sullivan said. "Again and again, both during and after the trial in this case, the Government was caught making false representations and not meeting its discovery obligations. And each time those false representations or unmet obligations came to light, the Government claimed that it had simply made a good-faith mistake, that there was no ill intent."

O'Brien had told the Judge that the Office of Professional Responsibility (O.P.R.) was investigating the behavior of the trial team in the Stevens case, but that was not enough for him. At the end of his remarks, Judge Sullivan said, "The Court shall commence criminal contempt proceedings against the original prosecution team, including William Welch, Brenda Morris, Joseph Bottini, Nicholas Marsh, James Goeke and Edward Sullivan." He went on to say that "the interest of justice requires the appointment of a non-government disinterested attorney to prosecute the matter" and named Henry F. Schuelke III, a Washington lawyer, to do so.

Ted Stevens dominated the brief marriage of Nick Marsh and Navis Bermudez. They had met in Washington in 2005. A New Orleans native, Bermudez had gone to George Washington University, got a master's in environmental studies at Yale, and spent several years working for an environmental organization before moving to the staff of a congressional committee. With short black hair and a trim physique, she could have passed for Marsh's sister. "We knew what our kids would look like," Bermudez told me.

After moving to Washington, Marsh bought a bungalow in Takoma Park, near the D.C. border with Maryland. It wasn't until shortly before their wedding, in 2008, that Marsh told her that the Alaska investigation led to Stevens. His frequent-flier miles took them to Argentina twice and on their honeymoon in Turkey. "He was really passionate about the work he did at Public Integrity. He left a lot of money behind to do it," she told me. "He felt very strongly about public-corruption cases--that people shouldn't be doing anything illegal on the public dime."

According to Bermudez, the Stevens case presented less than ideal working conditions for Marsh. "He was not happy about Brenda Morris being brought in," she said. "It was hard for him, because he put so much time in it. There was a lot of talk about who was going to be allowed to do what, a difficult situation. The morale of the team was not great." Now, with the appointment of a criminal prosecutor, Marsh had to hire his own defense attorney. (The Justice Department provided a stipend for legal fees.) Marsh chose Robert Luskin, an experienced Washington hand best known for his representation of Karl Rove during the Valerie Plame investigation.

The divisions within the Stevens trial team deepened when Marsh and Edward Sullivan were transferred out of the Public Integrity Section, in June, 2009. Marsh wrote in an e-mail to a group of friends, "As you all know I've been exiled from the public integrity section to the criminal division of the office of international affairs." In his new role, Marsh would no longer appear in court as a criminal prosecutor. "He saw anything that ended with him not being a prosecutor as apocalyptically bad," Luskin said.

What's more, Morris and Welch, the senior people in the Stevens investigation, did not receive, in Marsh's mind, equal punishment. Morris moved to Atlanta, and Welch went to his home town of Springfield, Massachusetts, but both worked in U.S. Attorney's offices and remained prosecutors. "It was upsetting that Brenda and Bill were treated differently," Bermudez said. Luskin told me, "The most junior guys, Nick and Sullivan, got moved. Nick clearly felt scapegoated, and it's hard to escape the conclusion that that is exactly what happened." (Citing Justice Department policy on the confidentiality of personnel decisions, officials declined to comment on the transfers, as did Welch. Morris could not be reached.)

As it happened, at the Office of International Affairs Marsh was made the Justice Department's primary point of contact with Switzerland, which meant that he was thrust unexpectedly into another high-profile assignment, the attempted extradition of Roman Polanski. The assignment drew some media interest; "FORMER PROSECUTOR OF TED STEVENS PURSUED POLANSKI" was the headline of a Times story on September 29, 2009. "Nick's whole attitude about O.I.A. was that at least he could just do his work and keep his head down," Bermudez said. "And then the Times picked it up. He was, like, are you kidding me?" According to his friend Josh Waxman, "That Times story made Nick feel like he would never get Stevens behind him."

The peculiar political crosscurrents of the late Bush Administration contributed to the disastrous course of the Stevens prosecution. The decision to indict Stevens was made after Alberto

Gonzales had to step down as Attorney General, largely because of his role in forcing out several U.S. Attorneys for insufficient fealty to Republican political goals. Michael Mukasey, the new Attorney General, took office pledging to rid the Justice Department of political influence. It fell to Mukasey and his team to decide whether to indict a senior Republican senator. In practice, that meant Mukasey was more or less obligated to defer to the judgments of career prosecutors like Marsh. If the leaders of the Justice Department had been more politically secure, they might have asked harder questions about whether the facts justified the criminal charges against Stevens. And they might have done everyone a favor by stopping the case before it began.

But the flawed case did proceed, and the prosecutors compounded its problems by failing to disclose sufficient evidence to the defense. And so, in the light of the two pending investigations, Marsh had to start answering questions that he was used to asking: What did he know, and when did he know it? This was difficult--practically and psychologically. "The Balkanized responsibility for preparing the case was a real problem," Luskin told me. "It was true that the 'government' had knowledge of certain facts and interviews, but no one individual knew all the pieces of information." Conducting an investigation from four thousand miles away also took its toll.

For months, Luskin heard nothing from Schuelke or from the O.P.R. investigators, but eventually both made arrangements to interview Marsh. Afterward, Schuelke told Luskin that he was most interested in Marsh's behavior in three areas. On March 31, 2010, in a letter to Schuelke, Luskin addressed the three areas. First, he acknowledged that the government should have turned over Allen's April 15, 2008, statement about the Torricelli note, but he explained that this decision was not Marsh's responsibility. Marsh did not prepare Allen for his trial testimony or put him on the stand. Second, regarding Rocky Williams, he, too, was not Marsh's witness, and his role in telling the defense about Williams's planned testimony was minor. The final issue involved the non-disclosure to the defense of a statement made by a former girlfriend of Bill Allen's. Marsh had made this decision, but only after consulting with the Justice Department's Professional Responsibility Advisory Office, which exists to advise line attorneys about their ethical obligations. "We were confident that Nick had good answers on all the areas of concern," Luskin told me. It seemed extremely unlikely that Schuelke would have sought any criminal prosecution of Marsh.

But more months passed, and there was no further word from the O.P.R. or from Schuelke. Marsh sent contradictory signals about how he was handling the wait. "Nick was very frustrated by the pace of the investigation," Josh Waxman said. "Someone like him, who had done everything on the straight and narrow, ethical to a T--to have to wait and sit back to hope that his name would be cleared, that really wore on him."

But Marsh also carried on with his job at the O.I.A., which included international travel, and made plans for the fall of 2010. The Washington Wizards basketball team had drafted John Wall, a celebrated rookie out of Kentucky, and Marsh bought a partial season ticket to their games. He obtained a DirecTV package to watch multiple N.F.L. contests. He purchased tickets to fly to a friend's wedding in California, in October, and to go to a Duke basketball game, in New Jersey, in December. At the same time, friends worried about him. "Over the summer, I started carrying my cell phone with me at home," Waxman said. "My wife thought I was crazy, but I wanted to be there for Nick in case he called." Marsh was not seeing a therapist or taking medication.

Marsh regularly asked his attorneys to try to find out when the investigations might conclude. Luskin let him know that he thought there might be a decision after Labor Day. Bermudez and Marsh took their dog, Bourbon, a rescue from Louisiana, to Maine over the long weekend. "He seemed really happy," she said. "All during that vacation, he had been given indications that he would be hearing something soon. He thought for sure it would be resolved the following week, then we'd have it behind us." But, when Marsh returned, there was still no word. " 'They think it'll be a few more weeks.' We heard that over and over again," Bermudez said.

In mid-September, Marsh took a weeklong business trip to Moldova and Portugal. Back in Washington on Thursday, September 23rd, he spoke to Waxman on the phone. "He was upset," Waxman said. "The strain of the investigation was getting to him. He just didn't know when he woke up every day that that was going to be the day that he was going to find out." The next day, Friday, September 24th, Marsh again called Luskin for news. "Nick was just checking in, to see if there was any word from Schuelke," Luskin said. As Bermudez recalled, "That Friday, Nick called me at work to say he had spoken to Luskin and we expect to hear something soon."

The Marsh-Bermudez home in Takoma Park looks like a lot of places where young professionals live, with comfortable, mismatched furniture. Marsh's pride was what he and his wife called his "man-cave," a partly renovated basement where he could sprawl on a beat-up sofa and watch sports on a big-screen TV. (A washer and dryer occupied the other, unfinished third of the basement.) On Saturday morning, Marsh headed to the basement soon after he woke up. Around ten, Bermudez went down to encourage him to join her upstairs.

"Nick got really upset when I went to talk to him," she recalled. "He said he was sorry he had ever taken the Stevens case. He was sorry that he had brought all this trouble into our lives, sorry that he had ruined our lives. I told him that his family and friends knew that he would never do anything wrong, that we all loved him, and that he should look to the future. He was really down but seemed like he'd be over it in a day or two." After their talk, Bermudez went out to do some errands. When she returned, Marsh was asleep in their bed. When she roused him, he went back to the basement to watch more TV.

The pattern repeated itself on Sunday. Marsh woke up and went downstairs to the basement. At around three in the afternoon, Bermudez went to check on him, but he wasn't in front of the television. He had hanged himself near the washer and dryer. There was no note.

Bermudez still lives in the home she shared with Marsh, and his voice still greets callers on the answering machine. "I don't think I understood the depths of how the allegations affected him," she told me. "He took his duties and his ethical obligations very much to heart. Even thinking that his career would be over was just too much for him. The idea that someone thought he did something wrong was just too much to bear."

Twenty months have passed since Judge Sullivan assigned Henry Schuelke to conduct the investigation of the Stevens prosecution. Schuelke has declined to comment on or provide any explanation for the extraordinary delay in producing his findings. The O.P.R. has circulated a draft report that concluded that Marsh and others committed professional misconduct, but the degree of misconduct, and the remedy for it, are unspecified; moreover, lawyers for the prosecutors are contesting the O.P.R.'s tentative version of what happened.

The long investigation obviously took a terrible emotional toll on Marsh. But the errors that he and his colleagues made caused real and lasting damage to Ted Stevens, and to his family as well. Marsh and his colleagues took an important but fairly routine political corruption investigation in Alaska and tried to leverage it into a prosecution of one of the leading political figures in the country. In doing so, they failed themselves and the Justice Department.

More than seven hundred people attended Marsh's funeral, at the First Baptist Church, in Washington. Senior Justice Department officials praised him to his surviving family members. Karen Loeffler, the U.S. Attorney in Alaska, travelled to Washington for the funeral, and later announced that her office had created the Nicholas A. Marsh award, to go to a non-Alaskan who makes the greatest contribution to justice in the state each year. Although Marsh's reputation had suffered a severe and largely deserved fall for his actions in the Stevens case, skilled lawyers have rallied from far worse professional disasters. There is every reason to believe that he would have gone on to a distinguished career, and perhaps even to the judgeship he sought. But something in Marsh could not let the official system for discipline play out, and instead he imposed an unfathomably harsh punishment on himself.

Sentencing Strategies

25

Jefferson County Court One of Six in the Country Selected for NHTSA Alcohol Anklet Case Study

The 23rd Judicial Circuit of Missouri is one of six programs in the country selected by the National Highway Traffic Safety Administration (NHTSA) to study the impact of SCRAM alcohol monitoring anklets on offender programs and communities. The study will focus on evaluating best-practice programs in an effort to assist other agencies looking to adopt the technology.

The courts in Missouri's 23rd Judicial Circuit utilize the 24/7 alcohol anklets, which sample sweat to see if a subject has been drinking, for repeat DWI, domestic violence and other serious alcohol-related offenses. According to Division 12 Associate Circuit Court Judge Stephen Bouchard, his court incorporates SCRAM into a comprehensive program that includes immediate consequence for violations and mandatory treatment for defendants on probation. "Mental health professionals have told us it is much easier to treat an alcohol abuser when the individual is clearly maintaining sobriety," says Bouchard. While the length of time a defendant spends on SCRAM varies, the average duration in the 23rd Judicial Circuit is 137 days.

According to Bouchard, SCRAM is an excellent method to ensure that defendants are not consuming alcohol. "With SCRAM, it's basically impossible to consume without detection, and defendants know that if they drink or tamper, they'll be caught," he says. "It's an excellent deterrent, and our ability to verify a repeat

Jefferson County Court One of Six in the Country Selected for NHTSA Alcohol Anklet Case Study. PR Newswire, Dec 2, 2010.

162

offender's abstinence while they are in the community, either on bond or probation, definitely promotes public safety," he adds. The cost of the system averages $12 per day plus a $75 installation fee. In the 23rd Judicial Circuit, the defendants pay for the cost of the SCRAM monitoring.

The use of SCRAM in the 23rd Judicial Circuit has increased steadily since January of 2007, when twelve defendants were on SCRAM. As of October, more than 130 offenders were being monitored daily with SCRAM, and to-date, the program has monitored 323 defendants using SCRAM bracelets.

Statewide, Missouri has monitored more than 5,000 offenders with SCRAM since early programs began in the St. Louis area in 2004. Just over 500 offenders in Missouri wear the anklets daily. Two Missouri companies, Eastern Missouri Alternative Sentencing Services (EMASS) and St. Joseph-based Private Probation Services , provide SCRAM monitoring throughout eastern and northeastern Missouri. Both companies have monitored nearly 3,900 offenders in the eastern part of the state to-date.

The NHTSA study is being conducted by the Pacific Institute for Research and Evaluation (PIRE) . According to PIRE, the other programs selected for the SCRAM study include the City and County of Denver Electronic Monitoring Program, the statewide North Dakota 24/7 Program; the Nebraska Supreme Court Office of Probation Administration, the New York 8th Judicial District Hybrid DWI Court and Wisconsin Community Services (a SCRAM Service Provider). The studies are intended to provide best-practice models and give courts a better perspective on both the challenges and the potential impact of 24/7 alcohol monitoring.

Nationwide, SCRAM has monitored 155,000 offenders in 48 states and monitors just under 12,000 every day across the U.S. The third generation of the system, SCRAMx, was released in February of this year and integrates home detention (or "house arrest") capabilities into the same anklet. The NHTSA study will focus exclusively on alcohol-only testing programs.

26

Commission Proposes Changes to Sentencing Guidelines

Marcia Coyle

After considerable public input, the U.S. Sentencing Commission recently voted to send Congress amendments to the federal sentencing guidelines that, among other changes, would increase the availability of alternatives to prison and would alter the sentencing of corporate offenders.

Although the sentencing guidelines are no longer mandatory, judges continue to look to them on a regular basis in determining appropriate punishment.

Under the alternatives-to-prison proposal, courts could depart from the guidelines when an offender's criminal activity was related to drug or alcohol abuse or significant mental illness and when sentencing options, such as home or community confinement or intermittent confinement, would serve a specific treatment purpose. The commission also recommends that courts consider the effectiveness of residential treatment programs as part of their decision to impose community confinement.

By adjusting offense levels, the proposed amendments would make more offenders eligible for alternative sentencing options, such as split sentences (half in prison, half in alternative), home or community confinement.

"The commission has heard from virtually every sector of the criminal justice community that there is a great need for alternatives to incarceration," said Chairman William Sessions III in an April 19

WASHINGTON, M. Commission Proposes Changes to Sentencing Guidelines. New York Law Journal, April 26, 2010.

164

statement. "Providing flexibility in sentencing for certain low-level, non-violent offenders helps lower recidivism, is cost effective, and protects the public." Mr. Sessions called the changes a "very modest step" in the right direction.

SENTENCING OF ORGANIZATIONS

The commission also has proposed changes on the sentencing of organizations. Most importantly for corporations, a larger number of offending organizations would be eligible for a credit for having an effective ethics and compliance program.

In a firm memo discussing the proposed changes, Gibson, Dunn & Crutcher noted that a number of groups had urged the commission to eliminate the "absolute bar" to getting that credit if "high-level personnel" had participated in, condoned, or were willfully ignorant of the offense. The term "high-level personnel" is defined to include a director, an executive officer and "an individual in charge of a major business or functional unit of the organization."

Although no statistics are available, the law firm noted that the per se disqualification applies to several convicted corporations annually. David Debold, of counsel to Gibson Dunn, is co-chair of the Sentencing Commission's Practitioners Advisory Group.

The commission eliminated the per se bar but attached certain conditions for the credit to apply, the most important of which is that "the individual or individuals with operational responsibility for the compliance and ethics program…have direct reporting obligations to the governing authority or an appropriate subgroup thereof (for example, an audit committee of the board of directors)."

The change, according to Gibson Dunn, would expand the direct reporting required between the person with day-to-day responsibility for compliance—often the general counsel—and the members of the board.

Under other changes, it would be appropriate to consider such factors as an offender's age, physical, mental and emotion conditions, and military service—currently considered "not ordinarily relevant"—in determining whether to sentence outside the guidelines. However, the factors in the particular case would have to be relevant to an unusual degree and distinguish it from the typical case.

"Through this amendment, the commission is providing the criminal justice system, and particularly judges, with the information they have long sought," said Mr. Sessions. "The more information we can provide on the use of specific offender characteristics during the sentencing process, the more consistency and uniformity will result and the more justice will be served."

Another amendment responds to the Matthew Shepard and James Byrd Jr. Hate Crimes Prevention Act of 2009 by broadening the guideline for offenses involving individual rights to include the new hate crime offense. The act makes it unlawful to willfully cause bodily injury to a person because of the person's race, color, religion, national origin, gender, sexual orientation, gender identity or disability. The act also made it unlawful to attack a U.S. serviceman on account of his service, and the sentencing amendment would incorporate this new offense. The commission also expanded the definition of a hate crime in its penalty enhancement for hate crimes to include victims who were targeted because of their "gender identity."

The amendments must be submitted to Congress by May 1 and will become effective Nov. 1 unless Congress rejects them.

The Miranda Rule

27

Supreme Court Cases 2009-2010 Term

Lisa A. Baker

I n the most recent term, the U.S. Supreme Court decided several cases of interest to law enforcement. Three addressed legal issues implicated in the taking of statements in criminal investigations. In these cases, the Supreme Court provided additional clarification and guidance concerning the long-standing requirements set forth in Miranda v. Arizona, including 1) the circumstances governing when law enforcement may initiate contact with a subject who previously has invoked the Miranda right to counsel; 2) what will constitute a waiver of the Miranda right to silence; and 3) what must be conveyed to a subject to satisfy Miranda. (1)

Another case considered the constitutionality of a warrantless entry into a residence due to concerns about the safety and well-being of occupants inside. The Supreme Court also addressed the reasonableness of a search conducted by a police department targeting an officer's department-issued pager, the constitutionality of a civil commitment statute allowing for the continued commitment of federal inmates determined to be sexually dangerous, and whether the Second Amendment applies to states.

This article provides a brief synopsis of these cases. As always, law enforcement agencies must ensure that their own state laws and constitutions have not provided greater protections than the U.S. constitutional standards.

Baker, L. Supreme Court cases 2009-2010 term. The FBI Law Enforcement Bulletin, Nov 2010 v79 i11 p21(11).

DECIDED CASES

Berghuis v. Thompkins, 130S. Ct. 2250(2010)

In this case, the Supreme Court addressed the impact that silence has on attempts to interrogate an in-custody subject and whether officers could proceed with a custodial interview in the absence of an explicit waiver of Miranda rights. The subject in this case was arrested for his involvement in a murder, and detectives, after advising him of his Miranda rights, attempted to interrogate him. The subject largely remained silent; then, about 2 hours and 45 minutes into the interrogation, a detective asked if he believed in God, which the subject indicated he did. The detective then asked, "Do you pray for God to forgive you for shooting down that boy?" The subject responded, "yes."2 Authorities sought to use this admission against him. The lower courts allowed the statement to be used, but the Sixth Circuit Court of Appeals ruled in favor of the defendant. (3) The Supreme Court reversed this decision and found no Miranda violation. (4)

The Supreme Court explained that the subject's mere silence in the face of questioning was not a clear and unambiguous invocation of his right to remain silent. Previously, the Court had ruled that to effectively invoke the Miranda right to counsel, a subject must do so clearly and unambiguously. (5) In Berghuis, the Court acknowledged that there was no reason to apply different standards, depending on whether the subject invokes the Miranda right to counsel or right to silence. Accordingly, the invocation of either the right to silence or the right to counsel must be clear and unambiguous to be effective.

The Supreme Court also considered the defendant's claim that his statement still should be suppressed because he never adequately waived his right to silence. At first blush, this argument appears to have merit in light of the language in the original Miranda opinion emphasizing the heavy burden imposed on the government to demonstrate that a valid waiver was obtained and that "a valid waiver will not be presumed simply from the silence of the accused after warnings arc given or simply from the fact that a confession was in fact eventually obtained." (6) However, the Supreme Court has clarified its position in post-Miranda cases, emphasizing that Miranda is designed to ensure that the subject is advised of and understands certain rights and that, if invoked, these rights are safeguarded. (7) In Berghuis, the Court held that "Where the prosecution shows that a Miranda warning was given and that it was understood by the accused, an accused's uncoerced statement establishes an implied waiver of the right to remain silent." (8) By responding to the detective's question, the suspect demonstrated a willingness to waive his right to silence.

The Supreme Court also rejected the defendant's argument that even if he provided a valid waiver, the detectives were not permitted to question him until they obtained the waiver first. The Court noted that there are practical reasons why a waiver should not be required for an interrogation to begin as the interrogation can provide the subject with additional information to help the subject decide whether to invoke or to talk with law enforcement. As stated by the Court, "As questioning commences and then continues, the suspect has the opportunity to consider the choices he or she faces and to make a more informed decision, either to insist on silence or to cooperate." (9) Miranda is satisfied "if a suspect receives adequate Miranda warnings, understands them, and has an opportunity to invoke the rights before giving any answers or admissions." (10) Accordingly, "after giving a Miranda warning, police may interrogate a suspect who has neither invoked nor waived his or her Miranda rights." (11)

Maryland v. Shatzer, 130 S. Ct. 1213(2010)

In Maryland v. Shatzer, the Court ruled on the legal significance and definition of a break in custody within the context of the Fifth Amendment privilege against self-incrimination. (12) Post-Miranda cases expanded on the protections afforded an in-custody subject. In Edwards v. Arizona, (13) the Supreme Court ruled that once defendants invoke their Miranda right to counsel, any interrogation must cease, and there can be no further police-initiated interrogation without the presence of counsel. Edwards creates a presumption that once in-custody subjects invoke their right to counsel, any subsequent waiver of Miranda rights prompted by police-initiated interrogation is itself the result of improper police coercion and, thus, not voluntary. (14) The Maryland v. Shatzer case presented an opportunity to clarify at what point the Miranda-Edwards protection would be lifted, permitting police-initiated interrogation following an invocation of the Miranda right to counsel.

In Shatzer, the defendant was serving a sentence stemming from a child sexual abuse prosecution. A detective attempted to interview the incarcerated subject regarding allegations that he sexually abused his 3-year-old son. Shatzer initially waived his rights, believing that the detective was there to talk with him about why he was in prison, but, upon realizing the detective was there to

172

talk about the new allegation, Shatzer declined to speak without his attorney present. Shatzer was returned to the general prison population. Nearly 2 1/2 years later and after developing new evidence, another detective went to the prison to talk with Shatzer about the allegations that he molested his son. The detective advised him of his Miranda rights, and, this time, Shatzer waived his rights in writing. Subsequently, Shatzer made incriminating statements. He later was charged with various sexual abuse charges and sought to have the statements he provided suppressed.

Shatzer argued that because he remained in continuous custody following his invocation of his Miranda right to counsel, law enforcement could not initiate any contact with him while he remained in custody and that any waiver of his Miranda rights provided at the request of law enforcement was not valid. The trial court disagreed with Shatzer's assertion, concluding that given the passage of time, a sufficient break in custody occurred, permitting detectives to reinitiate contact with Shatzer despite his continued incarceration. (15) The Maryland Court of Appeals reversed the trial court's ruling, holding that the passage of time alone will not suffice to create a break in custody for purpose of the Miranda-Edwards rule. (16) The Supreme Court agreed to hear the case to clarify what will constitute a sufficient break in custody and the impact of incarceration on the Miranda-Edwards protection.

The Supreme Court ruled that a break in custody alone will not end the Miranda-Edwards protection. The Court instead called for a "cooling off period, prohibiting law enforcement from attempting to interview a subject who previously invoked his Miranda right to counsel for 14 days from his release from custody. According to the Court, 14 days gives "plenty of time for the suspect to get reacliminated to his normal life, consult with friends and counsel, and shake off any residual coercive effects of prior custody." (17)

Applying this principle to Shatzer who was incarcerated, as opposed to pretrial detention, the traditional freedom-of-movement test does not resolve the issue of custody. The Court distinguished between incarceration in the general prison population and pretrial detention and found that there was a sufficient break in custody (over 14 days) following Shatzer's initial interrogation until the detective reinitiated contact with him. (18) Thus, the waiver obtained from Shatzer was not the product of coercion, and his statements were admissible.

Florida v. Powell, 130 S. Ct. 1195 (2010)

In this case, the Supreme Court addressed the adequacy of Miranda warnings contained within standard advice-of-rights forms used by the Tampa, Florida, Police Department (TPD). The defendant alleged that the form insufficiently advised him of his right to have counsel present during an interrogation. In Miranda, the Supreme Court held that prior to custodial interrogation, a defendant must be advised that he has, among other rights, "the right to consult with a lawyer and to have the lawyer with him during interrogation." (19) The TPD form did not expressly state this, but, rather, advised the defendant of his right to talk with an attorney before answering any questions and that he could invoke this right "at any time ... during the interview." (20)

The Florida Supreme Court concluded that the form did not satisfy the mandate of Miranda. (21) The U.S. Supreme Court reversed, holding that the form communicated the essential message of Miranda despite the lack of adherence to its precise language. The Supreme Court again refused to require rigid compliance to precise language, instead focusing on whether, taken as a whole, the language adequately communicated to the defendant that he had the opportunity to consult with counsel during the interview. (22) The defendant was advised of his right to consult with counsel before answering any questions and that he could invoke this right during the interrogation. The Supreme Court stated, "in combination, the two warnings reasonably conveyed [the] right to have an attorney present, not only at the outset of interrogation, but at all times." (23)

Michigan v. Fisher, 130 S. Ct. 546 (2009)

Police officers responded to a disturbance call, and, as they approached the area, a couple directed them to a residence where they said a man was "going crazy." The officers continued to the home and found property damaged, as well as drops of blood on the hood of a pickup truck parked in front, clothes sitting inside of it, and one of the doors leading into the house. Through a window, they could see Jeremy Fisher inside the house, yelling and throwing objects.

The officers knocked on the door, but Fisher refused to answer. He also ignored their inquiries as to whether he needed medical attention and directed them to get a search warrant. One of the officers then pushed the front door partially open and saw Fisher pointing a gun in his direction. Eventually, the officers gained control over Fisher and secured the premises.

174

Fisher was charged with assault with a dangerous weapon and possessing a weapon during the commission of a felony. (24) The trial court granted Fisher's motion to suppress the gun, agreeing with him that it was seized in violation of his Fourth Amendment rights. This was upheld by the Michigan Court of Appeals after it concluded that the warrantless entry violated Fisher's Fourth Amendment rights as the situation "did not rise to the level of an emergency justifying the warrantless intrusion into a residence." (25) The court continued by noting that while there was some indication of a possible injury, "the mere drops of blood did not signal a likely serious, life-threatening injury." (26) The Michigan Supreme Court agreed to hear the case, but, after hearing oral arguments, vacated its order and let the lower court ruling stand.

The Supreme Court reversed, concluding that the state courts rulings were inconsistent with its long line of cases interpreting the Fourth Amendment in the context of exigent circumstances, particularly the Court's recent ruling in Brigham City v. Stuart. (27) In Brigham City, the Supreme Court recognized the need for law enforcement to make warrantless intrusions into a person's home "to render emergency assistance to an injured occupant or to protect an occupant from imminent injury." (28) In considering the reasonableness of the entry, the officer's subjective motivation behind the entry--what did the officer really want to look for--and the seriousness of the crime for which they were originally investigating are not relevant. The relevant consideration is whether the officer has an "objectively reasonable basis for believing that a person is in need of aid." (29)

Applying this standard to the facts of the case, the Court found ample support for application of the emergency aid exception, stating, "Officers do not need ironclad proof of a likely serious, life-threatening injury to invoke the emergency aid exception." (30) The Court concluded by stating:

It does not meet the needs of law enforcement or the demands of public safety to require officers to walk away from a situation like the one they encountered here. Only when an apparent threat has become an actual harm can officers rule out innocuous explanations for ominous circumstances. But '[t]he role of a peace officer includes preventing violence and restoring order, not simply rendering aid to casualties.' (31)

City of Ontario v. Quon, 130 S. Ct. 2619 (2010)

A police officer sued his agency and the city he worked for on the grounds that the department's review of text messages sent to and from his department-issued pager violated his Fourth Amendment rights. The Ninth Circuit Court of Appeals concluded that the officer maintained an expectation of privacy in the contents of the pager and that the review of the messages constituted an unreasonable search. (32) The Supreme Court agreed to hear the case.

The pager at issue was provided to the officer by the department to facilitate communication among SWAT team members. The agency had a "Computer Usage, Internet and E-Mail Policy" that did not specifically include pagers, but the department made it clear to employees that it would treat text messages the same as e-mails. (33) The department's contract with the service provider covered a specific number of characters. For several billing cycles, the officer exceeded his allotted character limit. His supervisor informed him that while he could review the messages, he would refrain from doing as long as the officer paid for the excess charges. After several months of exceeding the character limit, management decided to review the messages to determine the necessity of a contract modification. The service provider supplied transcripts of the messages, which, with respect to Officer Quon, were found to contain numerous nonwork-related, inappropriate messages. (34)

The Supreme Court refrained from addressing the issue of whether the officer had an expectation of privacy in the messages sent to and from the pager. The Court noted that the department made it clear that the pager was considered within the scope of the computer use policy. However, it recognized that whether an expectation of privacy existed was uncertain given the impact of statements by the officer's supervisor that he did not intend to review the pager's messages as long as the officer paid the overage. The Supreme Court stated:

Prudence counsels caution before the facts in the instant case are used to establish far-reaching premises that define the existence, and extent, of privacy expectations enjoyed by employees when using employer-provided communication devices. (35)

The Supreme Court instead based its holding on the reasonableness of the search, assuming there was an expectation of privacy in the contents of the pager. Applying the long-standing workplace search principles set forth in O'Connor v. Ortega, (36) the

Court concluded that the review of the text messages was reasonable in light of the work-related, noninvestigatory purpose--to determine the adequacy of the contract with the service provider--and that it was conducted in a reasonable manner. The Court saw the review of the transcripts as "an efficient and expedient way to determine whether Quon's overages were the result of work-related messaging or personal use" and not overly intrusive. (37)

United States v. Comstock, 130 S. Ct. 1949(2010)

Federal inmates challenged the constitutionality of a federal civil-commitment statute authorizing the U.S. government to detain a federal inmate certified as sexually dangerous beyond the time the individual otherwise would be released. The Supreme Court concluded that the statute is consistent with Congress' authority to enact laws that are "necessary and proper" for carrying out the powers vested to the federal government by the Constitution.

The statute at issue passed as part of the Adam Walsh Child Protection and Safety Act and codified at Title 18, U.S. Code, section 4248 and allows a federal district court to order at the government's request the civil commitment of an inmate determined to be sexually dangerous. (38) The inmate is afforded a hearing in which the government must support the claim by presenting clear and convincing evidence.

Inmates targeted by this statute challenged its constitutionality on a number of grounds, including that it amounted to a criminal, not civil, action, thus violating the Double Jeopardy Clause, and contained an insufficient legal standard asserting this type of action required proof beyond a reasonable doubt. In addition, they asserted that it exceeded Congress' authority under the Commerce Clause. (39) The district court agreed with the challengers' contentions. (40) On appeal, the Fourth Circuit Court of Appeals declined to address the standard-of-proof question, instead agreeing that the statute exceeded congressional authority. (41) The government sought Supreme Court review. (42)

The Supreme Court rejected the Commerce Clause challenge to the statute, holding that the Constitution provides Congress with ample authority to enact the civil commitment statute at issue. (43) The Court concluded that consistent with congressional authority under the Commerce Clause, the statute is "rationally related to the implementation of a constitutionally enumerated power." (44) The Court referenced the inherent authority Congress has with respect to matters relating to the handling of federal prisoners, including decisions pertaining to the provision of mental health care and the need to act to protect the public from the dangers these prisoners may pose, and concluded that the statute in question is rationally related to Congress' authority. (45) In addition, the Court rejected the argument that the statute violated the Tenth Amendment to the Constitution, which states: "The powers not delegated to the United States by the Constitution, nor prohibited by it to the States, are reserved to the States respectively, or to the people." Finding that the statute is within the scope of congressional authority, this area, thus, is not within those matters "not delegated to the United States." Further, the statute takes into account the interests of the states by requiring coordination with the state in which the prisoner is domiciled or tried and encourages the state to assume custody of the individual. (46)

McDonald v. City of Chicago, 130 S. Ct. 3020 (2010)

In this case, the Supreme Court ruled that the Second Amendment right to keep and bear arms for the purpose of self-defense applies not only to the federal government, as determined by District of Columbia v. Heller, (47) but to the states under the Due Process Clause of the Fourteenth Amendment. In reaching this decision, the Court concluded that the right to bear arms for self-defense is "fundamental to our scheme of ordered liberty" and "deeply rooted" in this nation's history. (48) Consistent with Heller, the Court emphasized that this right is not absolute and that the holding "does not imperil every law regulating firearms." (49)

CASES FOR NEXT TERM

Several cases of interest to the law enforcement community are already scheduled to be heard by the Supreme Court. These include the five presented here.

Thompson v. Connick, 578 F.3d 293 (5th Cir. 2009), cert. granted, Connick v. Thompson, 130 S. Ct. 1880 (2010)

In a lawsuit brought against the New Orleans District Attorney's Office, a former criminal defendant sued and was awarded 14 million dollars after a jury determined that the prosecutor's office failed to adequately train the prosecutor in the handling of exculpatory evidence. The Supreme Court will consider whether liability imposed on the D.A.'s office for failing to train the prosecutor in a single case is contrary to the traditional strict culpability standards by the Court in Canton v. Harris (50) and Board of Commissioners of Bryan County v. Brown. (51)

People v. Bryant, 768 N.W.2d 65 (2009), cert. granted, Michigan v. Bryant, 130 S. Ct. 1685 (2010)

The Supreme Court again will address the parameters of the accused's Sixth Amendment right to confront witnesses against him in a case involving statements made by a victim shortly after a shooting. The defendant was prosecuted for shooting the victim, who died shortly after being shot and after telling the police that it was the defendant who shot him. The Michigan Supreme Court held that the statements made by the victim were testimonial in nature within the Supreme Court's rulings in Crawford v. Washing-ion (52) and Davis v. Washington (53) and, thus, could not be used against him in his trial given he could not confront the witness against him.

Staub v. Proctor Hospital, 560 F.3d 647 (7th Cir. 2009), cert. granted, 130 S. Ct. 2089 (2010)

This case explores the scope of liability under the Uniform Services Employment and Reemployment Rights Act. The Court will consider whether a supervisor's discriminatory animus against an employee's military service should be imputed to the employer, even if that supervisor is not the ultimate decision maker with respect to the employment action taken against the employee claiming discrimination.

Thompson v. North American Stainless LP, 567 F.3d 804 (6th Cir. 2009), cert, granted, 130 S. Ct. 3542 (2010)

In recent terms, the Supreme Court has taken a number of cases to clarify what constitutes unlawful retaliation within the meaning of Title VII of the Civil Rights Act. (54) For the next term, the Supreme Court has agreed to hear another retaliation case to address who may claim retaliation within the meaning of the statute. The Court will consider whether the Sixth Circuit Court of Appeals was correct in ruling that the statute requires a party claiming retaliation to have actually been engaged in a protected activity within the meaning of the statute. This would require a showing that the person either complained of discrimination or opposed the employer's discriminatory practices. In this case, an employee complained of discrimination, and, 3 weeks later, her fiance was fired. The fiance filed his own action alleging retaliation. The Sixth Circuit Court of

Appeals dismissed his suit, finding that he did not engage in a protected activity and rejecting a theory of associational retaliation.

Snyder v. Phelps, 580 F.3d 206, cert. granted, 130 S. Ct. 1737 (2010)

This case stems from protest activity by members of the Westboro Baptist Church at the funeral of a soldier killed in combat. This group contends that the deaths of U.S. soldiers are punishment for this country's tolerance of homosexuality and presence of gays in the military. The father sued for the pain the protest activity at his son's funeral caused him. A federal judge awarded the father 5 million dollars. The Supreme Court will consider whether a private individual is permitted state protection from this type of activity and the scope of the First Amendment protection afforded.

ENDNOTES DELETED

28

High Court to Hear Appeal in Murder of Toddler, Young Woman

Judy Harrison

The Maine Supreme Judicial Court will hear oral arguments Thursday in an appeal from convicted murderer Jeffrey Cookson, who is serving consecutive life sentences for the slayings in December 1999 of his ex-girlfriend Mindy Gould, 20, and the boy she was baby-sitting, Treven Cunningham, 21 months old, both of Dexter.

Cookson's attorney, Karen Wolfram of Portland, is asking that clothes and a wig worn by a man who claimed to have killed the woman and toddler but later recanted that statement be tested for DNA. Results of those tests could lead to a new trial, she said in briefs filed with the court. Wolfram did not represent Cookson at his trial. Superior Court Justice Roland Cole in October 2009 properly denied a request for the testing of the items, Assistant Attorney General Donald Macomber, who represents the state, said in a brief to the justices. He argued that the clothes should not be tested, because Wolfram has failed to show the items had any association with the murders. Macomber also maintained that because the clothes were not given to police until two years after the slaying, the chain of custody, as defined by Maine law, was not maintained. Cookson, now 47 and incarcerated at the Maine State Prison in Warren, continues to maintain his innocence.

He was convicted in December 2001 by a Penobscot County jury of shooting the two execution-style on Dec. 3, 1999, at the Dexter home of Gould's sister. A few days before her death, Gould had taken out a protection from abuse order against Cookson of

Harrison, J. High court to hear appeal in murder of toddler, young woman. Bangor Daily News (Bangor, ME), Jan 12, 2011.

Dover-Foxcroft, according to previously published reports. The
appeal before justices Thursday deals with information given to
Cookson's trial defense attorney, William Maselli of Auburn, but not
shared with law enforcement officials or Justice Cole, who presided
at Cookson's trial, until shortly after the verdict was announced. In
2001, Maselli said that David Vantol, then 21 and living in Guilford,
had admitted to him that he committed the murders. Vantol later led
investigators to the murder weapon, which until then had not been
found, and the clothes and wig he said he had been wearing when he
killed the boy and Gould, the briefs in the current appeal agreed.
Vantol repeatedly told police in December 2001 that he committed
the crimes at Cookson's request and an offer of $10,000. Two months
later, at a hearing on Maselli's motion for a new trial, Vantol, who
was described in court as a man with a history of mental illness and a
limited education, recanted his confession. Records showed that
Vantol visited Cookson in jail in 2001. Investigators and prosecutors
speculated in 2002 that that was how Vantol learned the details of the
murders. "Whether you believe David Vantol's repeated confessions
to the murders or not, the evidence sought to be tested was taken into
police custody as part and parcel of the police investigation into the
murders from the same person who confessed repeatedly to the
murders and provided the actual murder weapon to the police two
years after the crimes were committed," Wolfram wrote in her brief.
"As such, the evidence is related to [the] underlying murder
investigation or prosecution that led to Mr. Cookson's conviction,
requiring an order of DNA testing in this case." In his brief,
Macomber said that all Wolfram has been able to show so far was
that the Maine State Police still have control or possession of the
clothing and other items Vantol provided them more than nine years
ago. She has not shown that the items were associated with the deaths
of Gould and Cunningham, which is required by Maine law before
they can be tested, according to Macomber.

"While [Cookson] would like this court to rely only on the
statements that Vantol made to the police when he turned the
clothing and other items over to the police on Dec. 8, 2001,"
Macomber wrote, "Cookson ignores that Vantol recanted those
statements, that the trial court expressly found Vantol's recantation
[and not his initial confession] was truthful, and that this court has
already found that the evidence supported the trial court's finding
discrediting the recanted statement."

The Maine Supreme Judicial Court in December 2003
unanimously affirmed Cookson's convictions and sentences. Justices
unanimously found that Maselli's decision not to tell police or the

judge that Vantol had confessed to the crimes was a "tactical" decision by the defense team.

In a related 2005 civil case, then Superior Court Justice Andrew Mead ordered Cookson to pay $1.5 million in damages to the slain toddler's mother, Cassie Cunningham, then 24 and living in Bangor. Cookson represented himself at the jury-waived trial. While Cunningham recognized it was highly unlikely she ever would collect the judgment, her attorney, Marie Hansen of Bangor, said in May 2005 that winning the lawsuit recognized her and her family's loss. Mead, now on the Maine supreme court, most likely will recuse himself from hearing Cookson's latest appeal.

There is no timeline under which Maine's high court must issue its ruling. Vantol, 30, now living in Hope, last fall was fined $1,000 and sentenced in Knox County to two years in prison for operating a vehicle after a habitual offender revocation, according to court news published in the Bangor Daily News. Details about that incident were not available Wednesday due to the snowstorm.

29

Prosecutors' Legal Strategy Advances in Murder Case

Kim Smith

One of two murder cases pending against a Tucson man has been dismissed at the request of prosecutors, who hope to overturn a judge's decision to throw out his police confession.

Michael Carlson, 54, told Pima County sheriff's deputies in June 2009 that he had recently killed two friends and that he had shot his sister to death in May 2003.

Carlson was indicted on first-degree-murder charges, and the two cases were assigned to separate judges, Christopher Browning and Richard Nichols.

Last month, Browning told prosecutors that they could not use Carlson's confession in the case involving Carlson's sister because deputies had violated his Miranda rights.

Prosecutors asked Browning earlier this week to dismiss the case so they could file with the Arizona Court of Appeals - knowing that Carlson would remain in jail in the double-homicide case.

Browning granted the motion Wednesday over the objection of defense attorneys.

The case should just be "stayed" until the upper court issues a ruling on the "special action" already filed by prosecutors, defense attorney Harley Kurlander argued.

Smith, K. Prosecutors' legal strategy advances in murder case. AZ Daily Star (Tucson, AZ), Dec 9, 2010.

Kurlander said he intends to ask Nichols to toss out the confession in the double-homicide case within the next couple of weeks. Originally, he had planned to wait until the higher court ruled on the special action.

The confession is considered a key piece of evidence in both cases. If Carlson is convicted in the double-homicide case, he could receive the death penalty.

Carlson was sentenced to 99 years in a Texas prison for aggravated armed robbery in the early 1980s. He was released on parole in May 2003 and moved in with his sister in Tucson, according to court documents.

Five months later, Carlson reported that his sister, Maria Thoma, 51, missing. Her body was found the same day, and she had been shot four times in the face and torso with a shotgun.

Her murder remained unsolved, and Carlson spent the next few years in and out of Texas prisons for violating his parole. He eventually absconded and ended up back in Tucson in December 2008.

Carlson was named a "person of interest" in June 2009 when Kenneth Alliman, 49, and Rebecca Lou Lofton, 52, disappeared.

Detectives picked Carlson up on the Texas fugitive warrant, and he allegedly confessed to killing the Marana couple and his sister.

When detectives began reading Carlson his rights, Carlson said he knew them, repeated some of them back and waived them, according to court documents.

Carlson didn't mention his right to have an attorney present during the questioning itself, so it isn't clear if he knew he had a right to an attorney at that moment in time.

Browning ruled the deputies should have read Carlson all of his rights, noting that the Miranda warnings consist of 55 words, and law-enforcement officers carry them around on a card.

Alternative Courts

30

Asylum Philadelphia

A Look at the Overburdened
Philadelphia Immigration Court

Julie Shaw

IN JUNE 2006, men in military clothes grabbed Maria, kidnapping her as she slept in a church shelter in Angola, bound and blindfolded her and dragged her away. They beat and raped her, and interrogated her about her boyfriend's human-rights work. Maria eventually escaped to the United States, where she sought asylum. But more than four years went by before a judge in Philadelphia heard her testimony. Separately in Philadelphia, "Esther," from Ghana, overstayed her tourist visa, fell in love with a naturalized U.S. citizen and married him in 2006. Then he turned abusive. "Esther" wants to stay here, and her attorney says that federal law permits it. But a backlog caused her hearing to be put off until Feb. 1, 2012, and now the matter appears headed out of the judicial system altogether. These two cases provide a glimpse into the highly emotional issues often brought before the overburdened Philadelphia Immigration Court, where applicants can remain in limbo for years and where the number of cases pending before just three judges skyrocketed to 4,573 in fiscal year 2010 -- a 20 percent increase from the previous year. It was the court's highest number of pending cases since at least 1998, according to the Transactional Records Access Clearinghouse (TRAC), a data-research center at Syracuse University -- and possibly its highest number ever. And it's not just traumatic for applicants. The judges themselves, because of the number and nature of the cases, "suffer from significant symptoms of secondary traumatic stress and more burnout" than prison wardens or physicians, according to a nationwide survey by the University of

Shaw, J. Asylum Philadelphia: A look at the overburdened Philadelphia Immigration Court. Philadelphia Daily News (Philadelphia, PA), Jan 12, 2011.

California, San Francisco. Last month, immigration lawyer Steven Morley was added to the Philadelphia court as its fourth judge, and he is to begin hearing cases Tuesday. The judges aren't allowed to discuss their work, but observers wonder whether the extra staffing will be enough to bear the burden triggered in large part by the Department of Homeland Security.

"I'm not even sure the fourth judge is going to make much of a difference, because enforcement [by Homeland Security] is cranking up, is still running full-tilt," said James Orlow, a veteran immigration lawyer in Philadelphia and past president of the American Immigration Lawyers Association. Even with more judges being sworn in, immigration judges nationwide "are still in a crisis phase," said Judge Dana Marks, of San Francisco, president of the National Association of Immigration Judges. New judges still have to go through training and don't take on full caseloads, she said. Maria's day in court Last month, more than four years after entering deportation proceedings in October 2006, Maria -- who asked that only her first name be used for this article -- finally testified before Judge Charles Honeyman. Honeyman, like the other Philadelphia immigration judges -- Miriam Mills and Rosalind Malloy -- has been more likely to deny than to grant asylum, according to Syracuse's TRAC. Summoning the horrible memory of the day she was kidnapped in Angola, in Africa's southwest, Maria told the judge that she had been dating a man who worked for a human-rights group. "They tied me -- my hands, my legs," she testified through a Portuguese interpreter. "They blindfolded me and took me to some location." During the four days that she was held captive, she was raped by several men and repeatedly beaten, she testified under questioning by her attorney, Troy J. Mattes, of Lancaster. Maria, 32, said that she was allowed to leave after agreeing to poison members of her boyfriend's group. But after she was released, she told her boyfriend what happened and he helped her escape from Angola. Two months later, in August 2006, she applied for asylum in the United States. Because of the high volume of cases in the court system and the time needed to locate, contact and get evidence from her former boyfriend, it took more than four years for her testimony to be heard. Mattes, who began representing Maria in 2007, found out that Amnesty International had written about her former boyfriend. Through his efforts, Maria was able to phone the man and get him to send a letter that was introduced in court as evidence of their past relationship. Ira Mazer, senior attorney in the Department of Homeland Security, cross-examined Maria on what appeared to be inconsistencies in her testimony. He questioned if the letter had been sent by her former boyfriend. But Honeyman said that he found her credible, and the evidence that she had submitted "genuinely plausible," and he granted asylum. Sitting in the back of the courtroom, Maria cried. Afterward, she said she was happy. Later, as Maria reflected on her case, she said that the hard part about waiting so long for a hearing was that she had to depend on others. "I can't work or anything," she said, speaking through a cousin who interpreted for her. "That's basically the downfall of that. I can't work, I can't study. I can't get any legal papers to do anything."

Her cousin said that Maria finally has received her legal papers to be in this country. Mattes said that the case was unusual. The hardest part of asylum cases, he said, is to back them up with evidence. Fortunately for his client, she was dating someone known to Amnesty International. And, he said, she was a witness who "didn't flinch."

Stepped-up enforcement

Philadelphia Immigration Court is a cog in a vast network overseen by the Justice Department: 271 judges in 59 immigration courts located in 27 states, Puerto Rico and the U.S. territory of the Northern Mariana Islands, in the Pacific Ocean.

Two of those courts are in Pennsylvania -- one in the federal building at 9th and Market streets, the other inside the York County Prison, in York, where U.S. Immigration and Customs Enforcement (ICE), an arm of Homeland Security, houses detainees accused of violating immigration law. Philadelphia's court was relocated Sept. 1 from cramped quarters at 16th and Callowhill streets, where the U.S. Citizenship and Immigration Services (USCIS), another agency under Homeland Security, remains.

Judges decide whether foreign-born individuals whom Homeland Security charges with violating immigration law should be ordered removed from the U.S. The Justice Department agency that oversees immigration judges was created in 1983, when the attorney general moved the judges from the former Immigration and Naturalization Service. Many immigration lawyers say that Homeland Security has been more aggressive in recent years in its enforcement, bringing cases before judges that previously wouldn't have been argued in court. Some attribute the increased enforcement to the terrorist attacks of Sept. 11, 2001. The Obama administration also has made it a priority to deport "criminal aliens," noncitizens convicted of crimes in the U.S. It recently touted its fiscal year 2010's record-breaking number of deportations -- more than 392,000. Lawyer Dave Bennion, of the nonprofit Nationalities Service Center, in Philadelphia, said that what would have been routine cases a few years ago -- such as a marriage to a U.S. citizen -- now may be disputed in immigration court. Often in the past an immigration officer at USCIS would have determined whether to grant a green card, without the case having to go before a judge. The stepped-up enforcement efforts by USCIS and ICE "have the result of increasing the backlogs in the courts," Bennion said. Bennion said that he's "a little bit reluctant to endorse" hiring more judges, because it "doesn't address the underlying problems that lead people to continue to come to this country and employers to continue to hire them." The case of 'Esther'

Ricky Palladino, the attorney representing "Esther," from Ghana, said that hers is an example of cases that shouldn't clog up immigration court. Under the Violence Against Women Act, Esther, 32, is "immediately eligible" for a green card because she is the abused spouse of a U.S. citizen, he said. He said that her marriage to her husband, also of Ghana, started off well but that he then lashed out about the "way she cooked, the way she cleaned," then began choking her. The abuse escalated to rape, the woman told Palladino. Esther and her husband filed for a green card for her in 2008, but failed to show up for their interview with the USCIS immigration officer, so the application was denied. Homeland Security placed the woman in removal proceedings in February 2009, after the green-card denial. At a hearing Dec. 13, Palladino told Judge Mills that USCIS had approved the woman's petition to be classified as an abused spouse. He explained afterward that the approval also meant that USCIS agreed that the woman's marriage was legitimate, not a sham. The Homeland Security attorney, Bruce Dizengoff, told the judge that he needed time to review the case and contended that it was properly before the court. Judge Mills sided with Palladino, referring to an August memo by ICE Director John Morton to have some cases returned to USCIS jurisdiction instead of remaining in the courts, in an effort to help unclog the courts. She instructed Palladino to file a motion to terminate the case, and to let the government's attorney respond. Palladino last week told the Daily News that the ICE chief counsel in Philadelphia, Kent Frederick, has agreed that the woman's removal proceeding should be terminated. Palladino also last week filed a joint motion indicating that both sides agree.

Once the judge grants the motion, as she is expected to do, Esther's request for a green card will be heard by a USCIS immigration officer, instead of languishing in the backed-up immigration-court system.

31

Wellness Courts Help Alaskans with Addiction Access Treatment

S ince a 2001 law establishing "therapeutic courts" has taken effect in Alaska, two "wellness courts"--one in Anchorage, and one in Fairbanks--have been successfully keeping some addicted offenders out of jail or prison. Applicants for the wellness court must first be approved for participation by prosecutors, public defenders, counselors, probation offices, judges, and the wellness court coordinator. After an evaluation, offenders are either recommended for outpatient treatment--in which case the probation officer visits the home to see if the applicant would be able to remain sober in that environment--or inpatient treatment--or incarceration.

Originally funded with the help of a National Institute of Justice grant, wellness courts in Anchorage and Fairbanks exist to help offenders with addictions obtain treatment. There are DUI (driving under the influence) wellness courts and drug courts, both for felony offenders. If they agree to follow the treatment plan for 18 months, offenders can receive reduced jail time.

People participating in the DUI wellness court are not allowed to drive at all. If someone is arrested three times for drunk driving, they face at least 120 days in jail, a $10,000 fine, and permanent loss of their drivers' license. There is also a wellness court for people who have committed their first or second DUI--a misdemeanor offense.

Michelle Bartley, the Therapeutic Courts coordinator for Alaska, told the News-Miner, which published an extensive article on the wellness courts last week, that the Fairbanks program cost $350,000 this past year. Compared to the average $44,000 a year the state pays per prison or jail inmate, that is a cost savings, according to a study by the Institute of Social and Economic Research at the

Wellness courts help Alaskans with addiction access treatment. Alcoholism & Drug Abuse Weekly, March 22, 2010 v22 i12 p4(1).

University of Alaska Anchorage states programs like therapeutic courts that keep people out of prison "save the state money right away, because they cost much less" than incarceration.

TREATMENT PROGRAM

Here are the steps the defendant must take to be a part of the wellness court treatment program:

1. Defendant has defense attorney contact the district attorney for wellness court.

2. Prosecutor decides whether to offer wellness court as a sentencing alternative.

3. Defendant observes wellness court in session at least once.

4. Defendant completes a substance abuse assessment to determine eligibility for intensive substance abuse outpatient treatment-- wellness court team must agree on the defendant's admission.

5. Defendant accept the offer.

6. Wellness court judge approves the agreement and the treatment plan.

7. Defendant enters a plea of guilty, and sentencing is set for 18 months later.

8. Defendant begins to follow the wellness court treatment plan, which includes a physical for the purposes of prescribing an anti-craving medication (if medically appropriate).

MISDEMEANORS

There's a similar court for misdemeanors related to DUI. The misdemeanor wellness court does not have the "stick" of incarceration, but does provide treatment and typically applies to the first DUI offense. Participation requires that the offender:

- Enter intensive outpatient substance abuse treatment with an approved treatment provider,

- Agree to be medically evaluated for the appropriateness of a medicine that stops cravings for alcohol (if indicated),

- Attend recovery support groups i.e. AA, NA or Na Tia Su Kan,

- Appear regularly before the wellness court judge for compliance hearings,

- Work or attend school a minimum of 32 hours a week,

- Undergo regular alcohol and other drug testing,

- Maintain sobriety,

- Attend Moral Reconation Therapy (MRT) *,

- Follow through with mental health services (if recommended), and

- Pay for treatment, the MRT course and some drug testing.

So far, 37 people have enrolled in the Fairbanks DUI program since it opened in 2007. Twenty are still active in the program, nine have graduated, three were discharged for violations, and one has died. An additional offender is awaiting approval. Many offenders want to get in the program, but space is limited. The prosecutor's office is strongly supportive of wellness courts, but some voters are not--they say criminal justice should be for punishment, not for treatment, according to the News-Miner.

For more information, go to www.courts.alaska.gov.

Moral Reconation Therapy (MRT) is a type of cognitive behavioral therapy targeting offenders. It was developed in the late 1980s by Kenneth Robinson, Gregory Little, and their colleagues at Correctional Counseling, Inc. For more information, go to http://moral-reconation-therapy.com/Resources/CBTR-%2019_1%202010GL.pdf.

32

DWI Court Offers Jail Alternative

Program Saves County Money

Jodie Jackson Jr.

"This is purely a voluntary program," Carpenter said, adding that the new court has funding for only 30 participants this year. A $50,000 grant will pay for testing and monitoring services, but the participants must pay for the $3,000 treatment.

"That is a limiting factor as to how many people can participate," said Carpenter, who has served on the 13th Circuit bench since 1999. "I don't think we'll have any trouble finding 30 people who can afford it."

When the grant funding was offered in October, court officials at first were inclined to decline the money because it could not be used to pay for treatment. "But it's better than nothing," Carpenter said. "It's not a lot, but it's getting us started."

DWI court will be Boone County's fourth specialty court, joining mental health, drug and reintegration courts. Carpenter said participants in the existing specialty courts have a 10 percent rate for committing another crime. According to the Bureau of Justice, recidivism among prisoners who serve jail time is 65 percent.

There are an average of 1,200 first-time DWI arrests in Columbia and Boone County each year. Roughly 100 of those offenders will have a second and third arrest, Carpenter said. "We

Jackson, J. DWI court offers jail alternative: Program saves county money. Columbia Daily Tribune (Columbia, MO), March 17, 2010.

made the conscious decision to try to intervene between that second and third" DWI conviction, she said.

The DWI court will result in an immediate savings of $1,000 to the county because the four participants will not each serve five days in the Boone County Jail at a cost of $50 per day.

"To me, that's a double benefit," Carpenter said. "The vast majority of these people are employed or students. They're not going to lose their job by going to jail."

She said the alternative sentencing programs are "problem-solving courts" that address mental illness or drug and alcohol abuse. "All of the alternative sentencing programs are cheaper than sending someone to prison," she said.

Mike Princivalli, the drug court coordinator, also will coordinate the DWI court. Princivalli formerly worked in the treatment and corrections fields and is convinced that the alternative sentencing programs are successful.

"I've been part of this going on 10 years," he said. "I swear by it."

Carpenter said the specialty courts keep extensive data and are closely monitored by state officials. And she will closely monitor program participants.

"When I have anyone in one of these programs for any length of time, I know their kids' names, how their mom's health is, where they work, if their dog's sick," she said. Still, Carpenter must sometimes tell participants, "You're going to jail" if they fail an alcohol test or don't follow all the program requirements.

The court has contracted with Reality House to conduct testing. Carpenter said unannounced visits are to be expected.

"It's 11 o'clock on a Friday night, there's a knock on your door, and there's somebody standing there with a portable Breathalyzer," she said.

Part IV

CORRECTIONAL SYSTEM

In Part 1 of this section, ethical behavior of corrections personnel is explored. In the first article, think about if the probation employees really have any culpability in this case or were they prevented from taking any action by policy, procedure, or law? Did they really have the authority to do anything? When deciding cases similar to the one presented in this first article, jurors are asked to place themselves in the officer's position, knowing only the information the officer knew at the time, no more. Given this, does your opinion change? The second article presents an interesting case of the systems theory introduced in the Preface of this Reader, the effect each branch of the criminal justice system has on the other branches. Are corrections officials left with no choice but to force feed an inmate? The final article in this section addresses the plight of an inmate. Did corrections officials do all they could to prevent the inmate from being victimized? Can you think of an alternative?

In Part 2 of this section, two distinctly different articles are presented. The first article is a comprehensive review on the use of conducted energy devices and their use on pretrial detainees. The article provides insight into real use of force incidents; it will expose you to an important issue in the criminal justice system, the use of force by corrections personnel. A case of an injured inmate is explained in the second article. As you read this article think about the viewpoints presented by the author of the article and their validity.

The theme of Part 3 of this section is evidence-based corrections. We cannot afford to continue to build more prisons and jails, and have high numbers of individuals who are released recidivate and return to incarceration. As you read the articles in this section, are any of the programs successful enough to make an impact on our correctional problems?

Continue to think about evidence-based corrections as you read the articles in Part 4. The articles present a host of potential programs to keep offenders from re-incarceration. Which programs seem to have the greatest chance of success? Which ones are destined to fail in your opinion? Part 5, special populations begins with a growing problem in the criminal justice field, providing care for the mentally ill. At which point do we decide that individuals with mental illness be diverted from the criminal justice process. In reality, most mentally ill individuals that begin the criminal justice process are not diverted and end up in the care and custody of the corrections branch. As you process the numbers presented in the first article, think about the enormity of the problem. Does the concept of the Crisis Intervention Team make sense? The last two articles in this Part present issues related to inmates with special needs. Are there any alternatives you can think of in handling special needs populations? What other special populations exist in the corrections environment?

Ethical Behavior of Correctional Personnel

33

Probation Workers Investigated in Carjacking

They Let Fugitive Felon Leave Office Before Fatal Incident in Citrus County Last Spring

Mark Douglas

A state inspector general is secretly piecing together actions by state probation employees that may have set the stage for a deadly carjacking in Citrus County last April.

But after eight months, the victim's son, Jason Haynie, said he hasn't heard a whisper about the review.

"For everything to still be left up in the air, it's hard for me to close the chapter on this thing," Haynie said. "I need some sort of closure."

On April 7, Jennifer Denise Marino, a 32-year-old fugitive and felony probation violator, walked out of a state probation office in Inverness and vanished into the surrounding neighborhood.

Hours later, she was arrested nearby in the death of Haynie's mother, Mary Haynie, a 64-year-old schoolteacher. The woman was fatally struck by her own car as her assailant drove it away.

Probation workers handling Marino's case had repeatedly told her to stay put while she paced in their lobby, but they made no attempt to arrest Marino when Marino picked up her bags and left.

DOUGLAS, M. Probation workers investigated in carjacking. The Tampa Tribune (Tampa, FL), Dec 4, 2010.

At the time, she was in violation of her probation for a violent carjacking in New York, a fugitive from Virginia, and behaving so strangely a probation worker later told a 911 operator, "I really do think that she's either gonna hurt herself or somebody else."

Local prosecutor Mark Simpson, who supervises the public interest unit for State Attorney Brad King, said he is reviewing the inspector general's preliminary report to determine whether criminal charges against state employees are warranted. "The public has a right to know what those employees have done," Simpson said. "But we have to be mindful that decisions we make affect people's lives."

Simpson said he may make a decision as early as next week.

Jason Haynie said it seems like his mother died just yesterday, even though it has been closer to eight months.

"No calls, no apologies, no insight, no news, nothing," Haynie said. "It's as if I don't exist."

Mary Haynie lived a quiet life surrounded by friends and family. She was active, healthy and still teaching young children. Marino had just been delivered to the probation office by a local shelter operator after checking out of a mental heath center in Miami.

Had they checked, local probation workers would have learned that Marino was in violation of her probation and was wanted on a fugitive warrant.

A probation officer called 911 to report that Marino "hightailed it" out of the office while her case files were still being sorted out. The same officer expressed concern to the 911 operator about what Marino might do next. "I don't know which direction she went, but I don't foresee her not hurting herself or someone else," the worker said.

Hours later, Haynie was dead. She had stopped by a grooming shop with her dog, Beans, when she happened to cross paths with Marino.

Gwendolyn Mobley, the probation office manager, refused to authorize Marino's arrest at the time she was there, according to office records. Mobley retired last summer. Her departure was unrelated to the carjacking, the corrections department said.

"If it was her fault, she needs to take a stand and own up to it being her fault and not let other people take the fall for it," Haynie said.

If Simpson declines to pursue criminal action against state workers, the inspector general will determine whether they should face disciplinary or administrative sanctions.

Until then, Jason Haynie waits. "With this report still lingering," Haynie said, "it's still as fresh as the day it happened."

34

Inmate Being Force-Fed, Lawyer Says

Mark Spencer

Prison medical workers have started force-feeding inmate William Coleman, who has lost more than 115 pounds during a yearlong hunger strike, one of his attorneys said Monday.

David McGuire, a staff attorney for the American Civil Liberties Union of Connecticut, said Coleman called him about noon and said he was about to be restrained and intravenously given liquids.

McGuire had met with Coleman, a 48-year-old British citizen, Monday morning at Osborn Correctional Institution in Somers. He said Coleman looked gaunt and was brought to the meeting in a wheelchair, although he stood up and sat in another chair on his own and was lucid.

"He's obviously very weakened," McGuire said.

The state received a temporary injunction in January from a Superior Court judge allowing the prison to force-feed Coleman, who stopped eating solid food to protest his 2005 rape conviction, for which he is serving an eight-year sentence. He maintains he is innocent and said in a statement the hunger strike is a protest against a "broken judicial system" that has victimized other innocent people.

McGuire said Coleman also stopped taking liquids Sept. 15, the one-year anniversary of his hunger strike.

Brian Garnett, the spokesman for the Department of Correction, declined to comment, citing the confidentiality of the medical treatment of inmates.

Spencer, M. Inmate Being Force-Fed, Lawyer Says. Hartford Courant (Hartford, CT), Sept 23, 2008

208

"We do have a court order in place to treat Mr. Coleman to protect his life if it's medically appropriate," Garnett said.

The ACLU initially sought to have a judge vacate the state's injunction, but has now decided to challenge the constitutionality of force-feeding in a bench trial scheduled for January.

"Every time an IV is inserted into Bill, a competent adult, the DOC will violate his right to deny medical treatment," McGuire said.

Coleman told McGuire he will not physically resist medical staff, but will remove the IV if he has the opportunity. In his statement, Coleman said being force-fed will only prolong his death because his organs will eventually give out anyway.

"I do not want to die," Coleman said, "but I am willing to die."

35

Ex-con Tells of Sex Forced On Him

Michael Biesecker

Even in prison, Dedric McDaniels could get the relaxer he needs to make his long hair straight and feminine.

Since he was 11, the New Bern native has thought of himself as transgender, a girl trapped in a male body. Now 35, McDaniels would be easy to mistake for a woman, especially when poured into a pair of his skinny jeans.

That made him a target for unwanted attention during the nearly six years he served in North Carolina's prison system for a drug conviction. In prison after prison, McDaniels said, he was harassed and assaulted by other inmates seeking sex.

Sometimes, he said, his tormentors were the very correctional officers who were supposed to help keep him safe.

One of those officers, Sgt. Ricky Campbell, is now awaiting trial on a felony charge of sexual activity by a custodian, punishable by up to two years in prison.

At a minimum security prison outside Lumberton last year, McDaniels said, the sergeant cornered him in a bathroom one Saturday afternoon and ordered him to perform oral sex.

"Penitentiary is a different world," said McDaniels, who was released on parole Oct. 1. "A sergeant with three stripes, his word is gold. If I didn't do as he said, he could have written me up for nothing, had me thrown into the hole. He could have said I hit him and had me arrested. Nobody's going to take my word over his."

Biesecker, M. Ex-con tells of sex forced on him. News & Observer (Raleigh, NC), Dec 5, 2010

That is why after it was over, McDaniels returned to his bunk, put a sample of the officer's DNA into a paper cup, and sealed it inside a latex glove.

"There's not much to do in prison, so I watched a lot of CSI," McDaniels said. "I knew that unless I had proof, nothing would happen to him."

A Correction employee since 1992, Campbell could not be reached for comment. His lawyer, Danny Britt of Lumberton, did not respond to messages left at his office.

83 SUBSTANTIATED CASES

The Prison Rape Elimination Act, a federal law passed in 2003, requires states to report annually to the U.S. Justice Department on incidents of sexual violence in prisons and jails. The law also dictates that states must have "zero tolerance" for employees who abuse inmates.

In the last three years, officials at the N.C. Department of Correction have investigated 835 reports of sexual misconduct and harassment by Correction employees. Of those, 83 cases were substantiated by the state as being true.

The federal law, known by its acronym PREA, does not require prison systems to disclose details about those cases. North Carolina officials have denied requests from The News & Observer for such information, citing the need to protect the privacy of the inmates.

Michele Luecking-Sunman, an attorney at N.C. Prisoner Legal Services, said her staff has lawsuits pending in state and federal court on behalf of 15 female inmates who say they were raped or sexually assaulted by Correction staff. The nonprofit legal aid group also filed a claim on behalf of McDaniels, seeking financial compensation for the assault he alleges.

Jennie Lancaster, chief operating officer and the prison system's point person on PREA compliance, said that in an organization with 40,000 inmates and more than 20,000 employees there will inevitably be cases of abuse and fraternization.

The majority of reported cases involve male staff at women's prisons. But Correction officials regularly receive reports of abuse and harassment between employees and inmates of the same sex.

"It doesn't matter if it's an inmate's word against an employee's word, we're going to investigate," said Lancaster, a 34-year veteran of the state prison system. "When you do that, the first thing you're trying to determine is whether there has been undue familiarity taking place, much less the breaking of the law. If we think a criminal act has taken place, we contact local law enforcement or the SBI."

EVIDENCE OFTEN LACKING

Luecking-Sunman said a major concern was for the nine out of 10 inmates who report being assaulted only to have the prison's internal investigation find insufficient evidence to substantiate the claim.

"It's hard to prove an officer said something or did something when it's the inmate's word against the officer's word," she said. "And then what often happens is the inmate gets disciplined for filing a false report. That completely deters many inmates from making a PREA report."

No data were immediately available as to how many Correction employees have been criminally charged with sexually assaulting inmates in recent years. But Lancaster acknowledged that many employees investigated for "undue familiarity" with inmates resign without facing prosecution.

Even when there is evidence of sexual misconduct, Lancaster said, local district attorneys sometimes hesitate to pursue criminal charges against prison staff if the sexual encounter was deemed "consensual."

The state law under which Campbell is charged specifically says it doesn't matter whether the sex was consensual, because of the immense power and influence prison guards have over those in custody.

'WE ARE RESPONSIBLE'

"We are responsible for the care and custody of these offenders," Lancaster said. "We also have a position of power and authority over offenders. There's absolutely no excuse for, or defense for, not maintaining your professional working relationship."

New correctional officers in North Carolina receive four hours of training on sexual assault and harassment. Once on the job, officers receive an annual review of the material.

McDaniels said he knows other inmates who were sexually victimized behind bars but who never filed a complaint for fear of retaliation or being labeled a snitch.

"There are a lot of people still inside going through what I went through," he said. "It needs to stop."

McDaniels is quick to admit that he is no choirboy.

First incarcerated at age 17, he has a record of at least two dozen convictions going back to 1991. All were for nonviolent offenses such as breaking and entering, larceny, credit card fraud and forgery.

His most recent stretch was for two 2004 convictions for possession of crack cocaine in Craven County. Because of his long history of run-ins with the law, prosecutors also charged McDaniels as a habitual felon, resulting in a prison sentence of nearly eight years.

His prison record shows he was cited for five rules infractions, including gambling, engaging in a sexual act and possession of contraband.

McDaniels, who describes himself as a "flamboyant homosexual," said that contraband was a pair of G-string panties he had crafted for himself out of a black stocking hat.

"I can't hide who I am," McDaniels said. "I shouldn't have to. I was born this way."

Lancaster said that safeguarding an inmate like McDaniels can be challenging.

"I've seen a lot of contraband in my 34 years, but I have never seen G-strings on a male inmate," she said. "Honestly, when you have an offender like him, where you know it's a fine line between him being a victim, and his clearly being seen as that, and on the other hand, what his risk behaviors might be by his drawing attention to himself."

Dr. Terry A. Kupers, a former prison psychiatrist from California who has written extensively about the issue of sexual violence against inmates, said housing people such as McDaniels in a general prison population full of "predators" all but ensures they will be victimized.

"It's predictable that he was going to be sexually assaulted," said Kupers, who has testified before Congress on the issue of prison rape. "It is the duty of prison administrators to protect these individuals."

ISOLATING GAYS, BISEXUALS

In some prison systems, Kupers said, there are special units for transgender, lesbian, gay and bisexual inmates to better protect them.

Lancaster said that in North Carolina, inmates are housed based on their "genital identity" but that administrators do their best to protect them. Transferring a prisoner to a new facility is one way to try to keep an inmate out of trouble, she said.

McDaniels' record shows he was transferred 23 times in less than six years.

"Does it cause the inmate more difficulty and does it cause the department more difficulty? Yes it does," Lancaster said. "That's why you try to keep your eye on them and ... you don't wait until the problems blow up around you to deal with it. But there's not a good solution to it."

A FREQUENT TARGET

Almost from the start of his incarceration in 2004, McDaniels said, he was targeted by both inmates and staff.

"The way I look, the way my body looks, I got a lot of unwanted attention," he said.

One night at Pamlico Correctional Institution in 2005, McDaniels said he awoke when three inmates somehow entered his locked cell and tried to sexually assault him. He said he screamed for help and managed to escape into the outside corridor.

At Lumberton Correctional Institution in 2006, he said an inmate assaulted him in the group shower. He was later attacked by an inmate at Hyde Correctional Institution.

Each time he reported being harassed or assaulted, McDaniels said prison officials simply transferred him.

At Wake Correctional Institution, McDaniels said, a male correctional officer made sexual advances on him.

"Every time I was in the shower, he would come in there and stare at me and talk about how I looked," McDaniels said.

McDaniels filed a written grievance against the officer in August 2009. Records show the officer denied "doing anything inappropriate" and the prison superintendent recommended "no further action."

The day after he filed the grievance against the officer at Wake, McDaniels was moved to the minimum security prison camp in Lumberton, where he was assigned to be a janitor.

INCIDENT AT LUMBERTON

On Saturday, Sept. 26, 2009, McDaniels said, Sgt. Campbell called him to his office and asked him to clean the staff rest room. Once he was in the rest room, McDaniels said, Campbell entered behind him, locked the door and began unfastening his uniform pants.

McDaniels said that he initially said no but that the officer insisted.

After the encounter, McDaniels kept the cup holding the DNA sample in a brown paper bag until Monday morning, when the prison superintendent returned to work. McDaniels then went to see the boss and told him what happened.

"He asked me if I had any proof," McDaniels said. "I held up the paper bag and told him what was in it. I tried to hand it to him, but he didn't want to touch it. He just told me to set it on his desk."

The superintendent called the Robeson County Sheriff's Department, which sent two deputies to take McDaniels' statement. The prison also launched an internal investigation. Two days later, on Sept. 30, 2009, Campbell resigned. He was arrested Dec. 14, according to court records.

Joseph Osman, the Robeson County prosecutor assigned to the case, said he could not discuss the details of McDaniels' account before Campbell's trial, which has not been scheduled. But he did confirm that there was "physical evidence" in the case. The next court hearing is scheduled for Jan. 10.

McDaniels, who now works at a Raleigh fast-food restaurant, said he looks forward to taking the witness stand against Campbell.

"Just because I'm a convict, just because I'm a homosexual, doesn't mean I deserve to be assaulted," he said. "I'm a human being, and no still means no."

Use of Force

36

An Examination of Legal Cases Involving the Use of Tasers and Stun Guns on Pretrial Detainees

Vidisha Barua and Robert M. Worley

Tasers and stun guns are conducted-energy devices used by jail and prison officers to subdue inmates. As nonlethal weapons, Tasers and stun guns are not designed to inflict serious injury or permanent harm, but they have nevertheless caused deaths when used on individuals with existing or potential health problems. The Taser was developed by Jack Cover, an aerospace engineer, in the 1960s, for the purpose of providing an alternative to the handgun (Ready, White and Fisher, 2008). It has been controversial since its inception (Kornblum and Reddy, 1991). In fact, when the Taser first appeared in law enforcement, it was banned by the state legislatures of New York and Michigan (Johnston, 1981).

Stun guns are weapons similar to Tasers. The stun gun is "an electrical self-defense device which sends out 50,000 volts to the body when pressed against the skin" (Kornblum and Reddy, 1991). Although it is commonly believed that Tasers and stun guns discharge 50,000 volts of electricity to the body, that may not be the case. According to Williams (2008), both the M26 and the X26 Tasers have 50,000 peak open circuit voltage at the main capacitor that allows a spark to go through a gap between clothing and a person's body. However, he asserts that the weapons do not deliver 50,000 volts into a person's body. Williams (2008) claims that once

Barua,V. & Worley, R. An examination of legal cases involving the use of Tasers and stun guns on pretrial detainees. Jailhouse Shock. Corrections Compendium, Summer 2009 v34 i2 p9(8). Reprinted with permission of the American Correctional Association, Alexandria, VA.

the weapon is applied to the body and the spark crosses a gap, the TASER M26 model delivers a peak loaded voltage of 5,000 volts, and the TASER X26 model delivers a peak loaded voltage of 1,200 volts. The 50,000 peak open circuit voltage at the main capacitator is used to produce a spark of a lesser voltage that is applied to a person's body. Tasers and stun guns cause victims to lose control of their muscles, collapse and remain immobile for a few minutes. The primary difference between the Taser and the stun gun is that the latter must be placed next to the subject's skin, while the former can be fired from up to a distance of 25 feet (Kornblum and Reddy, 1991; Williams, 2008).

Excessive use of force is embedded in the correctional officer subculture (Marquart, 1986). During the hands-off era courts were reluctant to try or decide cases filed by prisoners. The position of the courts during this era is best reflected in an infamous Virginia Court decision, Ruffin v. Commonwealth (1871), where an inmate was declared to be a "slave of the state." This changed with the coming of the hands-on era between the late 1960s and early 1970s when issues like equal protection and due process revolutionized the attitude of the courts. Since this time, use-of-force lawsuits have become a major part of all inmate litigation (Robertson, 2006).

While there has been at least some discussion devoted to the use of electronic energy devices by law enforcement officers, very few studies have exclusively examined the use of these devices on pretrial detainees in jail settings. Unlike inmates who have already been convicted, pretrial detainees are presumed innocent, and they therefore retain their constitutional right to be free from punishment even though they are confined (Bell v. Wolfish, 1979). While the excessive force claims of inmates are examined under the Eighth Amendment, those for pretrial detainees are usually governed by: the Fourth Amendment's objective reasonableness standard, as established in Graham v. Connor (1989); the governmental policy or custom standard, as established in Monell v. Department of Social Services of the City of New York (1978); and the failure to adequately train standard under City of Canton v. Harris (1989). This article explores jail officer liabilities for the use of Tasers and stun guns with regard to pretrial detainees.

A PRIMER ON THE RIGHTS OF DETAINEES

As Rosen (1990) writes, in the landmark case Bell v. Wolfish, "the Supreme Court for the first time explored the constitutional rights of pretrial detainees as a distinct group and articulated the principles that presently govern constitutional claims of jail inmates." The court ruled in Bell v. Wolfish (1979) that pretrial detainees retain their constitutional protections under the Fourth, Fifth and 14th Amendments, despite their confinement. This is because these detainees have not been found guilty beyond a reasonable doubt. Instead, pretrial detainees are held on the basis of probable cause that they have committed the crimes for which they have been arrested. This is not the same as being proved guilty; therefore, pretrial detainees retain most of their constitutional rights. However, the U.S. Supreme Court has pointed out that "[a] detainee simply does not possess the full range of freedoms of an unincarcerated individual" (Bell v. Wolfish, 1979). Most pretrial detainees are placed in jail to ensure their presence at trial rather than to punish them (Rosen, 1990).

In the Bell case, pretrial detainees at the New York City Metropolitan Correctional Center filed a suit alleging that their constitutional rights had been violated because the facility had been filled beyond its capacity and single bunks were replaced by double bunks in the cells and dormitories. The detainees alleged that their constitutional rights were violated because of crowding, undue length of confinement, improper searches, inadequate recreational facilities and lack of educational and employment opportunities. The court held that double-bunking, body-cavity searches and searches of detainees' quarters in their absence did not deprive pretrial detainees of their due process rights under the Fifth Amendment and their Fourth Amendment rights to be free from unreasonable searches and seizures. The court ruled, absent a showing of an expressed intent to punish, if a particular condition or restriction is reasonably related to a legitimate nonpunitive governmental objective, it does not amount to punishment and hence does not violate a pretrial detainee's due process rights under the Fifth Amendment. In fact, the core distinction between detainees and inmates with regard to their constitutional rights is that under the due process clause, detainees may not be punished without a prior adjudication of guilt (Bell v. Wolfish, 1979).

In Turner v. Safley (1987), the Supreme Court ruled that in order to determine if a prison regulation that burdens constitutional rights is valid, a court has to examine whether it is reasonably related to legitimate penological objectives or whether it represents an exaggerated response to those concerns. In Turner, state inmates brought a class-action suit challenging regulations of the Missouri Division of Corrections that restricted inmate-to-inmate correspondence and allowed inmates to marry only if there were

compelling reasons to do so. The court laid down a four-pronged test
to determine reasonableness:

- There must be a valid rational connection between the
  prison regulation and the legitimate governmental interest
  put for ward to justify it;

- Whether there are alternative means of exercising the
  right that remains open to prison in mates;

- The impact that accommodation of the asserted
  constitutional right will have on correctional officers and
  other inmatcs and on the allocation of resources
  generally; and

- The absence of ready alternatives to the prison regulation.

Accordingly, the court ruled that while the inmate-to-inmate
correspondence was reasonably related to legitimate security
concerns, the inmate marriage regulation was not related to any
legitimate penological objective.

In Hause v. Vaught (1993), the 4th Circuit applied Turner v.
Safley (1987) to pretrial detainees as the "Turner test still remains the
default standard in First Amendment cases" (Robertson, 2007). In
this case, Hause challenged the detention center's policy that did not
allow detainees to receive books and periodicals in the mail as an
infringement of his First Amendment rights. The policy was put in
place to prevent the smuggling of contraband. Hause argued that
receiving material sent by publishers provided an easy alternative.
The 4th Circuit ruled that considering the brief period of time that
detainees are confined, publications are likely to arrive in most cases
after the detainee has been transferred to other facilities, thus causing
an unnecessary administrative burden on the jail officers. Moreover,
even though a publisher-only rule would prevent the smuggling of
contraband, publications could still be used to start fires, the court
pointed out. Applying Turner, the court ruled that the detention
center's ban on outside publications was reasonably related to
legitimate penological interests.

A standard for individual jail officer liability that is applied in
cases of pretrial detainees by lower courts was set by the Supreme
Court in Graham v. Connor (1989). In this case, there was evidence
that Graham was physically hurt by law enforcement officers during
an investigatory stop. Graham was a diabetic suffering from an
insulin reaction. During the traffic stop, Graham passed out briefly,
and one of the officers who arrived at the scene rolled Graham over

on the sidewalk and cuffed his hands tightly behind his back, ignoring the pleas of Graham's friend that he was diabetic. (1) During the encounter, Graham sustained a broken foot, cuts on his wrists, a bruised forehead and an injured shoulder. Thereafter, Graham filed a Section 1983 action, claiming his Fourth Amendment rights were violated. The court ruled that excessive force claims against the police should be analyzed under the Fourth Amendment's objective reasonableness standard, not the 14th Amendment's substantive due process standard. Under objective reasonableness, the question is what an ordinary prudent police officer at the scene would have done in the same or similar situation. Because the standard for liability is objective reasonableness, not subjective reasonableness, the specific officer's mindset at the scene is irrelevant. The court held that the relevant inquiry focuses on what the hypothetical reasonable officer with the proper training, experience and foresight would have done. Although they are confined, pretrial detainees retain their constitutional rights and, hence, the Fourth Amendment's objective reasonableness standard affords protection to them.

Departmental liability for the use of Tasers and stun guns against detainees is deficient policy, procedure and custom, leading to constitutional deprivations. Lower courts have followed Monell v. Department of Social Services of the City of New York (1978), which established that a Monell violation occurs when an agency articulates an official policy and that policy causes constitutional injury. In addition, nonofficial customs and procedures have the same weight as official policies when causing constitutional violations. In this case, female employees of the Department of Social Services and the Board of Education of the City of New York objected to official policies that required pregnant employees to take unpaid leaves of absence before those leaves were required for medical reasons. The district court and the U.S. Court of Appeals for the 2nd Circuit found the policy unconstitutional, but denied claims for back pay. The Supreme Court observed that the touchstone for a Section 1983 action to succeed against a governmental entity is that the official policy must be responsible for the constitutional deprivation. In Monell, the deprivation arose out of an official policy; thus, the local government was held liable. Monell was highly significant because it opened the liability floodgates for lawsuits against cities and counties (del Carmen, 1991; Kappeler, 2001).

Failure to adequately train jail officers may result in governmental liability, especially for the use of Tasers and stun guns. The Supreme Court's leading case on failure to train is City of Canton v. Harris (1989). The issue before the Supreme Court was whether the training program provided by the city of Canton, Ohio,

224

to its police officers was adequate. In this case, the facts showed that Geraldine Harris was in need of medical attention when she was arrested and taken to jail. Harris was found sitting on the floor of the patrol wagon, she slumped to the floor twice inside the station, and after her release from police custody without any medical care Harris was taken by an ambulance (provided by her family) to a nearby hospital. There, Harris was diagnosed with several emotional ailments, resulting in hospitalization for one week and outpatient treatment for a year. Harris sued under the legal theory that a person has a right to receive medical attention while in police custody. Citing Monell's rule, that a city may be liable under Section 1983 when policies or customs cause constitutional deprivations, the court held that the training provided to the city's police officers was clearly inadequate. The court ruled that such lawsuits can only yield liability against a municipality when the city's failure to train reflects deliberate indifference to the constitutional rights of its inhabitants.

Despite most courts following the objective reasonableness standard laid down by Graham, some courts have refused to apply this standard to pretrial detainees. The 4th Circuit Court of Appeals observed, "The point at which Fourth Amendment protections end and Fourteenth Amendment protections begin is often murky" (Orem v. Rephann, 2008). According to the 4th Circuit, once arrested, the Fourth Amendment protections cease and the 14th Amendment due process clause applies (Orem v. Rephann, 2008). Courts have also used the de minimis injury standard to Find jail officer's liable. Where the injury is de minimis, officers cannot be found liable (Valentine v. Richardson, 2008).

METHODS

A sample of 19 cases on jail officers' use of Taser and stun guns under Section 1983 is examined in this paper. The cases were obtained by cross-referencing Westlaw Campus and LexisNexis. Searches were performed on the terms "taser" "Section 1983," "jail" and "stun gun." The search terms were executed for all federal cases. Not all the cases returned by the searches were Taseror stun-gun-related cases. These were immediately eliminated from further consideration in this analysis. Additionally, cases that involved Tasers or stun guns but did not relate to jail officers were not considered in this analysis. The researchers systematically examined the summaries of each of the cases returned by the searches to select the appropriate ones for this study. So far, none of the cases has reached the Supreme Court. The cases examined in this article are lower federal court cases decided in the U.S. District Courts and U.S.

Courts of Appeals. They are broadly divided into cases in which the courts ruled against jail officers at this stage of the proceedings and cases in which they ruled in favor of jail officers.

COURT RULINGS AGAINST JAIL OFFICERS

Excessive use of force: Objective reasonableness standards and conflicting versions of events.

Tasering of an arrested person by police officers for being verbally unruly and refusing to wear a jail uniform is objectively unreasonable. In Stephens v. City of Butler, Alabama (2007), an arrestee was tasered four times by two police officers after he was brought to jail. The U.S. District Court for the Southern District of Alabama applied the Fourth Amendment's objective reasonableness standard to this case as the plaintiff, a pretrial detainee, was under the control of the police officers who were making the arrest report. Applying Graham, the court looked at the reason for the application of the Taser. Although the plaintiff was charged with running over senior citizens and handicapped persons in his vehicle, the event that triggered the tasering was the plaintiffs refusal to wear a jail uniform. Considering the second factor (2) laid down by Graham, the District Court observed that the plaintiff did not pose an immediate threat to the safety of the officers or others. He was unarmed and confined in a small room in the jail surrounded by three police officers. Third, the plaintiff was not actively resisting arrest nor was he attempting to flee from the interior room of the jail. Examining the totality of the circumstances, the court ruled that repeatedly applying a Taser on an unarmed person in police custody, surrounded by three police officers within the confines of a jail was "objectively unreasonable and excessive, particularly where the use of force was over something as minor as being verbally unruly and refusing to don jail garb." The plaintiff after all had made no effort to escape and was posing no threat to the safety of any officer. Accordingly, the District Court refused to grant summary judgment to the defendants.

Although the Supreme Court is not clear at which point after arrest the Fourth Amendment ceases to protect an individual, the 6th Circuit has held that the protection extends to the entire time the individual is in the custody of the arresting officers (McDowell v. Rogers, 1988). In Harris v. City of Circleville (2008), Harris, a pretrial detainee, sustained a spinal cord injury while being booked at the Circleville Jail. Passively resisting the officers, Harris refused to allow them to take away his belongings. Once Harris was on the ground, the officers used Tasers on his back. He could not move. The officers ignored his protests and removed the arrestee's belongings from his person. Harris was left on the floor for 80 minutes, after which he was taken to a hospital. He underwent surgery, but there was permanent injury to his spinal cord. Harris filed a Section 1983 action for excessive use of force against the officers. Since Harris was injured at the very beginning of the booking process in the presence of the arresting officers, the U.S. District Court for the Southern District of Ohio held that Harris' excessive force claim would be governed by the Fourth Amendment. Applying Graham to this case, the court found that the actions of the officers were objectively unreasonable. The court observed that Harris was not accused of a serious crime. He did not pose an immediate threat to the safety of the officers or others and was already handcuffed and inside a jail cell surrounded by several officers. Although Harris was verbally protesting, there was no evidence showing that he was violent or combative. Ruling the defendants were not entitled to qualified immunity, the court cited McDowell (1988), where the 6th Circuit held that the need for force is nonexistent when a handcuffed arrestee is not trying to escape or hurt anyone.

Whenever a plaintiff alleges that he or she presented no threat and that the use of force on the plaintiff was excessive, while the defendant claims that the force used was as per departmental policies, there are genuine issues of material fact, and summary judgment cannot be granted. Issues of material fact exist when there is a dispute about important facts of the case; that is, when the two parties have different versions of the relevant events. Summary judgment is usually granted when there are no factual disputes and the parties agree as to the relevant facts of the case. Once the court is convinced that there are no factual disputes, it will apply the law and rule on the motion for summary judgment. Such judgments are resorted to for the sake of speedy justice.

In Pipkins v. Pike County, Arkansas (2007), the plaintiff alleged that her constitutional rights were violated while she was incarcerated in the Pike County Jail. At about 1:40 a.m. on the night of the event, the defendants allegedly entered the plaintiffs cell. She was lying on the floor. The plaintiff alleged that the defendants used a Taser on her several times even though she was not presenting any threat. The department conducted an investigation and concluded that the officers were acting as per departmental policies. The plaintiff filed a Section 1983 action for excessive use of force by the defendants. The U.S. District Court for the Western District of Arkansas applied Kuha v. City of Minnetonka (2004), which held that an excessive force claim is analyzed under the Fourth Amendment's objective reasonableness standard. According to Kuha, the relevant inquiry is whether the plaintiff provided sufficient proof to show that the defendant's use of force was objectively unreasonable. In examining the case at hand, the District Court found that the plaintiff did provide documents showing that she was not acting in an uncontrolled or dangerous manner. Moreover, the court found that there were genuine issues of material fact as to the events that led up to the defendants using the Taser on the plaintiff. As such, viewing the plaint in the light most favorable to the plaintiff, the court denied summary judgment to the defendants.

Summary judgment cannot be granted when there are genuine issues of material facts. In Ndaula v. Holliday (2007), Ndaula, an immigration and customs enforcement detainee, considered equivalent to a pretrial detainee, alleged that excessive force was used against him by a "gang" of correctional officers when he was in his dorm drinking coffee while two wardens were present. Ndaula claims he was beaten and shocked with a Taser. After the incident, he was denied medical care. Analyzing the facts of the case, the U.S. District Court for the Western District of Louisiana held that since the affidavits submitted by Ndaula and the medical record reflecting complaints of pain refute the affidavits submitted by the defendants, there are genuine issues of material fact that preclude a summary judgment in favor of the defendants.

Use of force by jail officials against an inmate for being a sex offender is excessive and unreasonable. In Burr v. Hill (2005), Burr was rearrested for failing to register as a sex offender. While Burr was housed in the Dallas County Jail, jail officials double-cuffed his hands behind his back, dragged him through the jail and threatened to use a Taser against him, saying that was the treatment a child molester got in prison. As a result of this incident, Burr suffered from serious injuries for which he had to be taken to the Parkland Hospital. Without judging on the merits, the U.S. District Court for the Northern District of Texas determined that Burr had sufficiently stated an excessive force claim against the jail officers. Accordingly, the court allowed Burr to proceed with his excessive force claim.

Where there is a genuine issue of material fact as to whether an individual is subjected to use of a Taser inappropriately, summary judgment cannot be granted. In Castaneda v. Douglas County Sheriff's Investigator Rory Planeta (2007), the plaintiff alleged that a Taser was used on him during the booking process at the jail even though he was compliant. Moreover, he was not told that he would be subjected to Taser. The defendants contend that the plaintiff was highly combative during the booking process and was repeatedly warned that a Taser would be used if he did not stop resisting. Once the Taser was used, the plaintiff became compliant and followed

228

orders. The plaintiff filed a Section 1983 action for inappropriate use of the Taser. Looking at the facts of the case, the U.S. District Court for the District of Nevada noted that a material issue of fact existed regarding whether the plaintiff was subjected to use of a Taser inappropriately. Accordingly, the court refused to grant summary judgment to the defendants.

When filing a Section 1983 suit for excessive use of force, a plaintiff must specify each individual responsible for the excessive force and show an affirmative link between the injury suffered and that conduct (Rizzo v. Goode, 1976). In Monroe v. Arpaio (2005), Monroe was tasered shortly after he was housed in a jail. Monroe asserts that he sustained scars on his back from the Taser. Monroe filed a Section 1983 action for excessive use of force. The U.S. District Court for the District of Arizona acknowledged that given the circumstances, Monroe could have a claim for excessive use of force. However, applying Rizzo, the court noted that for Monroe's claim to survive, he must connect the claim to the named defendants. Accordingly, the court advised Monroe to name the defendants in their individual capacities and mention what each individual did or failed to do.

In Orem v. Rephann (2008), the 4th Circuit Court of Appeals applied the 14th Amendment's due process clause instead of the Fourth Amendment in an excessive use of force claim against Officer Rephann. Orem was arrested for disrupting and assaulting an officer after being served with a family protective order. While Orem was being transported to the West Virginia Regional Jail, Rephann tasered Orem twice, underneath her left breast and on her left inner thigh. During this time, Orem, 27 years old and 100 pounds in weight, was in a police car with handcuffs and a foot restraint device on her. Rephann, on the other hand, weighed 280 pounds. The District Court found the use of force unreasonable and in violation of Orem's Fourth Amendment rights. Accordingly, the court denied summary judgment to Rephann. Rephalm appealed to the 4th Circuit Court of Appeals. Citing Riley v. Dorton (1997), the court pointed out that Fourth Amendment protections did not extend to arrestees and pretrial detainees. Considering the factors laid down in Johnson v. Glick (3) (1973), the 4th Circuit concluded that Rephann's actions were not a good faith attempt to restore order, but unnecessary and wanton.

COURT RULINGS IN FAVOR OF JAIL OFFICERS

Actions reasonably related to a legitimate goal.

Pretrial detainees are not considered guilty beyond a reasonable doubt, and they therefore retain their constitutional right to be free from punishment, even though they are confined (Bell v. Wolfish, 1979). In Davis v. Lancaster County, Nebraska (2007), Davis, a pretrial detainee, was allegedly kicked, punched and tasered while he was taken to his holding cell. The defendants argued that Davis was restrained to maintain order and security at the jail. In Bell v. Wolfish (1979), the Supreme Court recognized that "Ensuring security and order at [an] institution is a permissible nonpunitive objective, whether the facility houses pretrial detainees, convicted inmates, or both." Thus, the U.S. District Court for the District of Nebraska found the defendants' actions reasonably related to furthering a legitimate purpose of maintaining order and security. Accordingly, the defendants were granted summary judgment.

Objective reasonableness, governmental policy or custom, and failure to train standard for pretrial detainees.

Excessive force claims of pretrial detainees are examined under the Fourth Amendment's objective reasonableness standard. In Bustamante v. Roman (2008), the plaintiff alleged that a Taser was applied by unidentified police officers on his testicles during the course of his arrest, which led to one of his testicles being removed. The plaintiff filed a Section 1983 action against the police. Citing Lolli v. County of Orange (2003), the U.S. District Court for the District of Arizona observed that the Fourth Amendment applies to excessive force claims of pretrial detainees. The court observed that the plaintiff failed to allege facts supporting his claim that the force used was objectively unreasonable under the circumstances. He also failed to connect any of the named defendants to the alleged excessive force. Citing Rizzo v. Goode (1976), the court noted that in an action under Section 1983, a plaintiff must allege that he or she suffered a specific injury as a result of the conduct of a particular defendant and must allege a link between the alleged injury and conduct of the defendant. Since the plaintiff failed to connect any of the defendants with the alleged injury, the court found that the plaintiff failed to state a claim for violation of his constitutional rights. Hence, the complaint was dismissed.

In Tyson v. Dykes (2007), inmate Tyson claims that he had called the sheriffs office as armed men were chasing him on his property. However, when the officers arrived, they used excessive force against Tyson and arrested him. Tyson filed a Section 1983 suit

230

against the sheriff for tolerating and encouraging civil rights violations by his officers. He alleged that Sheriff Dykes was on notice about the tasering of pretrial detainees but chose to ignore it. Citing Burge v. St. Tammany Parish (2003), the court noted that claims of inadequate training and supervision generally require a showing of more than a single incident (Monell, 1978). The court observed that Tyson has not presented any evidence showing a pattern in Dykes' conduct to defeat his plea for qualified immunity.

If a violation of constitutional rights takes place, it is imperative for a plaintiff to specify whether this act occurred before or after he or she was taken into custody. Accordingly, different legal standards apply. In Poteet v. Polk County, Tennessee (2007), inmate Poteet was tasered by McMinn County officers for giving chase, and Poteet was subsequently hospitalized and incarcerated. The officers stated that Poteet was intoxicated at the time he was booked. In fact, the officer at the county jail could not complete the booking process because of Poteet's drunkenness. Poteet filed a Section 1983 suit for excessive use of force in arresting and detaining him, claiming that his constitutional rights were violated. The defendants moved for summary judgment, claiming that they were shielded by the doctrine of qualified immunity. The U.S. District Court for the Eastern District of Tennessee observed that the predicament of the plaintiff at the time of the incident has to be taken into consideration. If the plaintiff was a free person at the time of the incident, the Graham standard would apply for a violation of Fourth Amendment rights. However, if the incident took place while the plaintiff was in custody after conviction, the Eighth Amendment's cruel and unusual punishment clause would apply. The court found no evidence to show that Poteet was abused or that there was excessive force used against him. Accordingly, the complaint was dismissed.

The standard that governs excessive force claims for pretrial detainees has not yet been made clear by the 8th Circuit. "Between arrest and sentencing lies something of a legal twilight zone" (Wilson v. Spain, 2000). In McBride v. Clark (2006), officers applied a stun gun to McBride, a pretrial detainee, for creating a disturbance in the detention center. The officers were trained in the use of Tasers and stun guns. McBride filed a Section 1983 suit against the officers for excessive use of force. The parties to the suit disagreed on the appropriate governing standard for the excessive use of force. While McBride contended that the Fourth Amendment's objective reasonableness standard applied, the defendant argued that the Eighth Amendment's cruel and unusual punishment standard applied. In this case, the plaintiff was being held on warrant for suspicion of drug-related offenses. As such, he was not technically a pretrial detainee.

Under such circumstances, the 8th Circuit has applied the Fourth Amendment standard. Accordingly, the U.S. District Court for the Western District of Montana applied the Fourth Amendment's objective reasonableness standard. Reviewing the facts of the case, the court observed that McBride was yelling vulgarities and, after being told that he had hepatitis C, he removed his IV and caused himself to bleed. Under the circumstances, the officer's action was objectively reasonable.

The use of stun guns by prison officials to subdue a violent pretrial detainee does not violate the detainee's constitutional rights. In Birdine v. Gray (2005), Birdine, a pretrial detainee, was incarcerated at the Lancaster County Jail. Due to violent behavior toward correctional officers, a stun gun was applied to Birdine on two occasions by an officer trained in its use. Birdine was first shocked soon after he was taken to a cell in the holding area. As the officers tried to take off his handcuffs, he started resisting them physically. Birdine was shocked a second time immediately after the officers left his cell in the holding area. He created a disturbance by banging and kicking the door. He refused to follow instructions and was attempting to destroy the light fixture in his cell. At that point, officers trained in the use of stun guns shocked Birdine for the second time in order to subdue him. Birdine filed a Section 1983 suit against the officers for excessive use of force. Citing Jasper v. Thalacker (1993), the U.S. District Court for the District of Nebraska concluded that the use of stun guns on Birdine did not violate the Constitution. Moreover, the court observed that in neither occasion did the stun gun use cause any significant injury to Birdine. Also, the force used was commensurate to the risk posed, and not excessive, observed the court. Accordingly, the court concluded that Birdine's constitutional rights as a pretrial detainee were not violated, and hence, his suit was dismissed.

For an excessive use of force claim under Section 1983, it is necessary to name the defendants who used excessive force. If the department is named, it will be a municipal liability case, and under Monell, a plaintiff must show a policy, custom, practice or procedure that can be linked to the constitutional violation complained of. In Goodwin v. Hamilton County (2005), Goodwin, an inmate of the Hamilton County Jail, was transported to a medical facility. Upon reaching the facility, the officers initially refused to release him. Later, they did let him out of the cruiser but with handcuffs. Goodwin alleges that soon after he got out of the cruiser, several officers tasered him, applied pepper spray, and kicked and choked him. Goodwin Fried a Section 1983 suit for excessive use of force against the sheriffs department. The U.S. District Court for the

232

Eastern District of Tennessee directed Goodwin to rile an amended complaint naming all the defendants who used excessive force against him. In the second amended complaint, Goodwin named the officer who transported him to the medical facility, but did not seek monetary damages, and did not clarify if he was being sued in his official or individual capacity. As such, the court assumed that the officer was being sued in his official capacity. In that case, the court must proceed as if Goodwin has sued the county itself. In order to prevail on a suit against a county, the plaintiff must show that the constitutional violation was a result of an official custom or policy adopted by the county. Goodwin failed to show that the alleged violation of his rights was a result of Hamilton County's official custom or policy. Accordingly, the defendants were granted summary judgment.

The principle of respondeat superior does not apply to Section 1983 actions. In Ramirez v. Johnson (2007), inmate Ramirez filed a complaint about an event that occurred while he was a pretrial detainee. Ramirez alleged that he was handcuffed, beaten and tasered for taking a sandwich that did not belong to him from the jail's food cart. He filed a Section 1983 suit for excessive use of force against the sheriff. Citing Polk County v. Dodson (1981), Cottone v. Jenne (2003) and Harris v. Ostrout (1995), the U.S. District Court for the Northern District of Florida observed that "respondeat superior, without more, does not provide a basis for recovery under Section 1983" (Ramirez v. Johnson, 2007). The mere right to control without any direct participation does not lead to Section 1983 liability. Accordingly, advising the plaintiff to file an amended complaint, the court held that unless the plaintiff alleges facts establishing a causal connection between the actions of Sheriff Johnson and the alleged constitutional violation, the complaint will fail.

In addition to the above holding, the court has also ruled that applying a Taser to a mentally ill inmate is not a violation of his or her constitutional rights as long as it does not amount to deliberate indifference to the inmate's serious medical needs. In Burkett v. Alachua County (2007), the mother of a detainee who died while in jail filed a Section 1983 suit for excessive use of force and deliberate indifference to the detainee's mental health. Mark Burkett, the detainee, was agitated in his cell when officers came to take him for his first appearance before the judge. The officers shot Burkett with a Taser to handcuff him. At court, the judge ordered that Burkett be given a mental health evaluation and a blood sample be drawn from him. Later, when officers and a nurse tried to take blood from Burkett at his cell, he was highly agitated and resisted the officers. An officer used a stun gun on him while other officers placed him into a three-point restraint. Soon after, Burkett stopped breathing. Medical personnel conducted CPR on him, but he was declared dead at the hospital. Burkett's mother filed a Section 1983 suit. The 11th Circuit, in assessing the standard for excessive use of force, quoted Lee v. Ferraro (2002), which stated that the inquiry should be to "ask whether a reasonable officer would believe that [the] level of force [was] necessary in the situation at hand." The 11th Circuit observed that considering Burkett's agitation when officers entered his cell, his earlier aggression and his altered mental state, an officer could have believed that the use of force was reasonably necessary. Accordingly, the court held that the use of force was not excessive in violation of the Fourth Amendment, even though the detainee died in the process.

The de minimis standard. For an excessive force claim to succeed under Section 1983, there must be more than de minimis injury. In Valentine v. Richardson (2008), Valentine, a pretrial detainee, claimed that he was severely beaten by officers using stun guns and billy clubs. He was taken to the hospital the next day after he had seizures. Valentine filed a Section 1983 action against the officers for excessive use of force. Relying on hospital reports, the District Court concluded that Valentine had not been subjected to excessive force since there was no evidence of any bruising or injuries from the alleged assault. The court noted that even if Valentine was assaulted, his injuries were de minimis. After reviewing the magistrate judge's report, the U.S. District Court for the District of South Carolina granted the defendants' motion for summary judgment.

Excessive force claims in prisons do not survive if the injury is de minimis. In Henderson v. Gordineer (2007), Henderson, a pretrial detainee, had a skin problem. He alleged that his whole body was itching and that the defendants were deliberately indifferent to his medical needs. On the day of the incident, Henderson claims that he was distressed and, so, snatched some pills from Nurse Hudson and swallowed them. Detention officers threatened to taser him if he did not stop running and spit out the pills. Since he refused to do either, he was tasered once. Soon after, the Taser prongs were removed, he was medically examined and there was no injury found from the Taser. Henderson later filed a Section 1983 suit for excessive use of force against the detention officers for misuse of the Taser. The U.S. District Court for the District of South Carolina applied the 4th Circuit decision of Norman v. Taylor (1994), which held that absent the most extraordinary circumstances, excessive force claims do not lie where the injury is de minimis. The Norman decision was based on a convicted inmate. The District Court ruled that the de minimis injury standard may also be applicable to pretrial detainees. Quoting

234

Norman, the court observed that with de minimis physical injury, an inmate may recover only if the conduct resulted in "an impermissible infliction of pain" or was "repugnant to the conscience of mankind" (Norman v. Taylor, 1994). The use of a Taser device was also reasonable under the circumstances to gain control of Henderson. Accordingly, the defendants' motion for summary judgment was granted.

CONCLUSION

There are eight cases in this study that show circumstances where the courts found the use of Tasers and stun guns by jail officers to be inappropriate. Tasering a pretrial detainee in the back that resulted in permanent injury to his spinal cord, when he was only passively resisting, is objectively unreasonable (Harris v. City of Circleville, 2008). Tasering a person without provocation when she was lying on the floor of her cell at night is objectively unreasonable (Pipkins v. Pike County, Arkansas, 2007). Being shocked by a "gang" of correctional officers when the plaintiff was in his dorm drinking coffee is objectively unreasonable (Ndaula v. Holliday, 2007). Dragging and threatening to taser a sex offender who was real Tested for failing to register as a sex offender is excessive use of force (Burr v. Hill, 2005). Where the plaintiff was tasered during the booking process at a jail even though he was compliant raises questions of inappropriate use of a Taser device (Castaneda v. Douglas County Sheriffs Investigator Rory Planeta, 2007).

In 11 cases, the courts ruled in favor of prison officials. Where a pretrial detainee was kicked, punched and tasered while being taken to his holding cell, the court found the officers' actions reasonably related to the legitimate purpose of maintaining order and security (Davis v. Lancaster County, Nebraska, 2007). The use of Tasers and stun guns to induce compliance by difficult inmates during strip searches is justified since it is reasonably related to legitimate penological interests.

In an excessive force claim for use of Tasers, a plaintiff must specify each defendant and link the injury to the action of the defendant (Monroe v. Arpaio, 2005). Where the plaintiff alleged that a Taser was applied by unidentified police officers on his testicles, the court held that the plaintiff failed to show that the force was objectively unreasonable under the circumstances (Bustamante v. Roman, 2008). A pattern of the sheriff's ignoring the tasering of pretrial detainees must be shown to find him liable for such a policy, custom or practice under Monell (Tyson v. Dykes, 2007). Whether an excessive force claim will fall under the Fourth or the Eighth Amendment will depend on the stage at which it was used, before or after being taken into custody (Poteet v. Polk County, Tennessee, 2007). It is objectively reasonable to use Tasers and stun guns to maintain and restore order where the plaintiff was creating a disturbance in the detention center (McBride v. Clark, 2006). The court found the use of a Taser to be reasonable on two occasions: first, when a pretrial detainee was physically resisting the officers, and second, when a detainee was trying to destroy a light fixture in his cell, thereby posing a threat to the officers (Birdine v. Gray, 2005). In order to rind a supervisor liable for tasering done by his subordinate under Section 1983, the plaintiff must show a failure to train that is responsible for the constitutional violation, as the principle of respondeat superior does not apply. Moreover, such failure must amount to deliberate indifference (Sparks v. Reno County Sheriffs Department, 2004; Ramirez v. Johnson, 2007). Where a mentally ill inmate who was agitated and resisting officers died after he was tasered to bring him under control in order to take a sample of his blood, the court found the use of force objectively reasonable (Burkett v. Alachua County, 2007).

Where a plaintiff is suing a county because he was tasered by several officers, he must show that the action of the officers was related to an official policy, custom or practice to find the county liable under Monell (Goodwin v. Hamilton County, 2005). A pattern of the sheriff ignoring the tasering of pretrial detainees may result in liability for such a policy, custom or practice under Monell.

Of the 19 cases discussed, the courts ruled in favor of jail officers in 11. However, the number of cases in which they did not at this stage of the proceedings is comparable. As such, the issues of individual officer liability, official custom or policy, and adequate training must be addressed at the policy-making level on the basis of court decisions that show instances where individual officers and the municipality can be held liable.

REFERENCES AND ENDNOTES DELETED

Vidisha Barua, Ph.D., Esq., and Robert M. Worley, Ph.D., are assistant professors of criminal justice at Penn State University, Altoona.

37

Inmate's Plight a Travesty

Ruth Sheehan

A picture in Sunday's paper showed prisoner Timothy Helms sprawled in a hospital bed, gown askew, eyes closed, his face obscured by a breathing mask. What readers couldn't see was the plastic ankle cuff and metal shackle that chained Helms to that bed. As if, by some miracle, the poor slob could get away. Helms has been a quadriplegic since August. Before then, he used a pair of batteries to start a mattress fire in the cell where he'd been kept in solitary confinement for 571 days, a place only prison staff could access. The next day he was escorted by correction officers to an emergency room near the maximum-security prison in Taylorsville. According to prison spokesman Keith Acree, Helms "appeared to have suffered only some minor scrapes" in the blaze. In the days following the fire, by Acree's account, "Tim became ill and was hospitalized." Sounds like the flu. The ER doc, though, described blunt trauma injuries and the impression of a billy club on Helms' upper chest and back. His nose and ribs were broken, his skull was cracked and blood had seeped into his brain.

While lying in the hospital, Helms was charged with two felonies: burning a public building and malicious damage to occupied property.

But the malicious damage to a human being? An internal investigation at the prison was unable to determine how Helms was injured. Seven months later, the incident is still being reviewed by the State Bureau of Investigation. Helms' family members were not informed of these events until they were contacted by my colleague, Michael Biesecker, in February. Michael Helms, Tim's brother, did not know about the fire, or the alleged beating, or the surgery, or his brother's paralysis. He did not even know where his brother had been moved. Only after sending more than 100 e-mail messages to the governor and prison muckety-mucks did Helms' brother finally

Sheehan, R. Inmate's plight a travesty. News & Observer (Raleigh, NC), April 6, 2009.

238

receive a one-line answer. Tim had been moved to Central Prison "where there have been no problems and no use of force." Prison officials have repeatedly denied family requests to visit. They claim Helms doesn't want visitors. They claim he hasn't signed the right form. Hard to do when you can't hold a pen. For those who believe Helms got what he deserved for his part in a 1994 drunken driving accident that killed three teenagers, consider a few mitigating factors. Consider that Helms was mentally retarded and suffered mental illness. Consider he was deemed competent to confess without an attorney present. Consider that, according to his brother, Tim was so drugged when he agreed to serve three life terms that he did not recognize his mama. For what it's worth, his family has always maintained that Helms was not the one driving his mother's 1968 pickup the night of that terrible accident. But even if Helms is guilty, no person deserves to be beaten so severely his body bears welt marks in the shape of a billy club. No one should be left incontinent at age 48. A disability rights group wants him released. Surely he's been punished enough. The question is what punishment will suffice for the guards who were present when Helms "became ill," and the prison officials who allowed this travesty to occur.

Evidence-Based
Corrections

38

Community Supervision in Oklahoma Goes Evidence-Based

Kenny Holloway

E vidence-based practice, evidence-based supervision, research-based supervision--all of these terms refer to a body of knowledge resulting from an analysis of criminal justice research that has been conducted during the past 30-plus years. This body of knowledge has produced validated "principles" that have demonstrated remarkable outcomes with correctional populations. Documented reductions in recidivism in some populations have exceeded 30 percent. The long-term goal of evidence-based supervision (EBS) is sustained behavioral change that results in reduced recidivism.

Oklahoma began implementing these practices in supervision during 2006. Probation and parole officers have worked diligently to use tools available to effect and support behavioral change in the offenders they supervise. Our preliminary outcome data demonstrates the dedication and tenacity of our officers in the application of these new skills for successful intervention with offenders. Since these practices have been implemented, Oklahoma's revocation rate for offenders supervised by probation and parole officers was reduced by 32 percent in the initial year and 16 percent for the fiscal year ending June 2009.

With the application of EBS, Oklahoma increased successful offender outcomes, thereby reducing recidivism. A successful outcome is measured by decreasing the number of offenders

Holloway, K. Community supervision in Oklahoma goes evidence based. Probation and Parole Forum. Corrections Today, June 2010 v72 i3 p76(4). Reprinted with permission of the American Correctional Association, Alexandria, VA.

242

accelerated or revoked to prison while under supervision. Intermediate measures of progress include:

- Percentage of employed offenders;

- Percentage of offenders participating in substance abuse treatment;

- Percentage of offenders participating in educational programs; and

- Percentage of offenders participating in cognitive programs.

While many of the principles of EBS have previously been identified as components of "what works," more recent research has found "statistically significant" reductions in recidivism when these practices are used. All the components of EBS have been demonstrated as valid practices to reduce recidivism when managing community-based corrections populations.

The principles of evidence-based practices are:

- Assess actuarial risk and need;

- Enhance intrinsic motivation;

- Target interventions;

- Offer skill training with directed practice;

- Increase positive reinforcement;

- Engage ongoing support in natural communities;

- Measure relevant processes/practices; and

- Provide measurable feedback.

TARGETED INTERVENTION: THE TOOLS

The components of evidence-based practice are directed toward identifying criminogenic risk factors of moderate- and high-risk offenders and applying corrections' scarce resources to these populations. Research documents that the best behavior change results are realized with moderate-risk offenders. High-risk offenders, or at least those on the far end of the risk spectrum, are least likely to benefit from therapeutic interventions. These are the offenders who, regardless of supervision techniques and interventions, are most likely to eventually re-offend and return to the criminal justice system. Supervision interventions with this population, termed "life course persistent," are directed toward control and containment in order to best protect the public. Intervention with low-risk offenders has been shown to be a poor use of correctional resources and, in many instances, has been documented to increase risk factors in this population.

Various tools allow probation and parole officers to work with targeted offenders in an effort to develop, or enhance, an offender's internal motivation to make behavioral changes. To support these major life changes, officers apply assessment and evaluation results and work with offenders to identify interventions available in support of changes to move an offender away from a criminal lifestyle and toward desistance.

In early 2000, Oklahoma began using the LSI-R (Level of Services Inventory-Revised) as the agency's primary risk assessment tool. This is a third-generation risk assessment tool that is administered by officers trained to incorporate motivational interviewing (MI) techniques in the semi-structured interview. These techniques enable the officer to better elicit responses from an offender. MI has proved to be an effective tool for use in brief behavioral interventions with offenders. More specifically, MI techniques are well-suited to help the officer challenge an offender's sometimes distorted thinking patterns and engage the offender in examining behaviors and their impact on not only the offender, but also on those around him or her. While the goal of supervision is to change an offender's behavior, the responsibility for that change rests solely with the offender. An officer can challenge and question, and provide advice and support, but only the offender can elect to make changes.

Interventions include drug and alcohol treatment, mental health treatment, cognitive restructuring programs, anger management programs, and educational and employment programs. All treatment programs are based on a cognitive model and target specific risk factors. Each offender has different risk and need factors and requires varying levels of intervention. Officers must take this into consideration and work with treatment providers to match each offender to appropriate programs.

As offenders learn new ways to deal with old behaviors, it is critical that the opportunity to practice new behaviors is provided-- and that those new behaviors are acknowledged and rewarded as appropriate. It is important for an offender to learn to recognize triggers to unhealthy behavior before they can implement and

244

practice newly acquired skills that serve to redirect their actions. Through gaining problem-solving skills, offenders are provided with tools for better decision-making.

Engagement in pro-social activities serves to increase protective factors and support an offender's long-term behavioral change. Protective factors are those skills, associations and learned behaviors that support individual risk reduction. As with all skills, repeated practice in everyday situations is critical for supported acquisition and retention.

HOW TO GAUGE SUCCESS

Since incorporating the principles of evidence-based practice, Oklahoma has seen outcome results not unlike those promised by the research. As noted, the long-term outcome is risk reduction and an increase in protective factors. Since this type of evaluation and measurement takes several years of outcome data, short-term and intermediate measures were identified that would provide an indicator of supervision success. Components for measure were identified as case status at discharge, employment status, program participation and the rate of offenders who absconded supervision. All data is based on monthly statistical reports submitted by six probation and parole operations units. The data was analyzed for each fiscal year, July through June, for 2007, 2008 and 2009.

In order to evaluate ongoing outcomes, a base rate was established by identifying each of the outcome components for FY 2007. Revocations were identified by the total number of probation and parole offenders who were accelerated or revoked to prison at the time their supervision was terminated. Table 1 reflects that 3,015 offenders were revoked from community supervision to a period of incarceration during FY 2007.

Table 1. Baseline Data Revocations for FY 2007

Technical/Absconders	801
Law Violations	1,824
Specialty Courts	390
Total	**3,015**

Revocations were divided into three distinct areas: 1) technical violations and absconders, 2) new law violations, and 3) revocations by specialty courts. Revocations are the most critical area for evaluation. Offenders who are revoked to prison take the most critical correctional resources that should be reserved for those who pose the greatest risk to the public. Technical violators are best suited for revocation reduction activities because sanctioning alternatives are available to manage these offenders. The most difficult population to impact is offenders who commit law violations. Law violations are committed by all offenders, not just those identified as high risk. Consistently identifying these offenders prior to the commission of a new crime is not always possible. Many times, the best result occurs when officers move quickly to intervene with an offender who has become noncompliant and with whom intermediate sanctions have not been successful. Probation and parole officers provide courtesy supervision for many drug courts, DUI courts, and mental health courts and for some community sentencing councils. In these specialty courts, failure to comply with strict guidelines often leads to revocation with few additional options for the participating offenders.

Employment. Although lack of employment is not a criminogenic risk factor for all offenders, stable and satisfying employment provides an offender the opportunity for developing pro-social relationships that support a crime-free lifestyle. Employment serves to provide structure to an offender and can serve as a basis around which to schedule an offender's time. Lack of consistent employment has been correlated to a higher risk for criminal behavior. Therefore, employment serves as a protective factor for an offender. For the use of outcome measures, the average employment rate is considered for each time period, calculated on the monthly average over the year. Offenders not required to be employed, such as individuals who are permanently disabled, are considered employed for the purpose of this measure.

Absconders. Offenders who fail to submit to supervision are classified as absconders. They can pose the most risk to the public (due to failure to comply with supervision directives) or they simply fade away never to be seen again by the criminal justice system. Until their status is resolved, their eventual risk cannot be adequately assessed.

Treatment programs. Participation in treatment programs has the greatest potential for risk reduction. It is in these programs that offenders are exposed to behavioral alternatives that lead to desistance. Consideration must be given to ensure only offenders with identified criminogenic risk factors are placed into targeted programs. Program participation is monitored through rigorous communication between the offender, the treatment provider, and the supervising officer. Probation and parole officers have become experts in assessing change readiness, which is the foundation for behavioral change. Baseline treatment participation is shown in Table 2.

Table 2. Treatment Program Participation FY 2007 by Program Type and Number of Offenders Participating

Substance abuse - outpatient	5,417
Substance abuse - inpatient	407
Cognitive behavioral	2,075
Cognitive - mental health	974
Cognitive - anger management	524
Employment	1,786
Education	461

Offender-officer relationship. Another critical factor contributing to successful offender outcomes is the supervision relationship. When an offender perceives the officer to be supportive in the offender's change process, outcomes improve. Officers who are "firm and fair" establish expectations and behavioral parameters that serve to guide the supervision process by providing the offender a roadmap to success. Inclusion of the offender in all planning processes is essential to improving desired outcomes.

MEASURING RESULTS

The base measures for FY 2007 were consistent with the previous year's results. With the implementation of evidence-based supervision, officers began to focus their supervision strategies toward activities that supported offender behavior change. This began a continued trend toward meeting expected and desired goals of supervision.

During the initial year of implementation, officers were able to focus their supervision activities on moderate- and high-risk offenders while realigning low-risk offenders to administrative levels of supervision, or by terminating supervision altogether. Low-risk offenders, identified by the LSI-R, were subject to closure upon completion of the assessment process. For continued supervision, an officer was required to develop a case plan that would target offender needs and develop a timeline with the offender in order to meet expectations for completion of supervision. Once those expectations were met, supervision would be terminated, or if justified, continued for an additional six months.

By realigning supervision resources to moderate- and high-risk offenders, caseload sizes statewide were reduced. This provides officers more time to direct their efforts to offenders most in need of supervision. At the close of FY 2008, the average statewide officer caseload was 77, down from 85 at the close of FY 2007. This was calculated based on the total number of offenders subject to active supervision, divided by the total number of officers statewide. Table 3 compares year-end active offender counts for each year.

Table 3. Year-End Active Count by Supervision Type

Type Case	Year-End Count June 2007	Year-End Count June 2008	Year-End Count June 2009
Probation	22,009	20,982	20,845
Parole	2,107	1,812	1,892
GPS/EMP	396	414	482
Total	24,512	23,208	23,219

This process does not take into consideration the actual caseload sizes in metro areas where specialization continues to consume a district's primary resource--the probation and parole officer. Commitment to specialty courts and designation of specialty caseloads (parole, GPS, sex offender) also impacts the district's allocated officer positions.

With the close of fiscal year 2009, initial outcome data was available for comparison to established baseline measurements and FY 2007 data, as outlined by Table 4.

Table 4. Revocations FYs 2007 - 2009 by Revocation Type

Type of Revocation	FY 2007 (Percentage of total)		FY 2008 (Percentage of total)		% Decrease from FY 2007
Technical/ absconder	801	(27%)	546	(27%)	32%
Law violations	1,824	(60%)	1,248	(61%)	32%

Specialty courts	390	(13%)	246	(12%)	37%
Total	**3,015**	**(100%)**	**2,040**	**(100%)**	**32%**

[Table 4 continued]

Type of Revocation	FY 2009 (Percentage of total)		% Decrease from FY 2008
Technical/ absconder	443	(26%)	19%
Law violations	1,021	(60%)	18%
Specialty courts	241	(14%)	2%
Total	**1,705**	**(100%)**	**13%**

The intermediate measures indicate a significant reduction in the number of offenders who were revoked to a prison term from a period of community supervision. At the close of FY 2008, the overall number of revocations was reduced by 975 from the base measure established from FY 2007, a 32 percent reduction. Interestingly, it holds steady across the range for technical/absconders and for new law violations. Specialty courts experienced a 37 percent reduction in revocations. Each year, the total percentage of each type of revocation class remained fairly constant. While revocation reductions continued in FY 2009, the decrease was less, but still significant. The data outlined in Table 5 show a com parison of revocation rates each year, as a component of overall case closures.

Table 5. Revocation Rate as Percentage of Closures

	FY 2007	FY 2008	FY 2009
Revocations	3,015	2,040	1,705
Closures	12,662	12,373	12,871
Revocation Rate	**23.81%**	**16.48%**	**13,25%**

While a reduction in the number of offenders revoked to prison is even more significant in light of the current economic crisis faced by the agency, it is not necessarily a reflection of long-term behavioral change. This measure is only reflective of the offender's status at the time of termination of supervision. Until there is at least three years of data available, the reduction of individual offender risk cannot be determined. Indicators that demonstrate movement toward this risk reduction include the other intermediate measures that have been previously identified: employment and program participation.

Employment rates of offenders increased by 2.95 percent from FY 2007 to FY 2008. For FY 2009, those rates decreased by more than 1.5 percent. When considering the economy and the population, this small drop does not seem too significant at this point.

Program participation is an indicator of an offender's active involvement in the change process. Most program areas reflect continuous improvement (Table 6), with the exception of inpatient substance abuse treatment, cognitive-behavioral therapy and education. While any reduction in program participation is a concern, other factors may contribute to this decrease, such as multiple program needs and program prioritization.

Table 6. Program Participation

Program Type	FY 2007	FY 2008	FY 2009
Substance abuse - outpatient	5,417	5,713	5,964
Substance abuse - inpatient	407	442	413
Cognitive behavioral	2,075	2,166	2,124
Cognitive mental health	974	1,126	1,237
Cognitive anger management	524	608	728
Employment	1,786	1,514	1,617
Education	461	411	393

OFFICERS MAKE THE DIFFERENCE

Oklahoma is fortunate to have officers and supervisors who exemplify excellence in all they do. These officers are committed to engaging offenders as partners in their supervision in order to provide an opportunity for life changes that will help lead them to not only lower recidivism rates, but also to desistance from a criminal lifestyle. When converted to dollars, probation and parole has diverted more than $20 million in incarceration costs since implementing evidence-based supervision. This is based on a reduction of 1,310 offenders revoked since FY 2007 at a daily cost of $43 per day (assuming a term of one year for each revocation). The cost savings realized by the state is significant, but are immeasurable to those citizens who could have been potential victims.

Kenny Holloway is deputy director of treatment and rehabilitative services for the Oklahoma Department of Corrections.

39

Investing in Healthy Communities

Together, in Partnership, We Have a Responsibility to Society and to Offenders to Continue Developing and Evaluating Efficient, Effective, and Cost-Conscience Methods of Delivering Valid, Evidence-Based Treatment and Programs

Elizabeth F. Gondles.

M any who commit crimes are unable to sustain healthy lives. They often come from poor neighborhoods and dysfunctional families and lack formal education, job opportunities, and quality health care. According to the Bureau of Justice Statistics, as of 2007 there were more than 7.3 million people in correctional systems (jails, prisons, probation, parole and community corrections). This population has a high prevalence of chronic medical and mental health issues, high rates of infections and sexually transmitted diseases, and substantial substance abuse disorders.

When I interview offenders, most of them say that they want help with their health problems, but have had limited or no access to

Gondles, E. Investing in Healthy Communities: Together, in Partnership, we have a responsibility to society and to offenders to continue developing and evaluationg efficient, effective, and cost-conscience methods of delivering valid, evidence-based treatment and programs. Corrections Today, Oct 2009 v71 i5 p6(1). Reprinted with permission of the American Correctional Association, Alexandria, VA.

health care throughout their lives. Time spent incarcerated may be the only time these men and women have access to adequate care.

The majority of the diseases and disorders found in correctional populations are contracted or developed in the community as a result of high-risk behaviors: substance abuse, unsafe sexual practices, violence, smoking and poor diet. This offender population with infectious or chronic diseases moves from the community, through correctional systems, and back to the community. Offenders in our correctional system today have been given the chance to improve their health through quality health care and to learn what they can do to support their continued wellness both "inside" and when they reenter the community.

Correctional health care professionals and public health agencies have a responsibility to reach this population. Together, in partnership, we have a responsibility to society and to offenders to continue developing and evaluating efficient, effective, and cost-conscience methods of delivering valid, evidence-based treatment and programs. We also have a legal, ethical and moral obligation to return offenders to the community in a reasonable state of health to facilitate their successful reentry.

In state correctional systems, at least 95 percent of all inmates will be released to the community--and more than 12 million people pass through our nation's jails annually. While incarcerated, inmates receive health care that requires continuity in community health systems. In order to optimize this care they receive in our facilities, inmates must not return to a society plagued with social disparities, exhausted community resources, poorly equipped health clinics, and economic disadvantages. To address these public health challenges and ensure continued wellness and quality of life, community leaders must work with correctional health professionals, nurses, and the allied health professions to improve access to health, mental health and support services to the correctional population in our charge.

Our professional and fiscal responsibility is clear: corrections, public health agencies, and community health programs must collaborate to promote continuity of care for the incarcerated and ex-offenders. Correctional systems should have access to public health services in the community, and more attention should be focused on preventive care, as well as connecting successful interventions to both correctional and communal settings. Using evidence-based research, we must develop innovative programs that involve community educators and stakeholders in these health care initiatives. Correctional health professionals can help improve the health of communities throughout the country when they address the health concerns of offenders.

Health care is an ever-growing and ever-changing field. Correctional health care is growing and changing as well. These developments are not only the concern of health personnel, they affect all corrections professionals from line personnel to wardens to agency directors. It is important for society to recognize that the health care and education of offenders is closely tied to improved community health. Investing in the health care of adult and juvenile offenders and returning them back home healthy is a key to overall public wellness. By reaching offenders in the criminal justice system, we in corrections have the ability to deliver vital messages about healthy practices and strengthen and improve the health of the overall community. We must continue to reinforce and develop new strategies, as well as revamp old partnerships and form new ones to improve the health of all.

40

Empirically Supported Reentry

Review and Prospects

The Community Corrections Research Team (1)

The number of individuals being released from U.S. jails and prisons into the community is growing at an unprecedented rate. In 2007, approximately 725,000 offenders returned to the community from prison (West and Sabol, 2008) and approximately 12 million offenders are released to the community from city and county jails (Harrison and Beck, 2006). Given that prison and parole populations are continuing to grow, the number of individuals released from incarceration back into the community is not likely to decrease.

Unfortunately, many individuals released from prison continue to engage in criminal behavior. For example, some research suggests that approximately two-thirds of released inmates are rearrested and 25 percent are reincarcerated for a new offense within three years of release (Bureau of Justice Statistics, 2007; Langan and Levin, 2002). In addition, many offenders are apparently ill equipped to meet the demands of society upon release. Substance abuse, limited education and poor job skills are well-documented among inmates, both pre-incarceration and post-release (e.g., Durose and Mumola, 2004; Petersilia, 2000), which likely contributes to the high rate of recidivism.

Given the number of inmates being released from incarceration back into the community, and the high rate of rearrest

Empirically supported reentry: review and prospects. Corrections Compendium, Fall 2009 v34 i3 p1(6). Reprinted with permission of the American correctional Association, Alexandria, VA.

among these individuals, offender reentry programs have received a good deal of attention in recent years. Reentry can be defined in various ways, but it typically means the process of preparing inmates to transition from incarceration to the community (Mellow et al., 2008). Although reentry has become the focus of increasing attention, there is little empirical research regarding the effectiveness of reentry programs.

OFFENDER REENTRY

The impact of reentry services is not limited to an exclusive focus on reducing recidivism. Although reducing recidivism is clearly an important goal, there should be other benefits as well. For example, released inmates account for a large proportion of the population with communicable health problems, including HIV/AIDS and hepatitis B and C (Mellow et al., 2008). Reentry services can assist inmates in obtaining needed health care. Moreover, reductions in recidivism and the provision of appropriate health care lead to significant cost savings, which is an important consideration for local and state governments dealing with crime and its associated costs.

The process of offender reentry may be conceptualized as beginning when an inmate enters a correctional facility and ending when that individual is no longer under any form of correctional supervision in the community. One model of reentry decision-making is based on the U.S. Department of Justice's three-phased reentry approach developed as part of its Serious and Violent Offender Reentry Initiative (SVORI) and the seven decision points identified by the National Institute of Corrections in its Transition from Prison to Community Initiative. This model is currently being used in several states.

These seven decision points are found in the phases of custody, release and community supervision/ discharge. The custody phase involves two decision points: first, assessment and classification, which involves measuring offenders' risks, needs and strengths upon entry to the correctional facility; and second, inmate programming, in which the correctional facility provides tailored interventions designed to reduce risk, address needs and build upon existing strengths. The release phase incorporates the next two decision points: inmate release preparation, which involves developing a parole plan to address supervision, housing, employment, drug testing and other considerations; and release decisionmaking, which is designed to determine the appropriateness of parole on a case-by-case basis. The community

supervision/discharge phase involves the final three decision points:
1) supervision and services; 2) revocation decision-making,
involving the use of graduated sanctions in response to infractions;
and 3) discharge and aftercare, which is when community
supervision is terminated and the inmate is no longer under
correctional supervision.

RELEASE DECISION-MAKING: PRISON TO COMMUNITY

Parole boards had wide latitude in deciding whether to release
offenders under discretionary parole prior to 1980. Parole was
granted in light of considerations such as rehabilitation, family
support and employment. Beginning in the early 1980s, however, the
impact of retribution and deterrence began to outweigh such
rehabilitative considerations. The use of determinant sentencing,
including fixed sentences and automatic release, further limited the
individualized decision-making capacities of parole boards. The
contemporary correctional decision to release an offender from
prison or jail and return that individual to the community is the first
of several that may be informed by empirical evidence regarding that
individual's readiness for reentry.

Approximately 200 state parole officials are responsible for
deciding the timing and release conditions for more than 120,000
offenders eligible for parole each year (Hughes, Wilson and Beck,
2001). These officials are also responsible for determining the
conditions of release for about 280,000 people discharged on
mandatory parole and conditional release, and for returning more
than 220,000 individuals to incarceration on the basis of parole
revocation (Harrison and Beck, 2005). The proportion of offenders
released unconditionally at the end of their sentence has been
estimated at 20 percent (Petersilia, 2001). The remaining individuals
are released under conditions involving assignment to parole officers,
who are responsible for ensuring that the parolee complies with the
terms of release, including housing, financial support and illegal drug
abstinence. About 400,000 of the 600,000 offenders who are released
on parole annually are rearrested within three years (Petersilia, 2001).
The process of "structured reentry" (Byrne and Taxman, 2004) has
both prison and community components, with the expectation that
greater structure, more intensive monitoring and more individualized
rehabilitation strategies will reduce this recidivism rate.

The community classification center is part of this trend
toward greater structure in reentry. Historically, those released from

258

prison have been largely responsible for their own aftercare; employment, housing, family and treatment needs were organized by the offender while still in prison or upon release (Taxman, 2004). The more recent emphasis on evidence-based practice in reentry, however, has prompted a shift in correctional programming and the community reentry process (Center for Effective Public Policy, 2007). Community-based classification centers and specialized programs can play an important part in both structured reentry planning (Wilkinson, 2001) and the delivery of targeted services that are particularly appropriate for that individual. Programs that target specific offender needs have been associated with lower recidivism rates (Seiter and Kadela, 2003).

Newer practice models, such as the five-step offender active participant model (Taxman, 2004), civic engagement intervention model (Bazemore and Stinchcomb, 2004) and critical time intervention (Draine and Herman, 2007), involve a different approach to reentry planning and service delivery. One component of this approach includes an aftercare discharge plan similar to that used for those on conditional release from forensic psychiatric hospitals (Draine and Herman, 2007). Another component includes enhanced communication using technology such as electronic tracking devices and records management systems, as well as the sharing of case management information (Burke and Tonry, 2006; Pattavina, 2004). The need for collaboration among parole agencies, law enforcement agencies and the larger community has been strongly emphasized (Bazemore and Stinchcomb, 2004; Sipes, 2008). It is also important to evaluate evidence-based reentry services to understand whether and how services are successful in reducing recidivism rates (Pattavina, 2004).

Numerous and wide-ranging changes in practice have coincided with the development of contemporary approaches to evidence-based reentry (Lowenkamp and Latessa, 2005). In his 2004 State of the Union address, President George W. Bush urged federal support for the development of new reentry initiatives focusing on job training, placement, housing and faith-based services (Burke and Tonry, 2006; Center for Effective Public Policy, 2007; Sipes, 2008). The Second Chance Act of 2007 provided funding toward improving reentry using approaches consistent with evidence-based policy (Burke and Tonry, 2006; Center for Effective Public Policy, 2007). Guidelines to assist in the reentry process (2) have been published (Sipes, 2008) and a number of local, state and national initiatives (3) have been created as well (Center for Effective Public Policy, 2007; Pattavina, 2004; Sipes, 2008; Taxman, 2004).

PROVIDING SUPERVISION AND SERVICES

Taxman et al. (2003) describe reentry as a process with three stages: institutional (at least six months prior to release), structured reentry (six months prior to release to 30 days after release) and integration (31 days following release). This section addresses the second of these stages. Taxman and colleagues identify two distinct models-- active participation and active receiver--that describe how offenders engage in reentry. The active receiver model involves formal assessment conducted by those who will decide what services the offender needs and should receive. The active participant model incorporates the offender as an important part of the decision-making process; it includes assumptions that the offender can be returned home, contribute to making transition arrangements while incarcerated and quickly transition from the dependency of incarceration to the relative independence of community life (Taxman, 2004).

During this stage, it is important for paroling agencies to collaborate with prison officials in the reentry transition process. Such collaboration might include using empirically supported decision tools, identifying risk level and targeting continuing rehabilitation needs. This promotes incentives for successful reentry and sets conditions based on risk, needs and indicated monitoring. Additional priorities for paroling authorities during this stage include developing strategies to handle parole violations, focusing on offender case management and supervision to engage offenders in change, and establishing new skills and competencies (Burke and Tonry, 2006).

There has been a limited amount of empirical research on parole services provided in the reentry process. In the early 1990s, California instituted a multidimensional, community-based program to facilitate parolee success for reintegration into society. The program (the Preventing Parolee Crime Program, or PPCP) provided six networks of service providers to support parolees in four domains: employment, substance abuse education and recovery, math and literacy development, and housing (Zhang, Roberts and Callanan, 2006). These investigators reported that non-PPCP group participants were 1.38 times more likely to be reincarcerated within 12 months of parole release. They also found that meeting treatment goals in the four domains was associated with the lowest reincarceration rate. Although these findings were significant, selection bias may offer an alternative explanation to the findings, which are attributed to PPCP. The absence of random assignment to

PPCP, with parolees selected according to rehabilitation need and program fit, means that those enter ing the program may systematically differ from those who do not on dimensions that affect these outcomes.

Another study (Martin, Lurigio and Olson, 2003) focused on a community-based supervision facility (the day reporting center), which provides supervision and services to participants (e.g., life-skills training, violence prevention, literacy classes, job-skills training, job placement services and GED preparation) during the day. Participants are usually permitted to spend their evenings at home (usually under electronic surveillance). This type of facility can be used as a condition of probation, a direct sentence or a "halfway-back" sanction for probation or parole violators. Investigators found that those participating in the program for less than 10 days had a significantly lower chance of remaining arrest free for 14 months or longer (14 percent) compared with those who spent more than 70 days in the program (25 percent). Although the day reporting centers have shown that offenders remain arrest-free, these positive findings may be explained largely by the impact of one particular intervention. Without a statistical measure of the contribution of each intervention, however, this question cannot be answered.

DISCHARGE AND AFTERCARE

Different approaches axe used for selecting individuals for participation in community-based reentry programs versus parole. Such reentry programs are now serving a number of post-incarceration individuals; in fiscal year 2004-2005, 43,843 paroled offenders were mandated to attend a reentry program (National Offender Management Service, 2005). One study evaluated individuals according to the risk-needs-responsivity model (Andrews, Bonta and Hoge, 1990), assessing risk levels and criminogenic needs designated in the reentry program. Those who appeared to represent a good "fit" with the program (with relevant risk, needs and responsivity consistent with what was offered) were more likely to be recommended for placement (McGuire et al., 2008). Another study evaluated a Serious and Violent Offender Reentry Initiative program in North Dakota (Bouffard and Bergeron, 2006), which consisted of three phases: institutional, transition and community-based. Program participation criteria included age (18-35 years old), a history of violent offending and a score of 24 or above on the Level of Supervision Inventory-Revised (LSI-R).

Aftercare services are intended to improve the community adjustment of released offenders and thereby decrease the risk of recidivism. Noncompliance with aftercare services is a substantial problem, however. One study (Schram and Morash, 2002) focused on a life-skills program for female inmates in Michigan targeting women with six to nine months remaining before they are eligible for parole. This program includes an aftercare component in which an aftercare agency serves as a community advocate for participants and provides limited financial assistance for housing and child care. Investigators reported extreme noncompliance with the aftercare component of the program and were unable to contact 77 percent of the program participants after their release. For those assessed at follow-up, the researchers found few significant differences between the treatment and comparison groups on the life-skills measures, which included self-esteem, anger and conflict management. Of the participants who completed the post-test measures, 37.5 percent indicated that aftercare services did not contact them; those who were contacted reported either very positive or very negative experiences. However, this high level of attrition makes it difficult to draw firm conclusions from these results.

Another study (Haas, Hamilton and Hanley, 2007) considered the West Virginia Offender Reentry Initiative, which also includes an aftercare component. The first phase of this program focuses on the transition from incarceration to the community, beginning six months prior to release. Offenders axe referred to various community programs, with planning in key areas (housing, employment and needed support services). At the end of this phase, an aftercare action plan is developed for the post-release reentry period. Investigators reported that only 12.9 percent of participants had actually received their aftercare plan, and even fewer sought those services post-release. Also, the evaluation focused on programming rather than recidivism, so very limited conclusions can be made regarding the effectiveness of the services for those who sought them.

A third study, describing the community phase of a reentry program for serious and violent offenders (Bouffard and Bergeron, 2006), indicated that program participants were referred to more community-based services than the comparison group. Despite this, they were less likely to have participated in most of those programs relative to the comparison group, including anger management and chemical dependency aftercare treatment. The results did indicate that participants were administered a significantly higher number of screens for drugs and alcohol than the comparison group and were significantly less likely to test positive for drugs. (Participants were also less likely to test positive for alcohol, but the re suits were not significant.) A survival analysis for recidivism indicated that offenders in the program were significantly less likely to be rearrested, but there was no significant difference with respect to revocation of parole. Though these results seem to indicate that the aftercare component may be effective for those who participate, it is important to note the small sample size of 71 participants in the program and 106 participants in the comparison group. The investigators also observed that the program operates in a "relatively small, racially homogenous, urban community," and that raises questions of generalizability.

Some programs are available to parolees on a voluntary basis, which may be more effective for certain individuals who are more motivated (Zhang et al., 2006). In one study (Pearson and Davis, 2003), clients were referred by correctional or community sources and received assistance with employment and child support. Participants of this program ranged from one month to more than 13 months post-release. Findings indicated that program clients were less likely to return to prison than individuals who scheduled a program appointment but never appeared. Clients also had a lower recidivism rate than that reported by the department of corrections for all inmates; however, the DOC population is not necessarily a representative comparison group. Pearson and Davis (2003), indicated that the client population resembled the parole population in some respects, but were typically less violent and lower risk. This may account for the difference in recidivism. In addition, clients experienced an initial increase in employment following a visit to the program, but the proportion began to decrease in the third fiscal quarter following the visit. It is difficult to draw conclusions about what aspects of the program were effective, given the attenuation of effects over time and the lack of a true control group.

California also has a network of voluntary programs to assist with post-release parolees. PPCP includes programs providing employment, substance abuse recovery, math and literacy skills, and housing services. Participants are referred by their parole officers. Participants who met the treatment goal of at least one of these programs had a recidivism rate of 33.6 percent, compared with a recidivism rate of 52.8 percent among non-PPCP parolees in the state (Zhang et al., 2006). Further analysis of the individual program effects revealed that parolees who met the treatment goals of the residential multiservice centers, which offer employment, math/literacy training and recovery services, had the lowest 12-month reincarceration rate (15.5 percent). Individuals who met the goals of the substance abuse network had a reincarceration rate of 25.7 percent, followed closely by the literacy program (26.5 percent)

and employment programs (28.5 percent to 33.1 percent). These
return rates were significantly lower than the rates of parolees who
did not meet the treatment goals of those programs. However,
motivation may have played an important role in the success of the
parolees who participated in the program and met treatment goals,
and it is an important alternative explanation to consider.

DISCUSSION

The present review suggests that reentry services are being provided
on a widespread basis in the U.S. If the trend of the past decade
continues, such services are likely to be provided to a growing
number of individuals during the late stage of incarceration, the
period immediately following release into the community and the
more extended period during which many individuals remain on
parole. This focus is a welcome addition to the rehabilitation and
management of offenders, given its potential to provide needed
services, reduce the risk of recidivism, and promote more responsible
and adaptive adjustment following release.

When reentry services are delivered in a way that is
standardized--when comparable services are delivered to similar
populations, with results measured--it becomes more feasible to
incorporate the use of empirical research in the investigation of
questions such as what works, in what intensity, over what duration
and at what cost. Unfortunately, judging from the present review of
the published literature on reentry, the provision of services is well
ahead of the formal investigation of such questions. If "effectiveness"
and "empirical validation" are to be important considerations in
reentry services policy, then this must change. The present review of
research on the reentry process is composed largely of studies
conducted at a single site, with modest numbers and using
interventions that are often a reflection of local practice preferences
rather than empirically supported interventions. It also suggests that
there is no dearth of conceptual thinking and practice descriptions
regarding reentry programming. The next important step, however, is
to integrate the conceptual and practice literature with effectiveness
research, much of which remains to be done. Research using multiple
sites, larger samples and uniform interventions selected as promising
(and also compared with a "practice as usual" group) will provide a
much stronger empirical basis for developing best practice standards
in this area.

In addition, reentry programs may include a number of
components. As this review shows, these include residential,

substance abuse, educational/literacy and employment services, among others. Currently, there is a tendency to evaluate the impact of a single reentry program. It will be important to conduct research on multiple sites, focusing on reentry programming that is fairly uniform, in order to empirically gauge the effectiveness of such programming.

One promising contribution to the reentry process appears to be the community-based classification center. Such a program is designed to receive individuals coming out of prison and provide assessment and targeted rehabilitation services to facilitate the transition from incarceration to community living within the first several months following release. Several potential advantages to such community classification centers include assessment of risk and rehabilitation needs in a setting that is based in, and more similar to, the community than a prison can be, and the linkage of assessment results with interventions beginning immediately. This allows observation of the individual's response to interventions that helps to inform subsequent placement and parole decisions. Such classification centers can provide important structure during the First 30 to 60 days following release, a period of relatively high risk for failure on parole (Heilbrun et al., 2008). They are well placed to conduct relevant research on risk, needs and intervention, perhaps in partnership with academic researchers (Heilbrun and Erickson, 2007). When research incorporates standardized measures of risk and needs, documents the impact of promising interventions and does so in different jurisdictions and over time, it can promote the development of empirically driven practice guidelines that would allow the reentry process to become more standardized, effective and efficient.

The increased emphasis on the reentry process wimessed in the past decade holds promise for the delivery of needed services and monitoring in a cost-effective fashion. The potential advantages to society are noteworthy and include decreased offending, a more effective criminal justice system, and inmates returned to society with better targeted and more appropriate services. More and better research, the implementation of interventions such as the community classifications center and the linkage of these results to more uniform reentry policy can help to realize this potential.

REFERENCES AND ENDNOTES DELETED.

Table 1. Summary of Key Findings and Practice Implications of Empirical Research on Reentry

Study	Summary of Findings	Practice Implications
Bouffard and Bergeron (2006)	* Reentry program participants were significantly less likely to be rearrested or test positive for drugs, but there were no significant differences on revocation of parole, relative to comparison group	* Importance of multiple outcome measures, including intermediate outcomes (e.g., family, housing, job, substance abuse) as well as new arrests and technical violations of parole or probation
Byrne and Taxman (2004)	* High-risk group had fewer overall arrests and new crime arrests within one year, and fewer probation violations * Moderate-risk group did not show difference relative to comparison group	* Importance of formal measurement of risk and dynamic needs * Use of risk-need- responsibility (RNR) principles recommended
Heilbrun et al. (2008)	* Rate of women rearrested during the six-month outcome period was lower for women released from prison into a community-based classification and treatment center; relative to sample returned directly to community on parole	* Importance of limited gender-specific programming * Importance of community-based classification centers in reentry
Lowenkamp and Latessa (2005)	* Residential programs were most effective for parole violators and high-risk offenders, but were associated with increases in recidivism for lower risk offenders (with the exception of parole violators); most effective programs were those that targeted criminogenic needs	* Importance of formal measurement of risk and dynamic needs. * Use of RNR principles recommended
Martin et al. (2003)	* Pretrial defendants who remained in the Day Reporting Center program at least 70 days had significantly lower recidivism rates than the pretrial defendants in the program for less than 10 days	* Possible dosage effect of community reentry programs should be investigated through research and program evaluation, and then implemented in policy
McGuire et al. (2008)	* Completion of a structured, community-based, offense-focused program predicted reduction in reconvictions	* Limited strength of the regression model and absence of comparison group make conclusions supporting treatment impact tentative

Pearson and Davis (2003)	* Clients of a program providing assistance with employment, child support and family reconnection had higher rates of employment and child, support payment, although effects attenuated over time; clients had a lower recidivism rate compared with the general DOC population.	* Importance of employment, child support and family reconnection
Schram and Morash (2002)	* Participants of program targeting problem-solving, anger management, self=esteem, parenting and employability more likely to use coping resources than were the comparison group; participants had a significantly lower 60-day return rate than the comparison group.	* Life-skills programs may be effective in helping female offenders cope in the community * Multiple obstacles to implementation of reentry programs, including variations among counselors
Zhang et al. (2006)	* Participants in the Preventing Parolee Crime Program who had access to employment, substance abuse, educational and housing services had lower levels of reincarceration than nonprogram parolees	* Programming more effective for individuals who met treatment goals or in a program for a longer period of time, consistent with minimum "dosage effect"

41

From Good Intentions to Evidence-Based

Paving the Right Road

R. Hugh Potter

O ne of the great mysteries of correctional practice is how a program or practice moves from one facility to become a standard part of the corrections world. In the world of social science, this is known as the "diffusion of innovations," the movement of an idea or practice from one setting across a variety of settings to achieve wide-spread adoption. (1) Of course, the difference between the diffusion of a fad and the adaptation of a productive correctional practice is important.

A definition of evidence-based practice was introduced in this column in the December 2006 issue of Corrections Today. (2) The authors offered that definition in terms of communicating program evaluation results, and this column takes a step back and propose some steps in that process to allow the readers to locate themselves on the road to proven practice. This column will examine the process by which individual research/evaluation studies move from a good intention to the ranks of evidence-based practice; or, just as important, why some good intentions should wind up in the "doesn't work" category.

Most ideas start from the observations of an individual or group of corrections professionals, corrections-associated academics or others associated with issues related to correctional populations and their families. Some ideas are purely observation-based, others

Potter, R. From good intentions to evidence-based: paving the right road. Research Notes. Corrections Today, June 2007 v69 i3 p74(2). Reprinted with permission of the American Correctional Association, Alexandria, VA.

268

are grounded in faith, some in academic theory and a good many are just well-intentioned. At a minimum, they are ideas that someone thinks will produce a desired outcome in a correctional environment.

Corrections professionals are very curious about what is working in different systems, and often seek out and share information with each other. When something being tried in one setting appears successful, others may adopt the practice if they think it will fit in their system. From these exchanges of ideas are born practice-based knowledge and operations. Knowledge and operations are often evaluated in terms of whether they make sense to those who conduct them or to other funding sources, such as legislators, who like the idea. One such practice-based program that made intuitive sense was Scared Straight, which brought children who were engaging in or at risk for criminal behavior to prisons to deter future criminal activity. The program was well intended, but in fact, was a consistent failure in evaluation studies.

Agency researchers or academics want to evaluate programs to see if they really work--or worse, to determine if they cause unanticipated harm. Program evaluation as a behavioral and social science criminal justice tool really took off in the 1970s as a way to determine whether the large sums of money being spent through the Law Enforcement Assistance Administration (LEAA) programs were actually accomplishing what the government wanted. In the early days of criminal justice evaluations evaluators often had to rely on pre- and post-test designs to see if knowledge or behaviors had changed from pre-intervention to some period following the intervention. At best, evaluators generally were able to conduct quasi-experimental designs with some sort of comparison or control group, often due to issues raised by attorneys and advocacy groups about rights to treatment and due process (procedural justice) issues.

During the next two decades, the science of evaluation changed rapidly, and the science community began to develop an idea of what constituted a strong research design to produce an "evidence base." The random assignment of individuals to treatment or control group has always been a hallmark of research. As legislatures and foundations began to ask how effective the programs they funded were, the importance of these designs became stronger. Some funding agencies began to demand that any program they funded have a random assignment of participants to treatment or control groups. Failure to promise to do so could result in not being considered for funding.

The question arose, however, whether one study was really enough to say something was the best practice in the criminal justice world. Thus, in the 1990s, the Office of Juvenile Justice and Delinquency Prevention funded the development of the Blueprints for Violence Prevention (3) at the University of Colorado to determine the strength of evidence among delinquency and violence prevention programs. Programs must satisfy three criteria for consideration: evidence of a strong deterrent effect, sustained effects beyond the treatment period and replication across multiple sites. Criteria such as cost effectiveness and consideration of mediating influences may also be assessed. Programs that satisfy two of the criteria may be put in the "promising practice" category, often due to a lack of replication studies. Those that satisfy more criteria move toward the "model program" category. The reader is encouraged to visit the University of Colorado Web site for more detailed information.

During the 1990s the science of "meta-analysis" was also developing as a statistical method for analyzing trends in evaluation data across multiple studies. This allowed the initiation of systematic reviews of evidence that attempt to look across the results of various studies in a statistically meaningful way. In the biomedical world, the Cochrane Collection (4) began subjecting medical studies to meta-analysis to determine whether practice-based procedures were truly effective when looked at broadly. On the criminal justice side, the Campbell Collaboration (5) evolved to subject a range of justice- and corrections-related programs to the same test. The Centers for Disease Control and Prevention also developed the Community Guides (6) process to test public health interventions, including violence prevention and even juvenile sentencing procedures. To date, only a relatively small number of corrections-related practices have been subject to the rigorous analyses of the Campbell Collaboration, while the Blueprints process has examined nearly 600 programs.

In the biomedical field, some cherished practices of physicians have not withstood the scrutiny of the Cochrane Collection or Community Guides process. As one might expect, this does not always sit well with the practice community that has faith in how it does things. There are dis-agreements between those who are "in the trenches" watching individual results and those in the "ivory tower" who simply crunch the numbers about whose methods are most appropriate. Even as the research community moves toward consensus about what it takes to move something into the evidence-based, best- or world's best-practice categories, researchers see that the practice community does not always agree with the assessments.

However, there are pressures to adopt the systematic review methodology for public policy decision-making and funding. This article has provided a cursory overview of the current thinking on establishing a practice as evidence-based. Readers are encouraged to explore the various schemes further at the Web sites listed below. For practical purposes, the message of the column is to be aware of what a particular funding organization or a legislator means by evidence-based. Language, even scientific language, is not always as specific as it should be.

This is an era with strong competition for scarce public resources for corrections-related programs. Knowing what it takes to move an idea, no matter how well-intended, to a promising practice to a model program, is a good starting framework for innovative ideas. Being evidence- or science-based is the new watchword for correctional programming. Just because it works in Rhode Island does not mean it will work in California. The days of "knowing what I'm doing" are gone; it takes evidence, not good intentions. Replication, sustained impact across multiple sites and repeated evaluations are the new requirements. It is important to share innovative practices with friends and colleagues, as this will help with replication studies.

ENDNOTES DELETED

Community Corrections

42

Leveraging the Criminal Justice System to Reduce Alcohol- and Drug- Related Crime

A Review of Three Promising, and Innovative Model Programs

Robert L. DuPont; Corinne L. Shea; Stephen K. Talpins; Robert B. Voas.

T he united states has both the highest incarceration rate and the highest prison population in the world; (1) while comprised of only 5% of the world's total population, it holds 25% of the world's imprisoned population. (2) Currently, more than two million people in this country are incarcerated, and the number of people on probation or parole totals more than five million. (3) Federal surveys show that approximately 75% of offenders under local, state and/or federal supervision are involved with alcohol or drugs (4) and that over 50% of them were "under the influence" at the time of their most recent offense. (5) Additionally, the estimated number of adult arrests for drug abuse violations has been increasing since 1970, with more than 1.6 million arrests made in 2006. (6)

The dramatic rise in the U.S. rate of incarceration over the past two decades from about 150 per 100,000 population where it had been for half a century to the current figure of about 700 per 100,000

Robert L. DuPont; Corinne L. Shea; Stephen K. Talpins; Robert B. Voas. Leveraging the criminal justice system to reduce alcohol- and drug-related crime: a review of three promising, and innovative model programs. Prosecutor, Journal of the National District Attorneys Association, Jan-March 2010 v44 i1 p38(5).

is associated with a dramatic--and continuing--drop in the rate of serious crime. (7) However, the crime reduction produced by incarceration comes at great cost. In the current tight budgeted environment, prison costs--both financial and human--are a major target for reduction. The goal for the future of the criminal justice system is to find cost-effective ways to extend the decline in crime while cutting the rate of incarceration. Achieving that goal will require a smarter criminal justice system.

Probation and parole agencies have the responsibility of tracking offenders under supervision in the community and the opportunity to reduce new crimes. Offenders released on probation and parole typically are not permitted to consume alcohol or illegal drugs or misuse prescription drugs as a condition of staying out of incarceration and in the community. However, typical community-based corrections, including drug-diversion programs, do not regularly monitor offenders for alcohol or drug use in part because they lack the resources to do so and in part because of a concern that doing so would increase rates of incarceration. Consequently, too many offenders continue their pattern of substance misuse and crime until re-arrested and imprisoned for new offenses. When alcohol or other drug use is detected, the consequences are often unpredictable, long delayed, and disproportionate to the offense and violation. When offenders test positive, most often there are no or minimal sanctions, but after a string of such violations a probationer may be sent to prison to serve long, possibly even draconian sentences. The high rates of recidivism and prolonged incarceration that result from this cycle can be overcome with the new approaches taken by a new model of community supervision that not only reduces drug and alcohol use but also reduces new crimes and--somewhat paradoxically--also reduces rates of incarceration.

The foundations of South Dakota's 24/7 Sobriety Project, Hawaii's Opportunity Probation with Enforcement, and Driving Under the Influence Courts are all based on the idea that the most effective way to reduce substance misuse and crime among offenders is to lay out clear expectations for alcohol- and drug-free behavior, provide opportunities for treatment and then to back up expectations with monitoring linked to swift and certain, but relatively mild punishments. (8) These programs leverage the criminal justice system to reduce substance misuse and recidivism among offenders in the community. They offer the nation an opportunity to substantially enhance public safety and improve public health simultaneously. There is good evidence that these programs--all using similar strategies that enforce the alcohol- and drug-free standard with random testing linked to meaningful consequences-reduce crime and reduce incarceration among criminal offenders in the community.

SOUTH DAKOTA'S 24/7 SOBRIETY PROJECT

As attorney general of South Dakota, Judge Larry Long started the 24/7 Sobriety Project to reduce the state's extraordinarily high rates of alcohol-related crime by targeting the DUI offense. The state provides all DUI offenders with treatment in a separate parallel program. Current Attorney General Marty Jackely is working with the National Partnership on Alcohol Misuse and Crime to evaluate an expansion of this program that would incorporate a formal contingency management system into the program.

The 24/7 Sobriety Project focuses on high-risk repeat DUI offenders; with rare exception all participants have been arrested at least one prior time for DUI, with 48% having three of more DUI offenses. (9) Unlike traditional approaches to DUI offenders that focus on separating the drinking from the driving through license restrictions, 24/7 Sobriety focuses on the root of the problem-- substance abuse. All participants in 24/7 Sobriety are prohibited from consuming alcohol and/or illegal drugs while under the supervision of the program.

Because alcohol is metabolized quickly by the body, participants must submit to either twice-daily alcohol testing, typically done at the local sheriff's office, or continuous transdermal alcohol monitoring. Participants who live distances from testing sites making it impossible for them to appear twice a day, so must wear transdermal ankle monitoring bracelets which track any alcohol use. Offenders are subject to random urinalysis testing or must wear sweat patches to monitor drug use. This combination of testing methods ensures effective monitoring of participant alcohol and drug use.

Any alcohol or drug use results in an immediate, shortterm jail stay. In addition, bench warrants are issued for any participant who does not report for testing. These clear expectations of program compliance and alcohol and drugfree behavior enforced by immediate sanctions have produced excellent results.

Results of the 24/7 Sobriety Project include: (10)

- 99% of twice-daily tested participants arrive on time to testing sites and test negative for alcohol

- 78% of participants monitored by bracelet are compliant and test negative

- 98% of urinalyses are negative

- 92% of sweat patch tests are negative

Contrary to initial concerns that 24/7 Sobriety participants would fail drug tests and flood local jails, 24/7 Sobriety has significantly helped these high-risk DUI offenders remain sober for the duration of their participation (an average of about 111 days). Preliminary data suggests that 24/7 Sobriety participants recidivate at approximately half or less the rate of regular DUI probationers." Additionally, recent state-level trends are promising. Since 2005, the number of 24/7 Sobriety participants has continued to steadily increase while the number of alcohol-related motor vehicle fatalities in South Dakota has decreased more than 50%. (12)

Although the 24/7 Sobriety Project was started with state funding, the probation portion of the program now is self-sustaining, paid for by participants. (13) With 56 counties in South Dakota participating in this successful innovative program, several other states are considering implementing similar programs to reduce DUI recidivism. Of particular note, North Dakota Attorney General Wayne Stenehjem commenced a pilot program in his state in 2007 and expanded it statewide with the legislature's support in 2009.

The 24/7 Sobriety Project breaks the mold of the historic license suspension policies that seek to stop drunk driving by preventing all driving or separating drinking from driving. License restrictions, while useful, are difficult to enforce and do not change behavior in the long-term because they do not address the root cause of the problem: substance misuse. Use of interlock devices on offenders' automobiles can be evaded by offenders who claim to have no cars and by using other cars that do not have interlock devices on them. Offenders in 24/7 Sobriety programs can obtain or maintain employment and support themselves and their families because they can continue driving, while close monitoring discourages alcohol consumption. This paradigm shift not only reduces pathological drinking of repeat DUI but all drinking of offenders while reducing DUI recidivism and decreasing the number of jail and prison stays.

DRIVING UNDER THE INFLUENCE (DUI) AND DRUG COURTS

DUI courts are based on the well-established drug court model, which now numbers over 2,000 in the United States. (14) DUI and drug courts continue to grow after the great success drug courts have demonstrated with both adults and adolescents. Though many drug courts and DUI courts take advantage of continuous transdermal alcohol monitoring or ethyl glucuronide (EtG) testing, most rely on random testing for alcohol and drugs. All drug and DUI courts provide extensive treatment opportunities supported by graduated sanctions and rewards. Participants are closely supervised and given guidance and support by judges to comply with the programs. These courts tend to be significantly less punitive than other courts.

DUI and drug courts offer alternatives to serving jail time for offenders who suffer from alcohol or drug problems. They provide a combination of case management, mandatory counseling, and alcohol and drug testing to individuals who plead guilty to a DUI or drug-related offense.

Repeat DUI offenders clearly are not in control of their drinking. The same is true for many repeat drug offenders, including those who drive after using illegal drugs. DUI and drug courts can identify these potential participants and through mandated treatment, ensure that these offenders receive help.

In a study of drug courts by the U.S. Government Accountability Office, (15) drug court participants were less likely to be rearrested or reconvicted than comparison groups, showing a lower rate of recidivism. While initial costs of providing services to drug court participants were higher than costs for the comparison group, drug court programs proved to be cost-effective in the long-term. Studies of well-run DUI Courts have shown similar outcomes. For example, a study of three Michigan DUI courts found that drug court participants recidivated 65% less often than probationers in comparison groups. (16) Several national organizations and associations recognize the courts' success and have passed resolutions formally endorsing them. These groups include the Governors Highway Safety Association, the Highway Safety Committee of the International Association of Chiefs of Police, the National Sheriffs Association, the National District Attorneys Association, and Mothers Against Drunk Driving. The major limitation of the drug court model for the DUI offense is that it is difficult to scale the drug courts to the enormity of the DUI problem. For this reason, some suggest limiting DUI courts to those offenders who fail at lower cost programs like 24/7 Sobriety.

HAWAII'S OPPORTUNITY PROBATION WITH ENFORCEMENT

Judge Steven S. Alm of the First Circuit Court of Hawaii brought HOPE Probation to life in Honolulu where it has flourished. Probationers who are drug-involved or committed crimes involving domestic violence of sexual abuse enter HOPE Probation through a warning hearing. HOPE participants are randomly and frequently tested for alcohol and drug use. Within 72 hours of a suspected violation, probationers attend a hearing. After the violation is confirmed, the offender immediately serves a short-term jail stay. Upon release, the probationer returns to the HOPE program. Offenders serving regular probation, unlike HOPE participants, are not randomly drug tested, but rather attend scheduled appointments with their probation officer and are given scheduled tests. When offenders violate probation, the probation officer must decide whether to recommend revoking probation or encouraging the offender to comply. Often these probationers are warned or otherwise lightly sanctioned rather than incarcerated.

Research demonstrates HOPE's potential. In an initial pilot study of HOPE, nearly half of the participants stopped using drugs immediately after participating in the formal warning hearing; more than half of the remainder stopped using drugs after a single experience of the jail sanction. A more recent evaluation of the hope program with a specialized unit of high-risk drug-involved probationers not supervised for domestic violence or sex offenses has yielded even more impressive results. (17)

At baseline, the HOPE participants had a significantly higher average number of positive drug tests (53%) than a comparison group of probationers (22%). However, at the three-month follow up, HOPE participants had fewer positives than the comparison group (9% vs. 33%). At the six-month follow up, the disparity between the HOPE participants and the comparison probationers was even greater (4% vs. 19%). At 12 months, 61% of all HOPE participants had zero positive drug tests; 20% had only one positive, 9% had two positives, and 10% had three or more.

The number of missed appointments followed a similar pattern for both HOPE and comparison groups. Of HOPE participants, 14% missed appointments at baseline, decreasing to 4% at three-month follow up and 1% at six-month follow up. Of the comparison group, 9% had missed appointments at baseline, 11% at three-month follow up and 8% and six-month follow up. Overall, 70% of HOPE probationers never missed an appointment in 12 months.

Finally, the percentage of probation revocations was significantly lower for HOPE probationers (9%) than for the comparison group (31%).These results demonstrate the key differences in the structure of HOPE probation that support probationers and hold them accountable without long-term jail stays and decreased costs.

Unlike other probation programs which mandate treatment for their participants, HOPE only provides treatment to offenders who request it and to those who demonstrate a need for it through persistent relapses in drug use despite implemented graduated sanctions. There are two direct benefits to limiting mandated substance abuse treatment. First, it cuts down on the expensive costs of treatment, saving the program and state money. Second, not all drugusing offenders require treatment to stop their pattern of drug use; many simply need a reason not to use. Rather than spending treatment dollars on every offender, HOPE ensures that those who need it the most receive it.

HOPE is now operating on a large scale in Honolulu, with over 1,200 clients representing more than one-seventh of all felony probationers. The challenge today is to test the model to other jurisdictions in the United States and to include parole and bail populations along with probationers. HOPE has already gained bipartisan support, with new legislation proposing funding for national demonstration programs under the title Honest Opportunity Probation with Enforcement Initiative Act of 2009, recently referred to Congress's Subcommittee on Crime, Terrorism and Homeland Security. (18)

FUTURE MANAGEMENT OF OFFENDERS IN THE CRIMINAL JUSTICE SYSTEM

Improving results within the criminal justice system starts with shifting the paradigm to one that sets clear expectations including no use of alcohol or drugs of abuse for offenders in the community and that helps them achieve this goal. These strict and closely monitored standards are also applied to keeping scheduled probation appointments and to participation in treatment when that is one of the conditions of release or supervision.

The 24/7 Sobriety Project, DUI/drug courts and HOPE models hold the promise of significantly reducing the demand for illegal drugs, crime, and prison populations across the United States. As representatives of the Institute for Behavior and Health, Inc. and the National Partnership on Alcohol Misuse and Crime, we support future development throughout the country of programs that manage alcohol- and drug-using offenders through close monitoring, swift, certain and graduated sanctions, as well as access to substance use treatment.

A central feature of this new strategy in all three of these innovative programs is sufficiently frequent random or continuous testing to prevent any significant use of alcohol or other drugs of abuse linked to swift and certain consequences, especially brief incarceration, for violations. These programs include substance abuse and well as treatment when appropriate. This new strategy is strikingly different from the usual practices in community corrections today where alcohol and drug testing is relatively infrequent and often scheduled so the offenders know when they will be tested. Even more distinctive is the imposition of incarceration for every single violation of the conditions of release to the community. Typically today the consequences of violations of parole and probation are unpredictable, often long-delayed and then severe. In this new model they are swift and certain, but not draconian.

Combining rigorous monitoring with treatment offers the best opportunity for long-term change in drug and alcohol-using behaviors among these high-risk populations. The standards set by these three program models are applicable to all stages within the criminal justice system when offenders are in the community from pre-trial through parole and probation. They can be branded and promoted as high-visibility, high impact improvements to the nation's current efforts to reduce alcohol misuse, illegal drug use and crime. Contrary to the expectations of many in the criminal justice field, these efforts have been shown to significantly reduce incarceration, a major goal of the criminal justice system today.

REFERENCES DELETED

Robert L. DuPont, M.D., President and Corinne L. Shea, M.A., Director of Communications, are with the Institute for Behavior and Health, Inc. Stephen K. Talpins, J.D., is Chairman and Chief Executive Office of the National Partnership on Alcohol Misuse and Crime. Robert B. Voas, Ph.D., is a senior research scientist with Pacific Institute for Research and Evaluation.

43

Toward Fewer Prisoners
& Less Crime

Mark A.R. Kleiman.

Mass incarceration can be approached from (at least) four perspectives: those of social science, cultural criticism, advocacy, and policy analysis.

The social scientist wants to know about causes and consequences, to employ theories to explain events such as the explosion of incarceration in America over the past generation, and to use events to develop new theories. The cultural critic strives to elucidate meanings, asking about the intentions behind the actions of participants in the social, administrative, and political processes that produce a given set of results; about how they justify those actions to themselves and others ; and about the character of the social order that produced those processes and their results. The advocate searches for persuasive means to the end of ameliorating an already identified evil. The policy analyst tries to figure out what course of action would best serve the public interest, all things considered, trying to take into account unintended as well as intended consequences.

Viewed through a policy-analytic lens, "mass incarceration" looks like only a partial problem definition; the other part of the problem is crime. If the crime problem were trivial, or if incarceration had only a trivial effect on crime, the solution to the problem of mass incarceration would be trivially obvious: release those currently locked up and end the practice of sending offenders to jail or prison. The policy analyst's work would then be complete, and the task of persuasion could then be turned over to the advocate, guided by the social scientist and the cultural critic.

Kleiman, M. Toward Fewer Prisoners & Less Crime. Daedalus, Summer 2010 v139 i3 p115(9).

282

But if crime is a real problem and if incarceration can be one means (among many) to control crime, then the situation looks more complicated. One would need to measure the harms done by crime as well as the harms done by incarceration, ask about the effects of alternative incarceration policies on the rates of different sorts of crime, and consider the likely results of making more use of other crime-control measures, including alternative forms of punishment, while reducing incarceration.

For example, it seems clear that increasing police activity can reduce victimization rates. Thus it ought to be possible in principle, given some target level of victimization, to "trade off" policing against incarceration: adding police while reducing imprisonment. Whether that tradeoff would be desirable is a different question. The extremely aggressive style of the New York Police Department, even if we credit it with reducing crime (and, consequently, reducing incarceration as well), seriously complicates the lives of poor, young African American, Dominican, Puerto Rican, and Haitian New Yorkers.

Is it better to live in a city with fewer prisoners but more police surveillance ? The answer is not obvious on its face: resolving the question would require both the collection of facts and the assignment of values to different outcomes. But it is the sort of question that a policy analysis starting from the problem of mass incarceration must try to answer, if crime matters and if incarceration is one means of reducing it. That analysis must also ask *which* offenders to release early or not to incarcerate at all.

Thinking about mass incarceration and crime control as twin problems can create two tactical advantages for those committed to reducing mass incarceration. First, since many political actors are concerned about crime and do think that incarceration helps control it, advocates of incarceration reduction will find a better hearing if they propose alternative means of crime control instead of simply ignoring the crime problem. Second, there is evidence that support for highly punitive approaches to crime varies--albeit with a substantial lag--with the crime rate, so that success in reducing crime will tend to facilitate the project of incarceration reduction. As the crime explosion of 1962 to 1994 helped produce the problem of mass incarceration, the crime collapse since 1994 might help ameliorate it, especially if victimization rates continue to fall.

Even at current levels, crime--especially in poor African American communities--remains a first-order social problem, comparable in magnitude to the problem of mass incarceration.

Merely reducing the prison head count without also making the lives of residents of dangerous neighborhoods safer would solve only half the problem.

T he measurable losses from crime do not seem to be especially large compared to the measurable losses from other sources of risk: surely not large enough to account for the level of public concern over crime. Across households, the average property lost to burglary comes out to about $4 per month, a small fraction of a typical utility bill. Homicide is a horrible event, but also a rare one; twice as many people die on the highways each year as are deliberately killed by others.

Victimization risk imposes costs on those who are never actually victimized, because of the costly efforts they make to avoid victimization and because of the "external costs" of victimization-avoidance measures taken by others. Crime, like incarceration, deprives people of liberty; it does so by making them afraid. The deprivation of liberty is, in general, less profound--though there are certainly people who feel trapped in their homes because they are afraid to go outdoors--but it extends to a much larger group of people. The costs of crime avoidance easily swamp the immediate costs of victimization.

If the bulk of crime-related loss is not victimization loss, then the rate of completed victimization--the crime rate--is not a good proxy for the seriousness of the crime problem. A neighborhood abandoned due in part to crime, or where residents stay inside behind locked doors for fear of muggers, or a park that many people are afraid to enter after dark, may have a lower rate of completed crime than a safer neighborhood or park simply because so many fewer people are at risk. Even before the spectacular post-1994 crime decrease, New York City had a relatively low burglary rate compared to other big cities. But the public impression that burglary risk was higher in New York was nonetheless probably correct: as a visitor could easily notice, New Yorkers were habituated to being much more careful about burglary-proofing their homes than was common in cities where burglary was less on residents' minds.

The extent to which the fear of crime reflects mass-media choices about what sort of "news" to emphasize remains an open question. Certainly, there is no strong tendency for measures of fear to shift quickly with, or even in the same direction as, measured crime. But this need not indicate that the fear itself is irrational or insensitive to the actual crime risks prevalent in various social milieux, since victimization might fall precisely as a result of increased precaution.

If the level of precaution tends to rise with the criminal riskiness of the social environment, and if precaution tends to reduce the rate of being victimized, then the measured changes in the rate of completed crime will tend to understate the changes in the underlying risk, especially when crime is increasing. For example, if the number of robberies doubles even as potential victims are taking greater precautions against being robbed, then the rate of robbery per exposed person-hour--imagining that such a quantity could be measured--must have gone up even more. The flow of population away from high-crime urban neighborhoods and into lower-crime suburbs and exurbs means that the measured crime rate could fall even as the level of risk in every area continued to rise.

The observation that the Great Crime Decline has left the country with "only" 250 percent of the crime rates prevalent in the early 1960s is less reassuring than it would seem. I am not very old, but I am old enough to recall when American storefronts, unlike European storefronts, did not have metal shutters, and when middle-class parents did not regard it as imprudent to allow their teenage children to ride late-night buses through tough neighborhoods. If Americans continued to be as careless about the risks of crime as they were forty-five years ago, the rate of completed crime would no doubt be substantially higher. The loss of that carelessness--or rather, of a social environment that made that carelessness rational--is not a small loss, and it becomes no smaller if we blame it on television news shows rather than on muggers.

The fear of crime deprives the residents of high-crime neighborhoods of economic opportunity by driving jobs away from the places where they live. Whether the "spatial mismatch" between the location of the unemployed and the location of unfilled jobs is an important cause of high minority unemployment remains a contested question, but there can be no doubt that having to commute farther to work is, at best, an inconvenience, especially for teenagers who would be working only part-time and whose attachment to the labor market may be weak. Those disadvantages tend to accumulate, since teenagers with less work experience become less attractive employees as young adults. Worse still, anything that makes licit employment less attractive will tend to make its illicit alternatives more attractive ; a criminal record can be a very substantial barrier to subsequent employment in the licit economy.

Poverty to crime to job loss to poverty to crime is a positive-feedback loop: poor neighborhoods are often high-crime neighborhoods, high-crime neighborhoods tend to be low-opportunity neighborhoods, low-opportunity neighborhoods encourage criminal activity by their residents, and criminal activity, in turn, makes the neighborhoods even less attractive places in which to live and do business and makes some of the residents less attractive as potential employees. Loss of residents, especially the relatively prosperous residents most likely to be able to afford to move out, makes a neighborhood less attractive to retail businesses, and the loss of retail services in turn makes the neighborhood a less attractive place to live for those who have other options.

The economic geography of every metropolitan area provides testimony to the importance of crime as a factor shaping residential and business location decisions. How else could one account for the coexistence of housing abandonment and new housing construction only a few miles apart? There are many reasons for moving to the suburbs, but crime ranks high on the list. The same applies to business-location decisions. It would be unconventional to insert a discussion of crime control in a treatise on reducing suburban sprawl, but it would not be irrelevant.

That poverty is a cause of crime is a commonplace, though the mechanisms involved are complex and poorly understood. That crime is a sustaining cause of poverty is no less true, though in the past it has been remarked on much less. The poor are victimized directly; the probability of criminal victimization falls with income. They are victimized again as a result of crime-avoidance behavior that limits their opportunities and blights their neighborhoods.

The picture is worst for African Americans; even adjusting for overall lower incomes, African Americans suffer much more crime than do members of other ethnic categories. Homicide provides the most dramatic example: representing less than 15 percent of the population, African Americans suffer more than 50 percent of the murders.

The problem tends to be self-sustaining. Given a constrained criminal justice system, punishment per crime tends to be lower where crime is more common. Assuming that the threat of punishment has some deterrent effect, growing up where that threat is smaller--and licit economic opportunity less available--should be expected, other things equal, to lead to a higher rate of criminal activity. Indeed, that is what we find. African Americans are far more

286

heavily victimized than others, but not as a result of cross-ethnic aggression; crime is overwhelmingly intraracial.

Paradoxically, then, efforts to reduce the racial disproportion in the prison population are likely to intensify the implicit racial discrimination among victims that results from lower per-crime rates of punishment, leaving African Americans even more exposed to victimization. The critique of the current system in terms of imposing prison sentences and the consequent social stigma on a much higher proportion of African Americans than of whites is fully justified by the facts, but the mechanisms involved are far more subtle than conscious, or even systemic, racial discrimination by officials against African American perpetrators.

In some ways it would be better if, as is often asserted, systemic racial bias, in the form of more severe punishment for African American offenders, lay at the root of the problem ; then eliminating racial bias could eliminate disproportionate incarceration. But if the actual problem is the positive-feedback loop from high criminal activity to low punishment-per-crime back to high criminal activity, no such fix is available. The standard critique portrays a melodrama; the reality is a tragedy.

I f crime and mass incarceration are both great evils, then we should look for ways to have less of both, for example by substituting some other form of punishment for incarceration to serve the twin functions of incapacitation and deterrence. If, as sociologist and anthropologist Bert Useem and economist Anne Piehl argue, the rising scale of incarceration has brought its marginal crime-control benefits down close to--or in some instances below--zero, then to some extent we could reduce mass incarceration without increasing crime. But the data do not suggest that 50 percent of current incarceration is useless, and cutting our incarceration rate in half would still leave it more than twice its historical norm and more than twice the level in any other advanced polity.

Probation and parole are the two systems that manage convicted offenders outside the walls of prisons and jails. Fines, community service, diversion to drug treatment or mental health treatment, and "restorative justice" programs all rely on probation and parole supervision as their enforcement mechanism, without which they are no more than helpful hints from a judge. Alas, that enforcement is generally very weak, and compliance with "alternative sanctions" spotty at best. In California's famous Proposition 36 drug-diversion program, only about one entrant in four completed the prescribed course of treatment, and virtually none of the rest faced any consequence for reneging on the bargain they had made with the court, other than the lost opportunity to have their convictions expunged and the risk that an outstanding bench warrant might complicate the aftermath of some future arrest. Those are precisely the sort of important but delayed consequences that impose suffering without changing behavior to any great extent.

That failure does not stem from the laxity or laziness of probation officers--though no doubt some probation officers, like some workers in any job category, are lax and lazy--but from the conditions under which they work. Typically, a big-city probation officer supervises more than one hundred clients and is expected to meet with each of them once a month. That schedule alone largely fills a working week, and the time required to prepare a violation report to send to the supervising judge is measured in hours. So the number of referrals is constrained by the officer's time. The judge and the judge's staff are also busy, and will not thank the probation officer for subjecting them to a flurry of revocation motions.

Short of the threat of revocation, a probation officer's leverage over a client is limited. Only the judge can order a term of confinement; the probation officer (generally with the concurrence of a supervisor) can only use moral suasion and impose additional requirements, such as more frequent meetings. But what if the client defies those requirements as well?

If a revocation motion is made, the judge, too, has a limited repertoire of sanctions. She can send the offender to prison or jail, usually for a period of months but sometimes for years. She can impose more onerous conditions of supervision (which, again, the probationer may well ignore). She can lengthen the period of supervision, which is a noticeable inconvenience but one that doesn't hit until sometime in the future.

None of these options is attractive. Jails and prisons are crowded, and whatever the probationer did to earn the conviction that underlies his probation term, the violation of probation conditions is likely to be relatively trivial: a missed meeting or a "dirty" drug test. To a judge who has just put someone on probation for a burglary, sending someone else away for a mere "technical" violation seems disproportionate, unless that violation comes at the end of a very long string. (Sometimes a new substantive offense is handled as a violation of probation rather than prosecuted afresh; in those cases, a term behind bars is a more likely outcome.)

As a result, the most likely consequence for a probationer caught breaking a probation rule is a warning, either from the probation office or (less often) from the judge. If the probationer keeps it up, at some point it will prove to be the case that his previous "last warning" really *was* the last, and he will be on his way to, or back to, a cell. But such deferred and low-probability risks, though they may cumulate to a great deal of punishment, do little to reduce the violation rate. The lack of an immediate and high-probability aversive consequence for a violation helps sustain the high violation rate, and the high violation rate in turn guarantees that most violations will not be sanctioned. This is simply the social trap of the neighborhood with a high crime rate and a low punishment risk per offense, writ small; the community corrections system reproduces the cruel and futile randomized draconianism of the larger criminal-justice system. (Parole supervision is tighter, though it, too, over-relies on severe sanctions, but there are about five times as many probationers as parolees.)

J ust as the threat of severe sanctions is largely impotent at controlling behavior if the sanctions are uncertain and deferred, the threat of even a mild sanction can be potent if the consequence follows the act swiftly and certainly. In Hawaii, a judicial warning that the next positive drug test would draw an immediate jail term measured in days succeeded in virtually ending drug use for more than three-quarters of a group of chronically defiant felony probationers, most of them methamphetamine users. The hard part was organizing the judge's staff, the probation department, the sheriff's office, the police, the jail, prosecutors, and defense counsel to deliver on that warning when the rules were broken. (That meant, for example, developing a two-page, check-the-box or fill-in-the-blank reporting form to replace the elaborate motion-for-revocation paperwork; since only a single violation is in question, very little information is needed.)

Half of the probationers in the program--dubbed HOPE (Hawaii's Opportunity Probation with Enforcement)--never faced an actual sanction; the warning alone did the job. On average, the group subjected to tight supervision spent about as many days in jail for probation violations as a comparison group, with more but shorter spells. But they spent only about a third as many days in prison after revocations or new convictions, and had only half as many arrests for new crimes.

The project now covers about 1,500 offenders, about one in five felony probationers on the island of Oahu ; the judge plans to expand it to 3,000, and intends to manage all of them himself, by contrast with a drug-court judge who typically manages a caseload of 50 to 75. Most of the participants, but by no means all, are drug abusers; the process works just as well enforcing different sets of rules on domestic violence offenders and on sex offenders. The underlying process isn't specific to drug abuse ; it applies basic principles of behavioral change relevant to a wide range of behaviors, as long as the behaviors can be easily monitored. South Dakota's 24/7 program, which requires repeat drunken drivers to submit to twice-a-day breathalyzer tests, has dramatically reduced their risk of winding up in prison for a third offense.

Commercial vendors now sell, for $15 per month, a service that tracks the whereabouts of a GPS monitor; parents place them in their young children's backpacks to be able to find them when they stray. One version of that service provides "exception reporting": after the parent enters a weekly schedule of where the child is supposed to be at given hours of given days, the system sends a text message to the parent's cell phone or email inbox if the child isn't where he is supposed to be.

Now imagine mounting such a unit on an anklet that can't be removed without setting off an alarm. That would make the whereabouts of an offender wearing that anklet subject to continuous monitoring. Comparing offenders' position records with the locations of crimes reported to the 911 system would make it difficult for anyone wearing an anklet to get away with a new predatory offense. Street gangs would not welcome the presence of members whose location is transparent to the police. Such a system would make it feasible to enforce curfews, stay-away orders, "community service" obligations, and requirements to appear as scheduled for employment or therapy, and to enforce home confinement as a sanction for violations of probation or parole conditions.

Unlike the expensive process of monitoring sex offenders, in which any straying constitutes a potential emergency and the system must therefore be staffed around the clock, for routine probationers and parolees there would be no urgency about responding to a mere schedule violation ; it would suffice for the probation or parole officer to be notified the next morning. As long as the offender is still wearing the device, finding him would pose no challenge, and the next day is soon enough for a sanction to be effective.

An emergency would arise only when an offender removed the device; usually that would mean he was planning either to commit a new crime or to abscond from supervision. But the police department, already staffed 24/7, could respond to those (presumably rare) events.

The operational challenges would be legion : developing rules about imposing and relaxing restrictions; figuring out what to do if the GPS unit loses contact with the satellite; dealing with false alarms; ensuring that the police respond quickly and vigorously to absconding; and managing the sanctions hearings. But given the results from HOPE, it's a reasonable guess that 80 percent, perhaps even 90 percent of probationers and parolees would comply with the system in the sense of not shedding the GPS device, and that they would be highly compliant with rules and commit very few new crimes. They would probably also find it much easier to secure employment--despite their criminal records--once employers found that they were not only certified drug-free but also showed up for work every day under pressure from their probation or parole officers. As a result, many fewer of them would wind up returning to prison.

Once probation and parole involved that sort of monitoring, only a limited number of cases would justify using incarceration : people who commit such heinous crimes that justice demands it (the Bernie Madoffs of the world), people whose demonstrated tendency for assault or sexual predation requires their incarceration to protect potential victims, and those who, in effect, *choose* incarceration by absconding. Everyone else could be adequately punished and largely incapacitated from reoffending with position restrictions alone, backed by monitoring and brief jail stays for violations. That could reduce the inflow to prison (both by reducing the number of revocations and persuading judges to sentence more felons to probation instead) and increase the outflow from prison by encouraging parole boards to make more early-release decisions. Moreover, converting probation into a real punishment, rather than the placeholder for an absent punishment that it now largely is, would be expected to deter crime, reducing the inflows to both prison and probation.

How far this process might go is anyone's guess. But it would not be utterly fantastic to hope that the United States might find itself a decade or two from now with a European incarceration rate and crime rates resembling those of the 1950s.

The change could not be made overnight; each jurisdiction that adopts such a system will need an operational "shakedown" period. Furthermore, it is essential that the program not outgrow its capacity to monitor and sanction ; once off fenders come to believe that the threat of quick incarceration is a bluff, their offending will so swamp the system that it will become a bluff.

But other than the need for shaking down and then phasing in, this approach has no natural upper limit. HOPE COSTS about $1,400 per year on top of routine probation supervision, which is to say that it costs about twice what routine supervision alone costs. Most of that excess goes to drug treatment for the minority that cannot comply without professional help. It pays for itself several times over in reduced incarceration costs alone, which means that cost need not be a barrier to expansion if some way can be devised to recycle the savings to the state budget from reduced incarceration into the county budgets that bear most probation costs.

The implementation of this idea will vary from jurisdiction to jurisdiction and from population to population. In various ways, it could be applied to juvenile offenders, probationers, parolees, and those released while awaiting trial either on bail or on their own recognizance. For juvenile probationers in particular, "outpatient" supervision under tight monitoring backed with the threat of forty-eight hours' solitary confinement for each violation might succeed in squaring the circle of finding a punishment aversive enough to deter but not so damaging as to risk pushing a juvenile toward persistent criminality by reducing his commitment to, and opportunities within, the world of school and licit work.

The project of what might be called "virtual" or "outpatient" incarceration cannot expect a universally warm welcome. In a criminal-justice-policy debate that sometimes seems to take place between the disciples of Michel Foucault and those of the Marquis de Sade, it will be too intrusive for the foucauldians and not retributive enough for the sadists. But for those not overly reluctant to punish lawbreakers with some months or years of a boring, go-to-bed-early-and-show-up-for-work middle-class lifestyle, and unwilling to accept current levels of incarceration or of crime, the virtual prison cell offers the prospect of having less of both.

With respect to the population not currently in prison, including pretrial releasees and those newly placed on probation who would not have gone to prison otherwise, there is no doubt that the proposed system represents a further extension of state control over individuals. Whether that is desirable could be debated, with the answer depending in part on the empirical results in terms of crime, days behind bars, and employment, family, and housing status, and in part on the value one assigns to the liberty and privacy of the recently arrested (including their liberty to commit fresh offenses with

292

impunity). In the somewhat longer run--over a period of a few years--
the result might be to reduce the scope of direct state control by
discouraging offenses and thus reducing the total size of the prison-
jail-probation-parole-pretrial release population.

Such a happy ending cannot be guaranteed. The program has
yet to be tried out on parolees; it is possible (though I would rate the
probability as small) that massive absconscion and consequent return
to prison would make it operationally infeasible. It is more plausible
that, in some jurisdictions, a combination of haste, under-resourcing,
and administrative noncompliance would lead to program
breakdown, with the supervised population discovering that, despite
the threat, violation did not in fact lead swiftly and predictably to
confinement. If that happened, violation rates would surely soar, thus
putting the program into a "death spiral" of increasing violation rates
and decreasing swiftness and certainty of sanctions. Preventing such
a breakdown is no easy task; managing the behavior of offenders is
straightforward compared to managing the behavior of officials, and
most of all the behavior of independent officials such as judges.

The other risk is that some offenders who, under the current
system of loose supervision, get away with minor violations, finish
their assigned terms, and then go straight would find the new system
of tighter supervision intolerable, commit repeated technical
infractions leading to short confinement terms, abscond, and wind up
in prison. That risk would be especially grave if the system were
applied to misdemeanants in addition to felons, since the
misdemcanants start out with a much lower level of prison risk.

But if the application of "outpatient incarceration" can be
restricted to those who would otherwise face, with high probability,
repeated spells of actual incarceration, then on balance it promotes
not only public safety but the liberty and life prospects of the
offender population. There are worse fates than being forced to live a
law-abiding life.

44

Stimulus Money to Fund Program for Residents On Parole, Probation

Jennifer Reeger

L ater this year, some criminals on probation or parole in Westmoreland County will be able to meet with a probation officer, receive drug-and-alcohol treatment and mental health services, and learn how to write a resume.

County commissioners yesterday accepted a $300,000 state grant to establish a Day Reporting Center in Greensburg as an alternative sentencing program that could alleviate jail overcrowding and lower recidivism rates. The grant, given to the county by the Pennsylvania Commission on Crime and Delinquency, is part of $748,000 in federal stimulus dollars being used to fund the program for the first two years, said Bruno Mediate, a supervisor with Westmoreland County Adult Probation who chaired a committee that has been studying the program since 2008.

The program, which will be housed at Southwestern Pennsylvania Human Services Inc.'s facility on South Maple Avenue, could open in late summer or early fall. As many as 200 offenders, who will be ordered to the program through the court system, will be served by the center, Mediate said. Many of them will be probation and parole violators who are having difficulty getting through drug-and-alcohol treatment, Mediate said. About 75 percent of those who fail to complete probation or parole have drug and alcohol problems, and half of those have mental-health issues as well. "We kind of call them the revolving door-type people," Mediate said. On top of that, some may have learning disabilities and haven't earned a high school diploma or GED. They also may need parenting and anger

Reeger, J. Stimulus money to fund program for residents on parole, probation.
Tribune-Review (Greensburg, PA), April 9, 2010.

management classes or need help finding a job. But getting those services often means traveling to different locations, something that may be difficult "We thought, why don't we bring all these fragmented services together, bring them under one roof, work together as a team and make a program where people could come together every day if needed to receive a multitude of services," Mediate said. Offenders ordered to the program will be evaluated on a case-by-case basis, Mediate said. However, violent offenders will not be admitted. The program will cost the county nothing for the first two years, but Mediate believes it can be self-sustaining even after the grant money dries up. Insurance payments for mental-health and drug-and-alcohol services would be tapped, and the offenders could be required to pay fees for the services, he said. The commissioners voted yesterday to save a grant program that was threatened by state budget cuts. The Local Arts Subgrants, which had been awarded since 1983, were in danger of being cut after the state budget slashed funding for the Pennsylvania Council on the Arts. The council had helped fund the local government grant program, providing a 50-50 matching grant to counties to dole out funding for local arts programs, said Dan Carpenter, program director for Westmoreland County Parks, which administers the grants. "I thought our program was going to come to an unceremonious end after all these years," Carpenter said when he heard the state was ending the funding. Instead, county commissioners decided to fully fund the program with county dollars when they had only previously had to provide half. So yesterday, 18 groups throughout the county were given a total of $9,430. That was the same amount as last year, Carpenter said. The grant awards were pared down from 20 applications requesting a total of $21,700. Grants were awarded to local governments and organizations for programs such as concerts and festivals. "It's a good way that our department and the county can support other organizations in the county that maybe our parks and recreation department can't serve," Carpenter said. Commissioner Chuck Anderson said the program was one that commissioners didn't want to see "fall through the cracks." "It's one of the programs we have that touches all areas of the county," added Commissioner Tom Ceraso. "We didn't want to see it go away because the state wasn't picking up their half." Chuck DeNunzio, second vice president of Derry Railroad Days, which received $290 for performing arts at the Sept. 25 festival, said he was pleased the county continued the grant program. "It's harder to get money every year," he said. "We're really going to try to take that a long way."

Special Populations

45

Crisis Intervention Teams Adapted to Correctional Populations

Jay Hodges

In fiscal year 2009, the Oklahoma Department of Mental Health and Substance Abuse Services (ODMHSAS) identified 38,222 individuals with serious mental illness (SMI) who were receiving ODMHSAS-funded mental health services in the state. The Oklahoma Department of Health, in its 2008 State of the State's Health Report indicated that 8.4 percent of adults have suffered at least one major depressive episode and 13.3 percent have serious psychological distress, ranking Oklahoma among the most mentally unhealthy states in the U.S.

At the end of fiscal year 2009, the Oklahoma Department of Corrections (ODOC) was incarcerating 6,276 offenders who were classified as seriously mentally ill. This accounted for 25.82 percent of the incarcerated population. During this time, there were 30,479 individuals who were under community-based correctional supervision. Based on the prevalence of psychological distress in the general population, there would be more than 4,000 mentally ill offenders under community supervision. If the percentages reflecting the incarcerated population held, there would be nearly 8,000 community offenders suffering from mental illness. Any of these scenarios would substantiate the fact that probation and parole officers frequently face the challenges of interacting with offenders with mental illness.

Hodges, J. Crisis intervention teams adapted to correctional populations. Probation and Parole Forum. Corrections Today, Oct 2010 v72 i5 p106(2). Reprinted with permission of the American Correctional Association, Alexandria, VA.

THE CORRECTIONS CRISIS RESOLUTION TRAINING

In response to the need for the development of specialized skill sets to successfully interact and manage these offenders, the Oklahoma Department of Corrections joined with various partners in the development of the corrections crisis resolution training (CCRT) in July 2009. This training program is an adaptation of the original crisis intervention team (CIT) training program developed by the Memphis, Tenn., Police Department. The program is designed to improve the outcomes of correctional officers' and probation and parole officers' interactions with people in crisis who also have mental illness.

This model of crisis intervention training is used by law enforcement agencies in communities across the nation and has now been modified for use with criminal justice populations. The Oklahoma project is a joint partnership between ODMHSAS, the Oklahoma City Police Department, the Midwest City Police Department, National Alliance of Mental Illness-Oklahoma, and numerous consumers and community mental health providers.

ODOC's venture into CIT was the result of a search for crisis de-escalation training to meet the needs of staff who were not experienced in working with mentally ill offenders. Although there was a great deal of information relating to agencies that had implemented training programs that targeted intervening with individuals in crisis situations, there were no specific training programs focused on correctional populations. After careful review, it was determined that the CIT training program could be modified to target the training needs of correctional staff, both inside the facilities and out on the streets.

In 2008, ODMHSAS offered a funding opportunity for programming that could help transform the culture of mental illness in Oklahoma. A grant proposal was developed that outlined the adaptation of the CIT model to a correctional intervention approach that would be delivered to probation and parole officers and institutional staff who work with SMI offenders. The grant was awarded and the partnership began the curriculum development phase as well as a plan for implementing the training program.

TRAINING OUTCOMES

The inaugural class of 22 probation and parole officers served as a testing ground for the modified curriculum. The anticipated benefits of the training included:

- An increased level of confidence in recognizing and responding to the needs of individuals diagnosed with a mental illness;

- The ability to safely and compassionately respond to individuals in crisis;

- New options for probation officers dealing with situations involving individuals in crisis; and

- An increased comfort level in discussing mental illness.

Since the implementation of the program, ODOC has trained approximately 65 probation and parole officers from across the state. These officers have acquired knowledge and skills necessary to successfully interact with offenders who are experiencing a crisis situation, due to a drug-induced state or as the result of mental illness. Correctional officers and unit staff from Oklahoma State Penitentiary, Mabel Bassett Correctional Center and Joseph Harp Correctional Center had experience working with the SMI offenders, as each of these facilities have specialized mental health units. This training, in many instances, was the first opportunity for these staff to receive specialized instruction in working with the mentally ill offenders. Their participation in the program and the exposure to the techniques of CIT has provided additional insight into working with this special population.

This program teaches participants techniques that will not only de-escalate individuals in crisis, but also how to develop and use a team to respond positively to the mental health needs of individuals. CCRT has a more limited focus than the original CIT program in that the application of skills is directed to a correctional population, either individuals under community correctional control or who are incarcerated within the agency. The program has served to meet a critical need for staff who are faced each day with the task of providing oversight of this challenging population.

Jay Hodges is a program specialist for Treatment and Rehabilitative Services for the Oklahoma Department of Corrections.

46

Dodge Correctional Hospice Program Gives 'Comfort Care' to Dying Inmates

Karen Rivedal

At 51, he looks two decades older. His thin body is swallowed up by the afghan that covers his bed. The blanket's vibrant colors, and the powder-blue paint on the walls, make his gaunt face look even paler. His chest is sunken, his limbs are fragile and doctors just found two new fractures in his spine. He is in some pain but says he's at peace in this place. "I'm very comfortable here," he said in a voice one must strain to hear. "I wouldn't wish this on anybody or anything, but I would never get treated like this anywhere else." Kaos Metz, who has end-stage liver disease, won't live to finish his 10-year sentence for causing injury while driving drunk and other alcohol-related crimes. But he's considered a success story, along with the 26 other prisoners who came here to die before him.

"They died well, and not alone," said Margie Barnes, coordinator for the hospice program that operates in one part of the prison hospital at Dodge Correctional Institution. The program, a first for Wisconsin prisons, was 2 years old last month. Funded by inmate fees and donations, it draws terminally ill inmates with less than a year to live from all 19 of the state's adult-male prisons. Specially trained inmate volunteers provide most of the "comfort care" for which hospice programs, inside of prison or out, are best known. That care includes sitting with patients, talking with them, writing letters for them, serving them meals, playing games and standing

Rivedal, K. Dodge Correctional hospice program gives 'comfort care' to dying inmates. WI State Journal (Madison, WI), March 1, 2009.

vigil around the clock -- literally standing at their bedside -- when death is imminent. On June 8, four inmate volunteers sang "Amazing Grace" as the hospice's youngest patient to date, Sellwyn Covington, a registered sex offender, died of cancer at age 28. "You try to comfort them, as much as a person can," said inmate volunteer Triru Dillie, 36, who is serving a life sentence for murder. "We don't try to force anything on them. We find it is a privilege to be with them when they die." 'Right thing to do'

To those who would oppose granting anything special or more comfortable to prisoners -- even on their death beds -- Dodge staffers say hospice care isn't an extra and any debate over it isn't their fight. "We don't consider ourselves the judge and jury," said Dodge prison guard Dawn Heeringa, who helps monitor the 62-bed infirmary, where two rooms have been dedicated for hospice patients, and a few more can be converted if needed. What's more, as hospice care becomes more common in prisons around the country -- 39 states offer it -- and in the community, where the hospice movement began in the mid-1970s, it would be wrong to withhold it, officials said. "This is the right thing to do," Warden Tim Lundquist said. Hospice care in any setting is aimed at giving dying people support and more say over their final days. It reflects a gradual societal shift from the desire to prolong life at any cost to achieving the best quality of life in what time is left.

Doctors and nurses focus on the relief of pain and other symptoms, rather than on finding a cure, with a team of professionals and volunteers to address any emotional, spiritual and psychological needs. At Dodge, prisoners entering hospice must understand they can't be cured and sign a form rejecting extraordinary methods to keep them alive. Officials believe that saves money, because it eliminates pointless tests and treatments, including visits to outside specialists and the security costs of transport. Dodge's infirmary psychologist, Lynn Stock, said hospice even made the prison safer. "When (other inmates) see staff demonstrate compassion toward dying patients, it creates more trust," Stock said. "It increases respect for staff." Andy Land, who runs a community-based hospice in Fond du Lac as part of Agnesian Health Care, helped prison staff start the Dodge hospice and continues to provide training for its staff and volunteers. He is paid through a surcharge on prisoner phone calls. "This is appropriate medical care," Land said. "This is not coddling." Security, skepticism

Even so, the success of Dodge's program hasn't come easy, staff members said. Planners faced unique security challenges and some skepticism from within. "We have to remember where we are," said Jim Hebel, a nursing supervisor who helped develop the hospice. "We are a medical facility, but we are in a maximum-security prison." Some on the medical staff were concerned about giving narcotics to inmates with a criminal history of drug abuse, even for end-of-life pain relief. And the inmates themselves have been a tough sell, because many believe the system will always try to shortchange them. "It's a constant education process," Heeringa said. "We have to sell hospice as a better way to die, and the rigidity of (prison) culture is a challenge we overcome daily." Security chiefs balked at the idea of open doors on dying patients' rooms and at letting inmate volunteers be in the rooms at all without a constant guard, even though two officers and a sergeant continually monitor the infirmary floor on foot patrol and by camera. Program planners eased security concerns by putting the hospice rooms near the floor's central nursing station for increased supervision, while convincing many nurses that the inmate volunteers could ease their immediate workloads. But one major limitation could not be helped, staff members said. To safeguard against abuse, inmate volunteers are only allowed to touch hospice patients on their hands, elbows and shoulders, Hebel said. Medical staff face the same restrictions, except as needed for specific procedures. "We don't allow hugging," Hebel said. "It's kind of difficult for us, but when it comes to hugging, which is typical in (community-based) hospice, we have to draw the line. We don't want to endanger our program by not having a very definite standard." The program does come with some extras that prisoners might otherwise not see, but they are either made by inmates or purchased through inmate fundraisers or donations from staff and patients' families. Extras includes the paint on the walls, white-lace curtains for the windows, quilts or afghans for the beds, special food, books, movies, fans, clocks and TVs. "I have not seen one instance of abuse of the program," consultant Andy Land said, "because the inmates own it." 'Looking for redemption'

Kaos Metz, who had lived in Jefferson and Madison, arrived at the hospice in late January from the state prison in Oshkosh. By mid-February, as he was failing, his main hope was that his daughter and her baby, whom he had never met, would visit soon. Hospice staff try to arrange for visits from outside friends and family. But for about one third of patients, no one comes, Barnes said. That makes the job of inmate volunteers even more important, as they are perhaps the dying patients' only real confidantes and confessors. "They serve a role that no other person can serve," Land said. "All the masks come off. Every single one of us has to answer the question, 'What have I done with my life?'Ce" And as the end nears, prisoners in hospice often look to reconnect with family and "make amends," Heeringa said. "No question they are looking for redemption," she said. To be hospice volunteers, inmates must have good conduct records and pass personality tests, followed by 16 hours of training. They aren't paid and must commit to the work -- typically in two-hour shifts -- for at least two years, on top of their required prison jobs. Inmate volunteer Dennis Gordanier, 37, who is serving a 20-year sentence for sexual assault, said volunteers get to be present for moments that range from sad to angry to harrowing to uplifting, sometimes all with the same person. "(One patient) flat-out came to me and said, 'Do you think I'm going to meet the Lord?'Ce" Gordanier said. "And it was the greatest feeling in the world to be able to tell him yes." It can be difficult when patients die, he said, especially if the death isn't an easy one.

"But you know they won't suffer anymore," he added. "They're going away from all that. It's a bittersweet thing." Metz died at 3:10 a.m. Wednesday. He never had a visit from his daughter, who lives in Michigan, or his nine-month-old grandson. Staff were trying to set it up, but bad weather and other circumstances got in the way. "Time ran out," Barnes said.

47

State No. 1 in Treatment of Pregnant Inmates

Tracie Mauriello

Pennsylvania prisons are the best in the nation when it comes to treatment of pregnant inmates, according to a report released Thursday. The National Women's Law Center and Rebecca Project for Human Rights analyzed policies related to prenatal care, shackling of women during childbirth and alternatives to incarceration that allow mothers to be with their children. In Pennsylvania state prisons, pregnant inmates receive regular medical exams, lab testing, prenatal vitamins, nutrition counseling, childcare education and postpartum care, said Susan McNaughton, spokeswoman for the Department of Corrections.

The state's female inmate population has grown from 1,947 in 2005 to more than 2,400 this year. On average, the state admits about 38 pregnant inmates each year. Between 2005 and 2009, 157 Pennsylvania Department of Corrections inmates gave birth. Another 36 pregnant inmates were released before their delivery dates. Pregnant inmates are housed at the State Correctional Institution Muncy in Lycoming County. They are housed in the general population until 10 days before their due dates, when they are moved to the infirmary. Pregnant inmates are not shackled during labor and delivery, Ms. McNaughton said.

That has long been the policy in the state prison system, but a new state law now also prevents county jails from shackling during childbirth.

State Sen. Daylin Leach, D-Delaware, introduced the legislation after reading about a shackled Philadelphia County inmate who was injured during childbirth. "I knew we had to make a change, and we did. It was a rare victory for human rights in Pennsylvania,

Mauriello, T. State No. 1 in treatment of pregnant inmates. Pittsburgh Post-Gazette (Pittsburgh, PA), Oct 23, 2010.

which is not always on the forefront of socially progressive legislation," Mr. Leach said. Even lawmakers who normally take a hard line on corrections supported the bill, he said. "They realized there is an innocent child just being born who is being placed at risk," he said. Reports of deputies shackling Allegheny County Jail inmates during childbirth at Magee-Womens Hospital drew public outcry in 2006. The new law gives Allegheny County inmates even more confidence that they won't be shackled, said Alison Colbert, assistant professor of nursing at Duquesne University who provides pre-natal classes at the jail. "It's something they all lived in fear of. The prospect of being shackled during labor was quite terrifying," Ms. Colbert said. "The Allegheny County Jail has maintained its commitment not to shackle, and it's wonderful, but before the legislation you never knew what might happen with a change in administration." The report gave Pennsylvania an overall grade of A-, the highest of any state. New Mexico, New York and Texas received overall grades of B+. The report's lowest grades went to Maine, Mississippi, Nevada, South Carolina, Virginia and Wyoming, which each received an F+. According to the report, Pennsylvania could improve by reporting outcomes of all pregnancies, by providing training to officers transporting pregnant inmates and by providing prison nurseries. Ms. Colbert identified one other area for improvement: "When an inmate is on the inside, we know they're getting good prenatal care. What we can do better is build a bridge to the outside." Ms. McNaughton said the Pennsylvania Department of Corrections strives to provide proper care for all inmates, and that pregnant women and mothers have unique needs. She said the department encourages caregivers to bring children to visit. Parents -- other than sex offenders -- are allowed to hold their children during the visit, she said. The purpose of Thursday's report was to encourage accountability and consistency in the treatment of incarcerated mothers.

InfoMarks: Make Your Mark

What is an InfoMark?

It is a single-click return ticket to any page, any result, or any search from InfoTrac College Edition.

An InfoMark is a stable URL, linked to InfoTrac College Edition articles that you have selected. InfoMarks can be used like any other URL, but they're better because they're stable – they don't change. Using an InfoMark is like performing the search again whenever you follow the link, whether the result is a single article or a list of articles.

How Do InfoMarks Work?

If you can "copy and paste," you can use InfoMarks.

When you see the InfoMark icon on a result page, its URL can be copied and pasted into your electronic document – web page, word processing document, or email. Once InfoMarks are incorporated into a document, the results are persistent (the URLs will not change) and are dynamic.

Even though the saved search is used at different times by different users, an InfoMark always functions like a brand new search. Each time a saved search is executed, it accesses the latest updated information. That means subsequent InfoMark searches might yield additional or more up-to-date information than the original search with less time and effort.

Capabilities

InfoMarks are the perfect technology tool for creating:

- Virtual online readers
- Current awareness topic sites – links to periodical or newspaper sources
- Online/distance learning courses
- Bibliographies, reference lists
- Electronic journals and periodical directories
- Student assignments
- Hot topics

Advantages

- Select from over 15 million articles from more than 5,000 journals and periodicals
- Update article and search lists easily
- Articles are always full-text and include bibliographic information
- All articles can be viewed online, printed, or emailed
- Saves professors and students time
- Anyone with access to InfoTrac College Edition can use it
- No other online library database offers this functionality
- FREE!

How to Use InfoMarks

There are three ways to utilize InfoMarks – in HTML documents, Word documents, and Email.

HTML Document

1. Open a new document in your HTML editor (Netscape Composer or FrontPage Express).
2. Open a new browser window and conduct your search in InfoTrac College Edition.
3. Highlight the URL of the results page or article that you would like to InfoMark.
4. Right-click the URL and click Copy. Now switch back to your HTML document.
5. In your document, type in text that describes the InfoMarked item.
6. Highlight the text and click on Insert, then on Link in the upper bar menu.
7. Click in the link box, then press the "Ctrl" and "V" keys simultaneously and click OK. This will paste the URL in the box.
8. Save your document.

Word Document

1. Open a new Word document.
2. Open a new browser window and conduct your search in InfoTrac College Edition.
3. Check items you want to add to your Marked List.
4. Click on Mark List on the right menu bar.
5. Highlight the URL, right-click on it, and click Copy. Now switch back to your Word document.
6. In your document, type in text that describes the InfoMarked item.
7. Highlight the text. Go to the upper bar menu and click on Insert, then on Hyperlink.
8. Click in the hyperlink box, then press the "Ctrl" and "V" keys simultaneously and click OK. This will paste the URL in the box.
9. Save your document.

Email

1. Open a new email window.
2. Open a new browser window and conduct your search in InfoTrac College Edition.
3. Highlight the URL of the results page or article that you would like to InfoMark.
4. Right-click the URL and click Copy. Now switch back to your email window.
5. In the email window, press the "Ctrl" and "V" keys simultaneously. This will paste the URL into your email.
6. Send the email to the recipient. By clicking on the URL, he or she will be able to view the InfoMark.